Eat, Drink & Be Vegan

Eat, Drink & Be Vegan

Everyday Vegan Recipes Worth Celebrating

DREENA BURTON

ARSENAL
PULP PRESS

VANCOUVER

ARSENAL PULP PRESS
Suite 200, 341 Water Street
Vancouver, BC
Canada V6B 1B8
arsenalpulp.com

The publisher gratefully acknowledges the support of the Government of Canada through the Book Publishing Industry Development Program and the Government of British Columbia through the Book Publishing Tax Credit Program for its publishing activities.

The author and publisher assert that the information contained in this book is true and complete to the best of their knowledge. All recommendations are made without guarantee on the part of the author and publisher. The author and publisher disclaim any liability in connection with the use of this information. For more information, contact the publisher.

Text and cover design by Diane Yee, Electra Design Group
Creative direction by Lisa Eng-Lodge, Electra Design Group
Production assistance by Andrea Schmidt
Editing by Bethanne Grabham
Photography by Pamela Bethel, *pamelabethel.ca*

Printed and bound in Canada

Library and Archives Canada Cataloguing in Publication:
Burton, Dreena, 1970-
    Eat, Drink & Be Vegan: everyday vegan recipes worth celebrating / Dreena Burton.

Includes index.
ISBN 978-1-55152-224-1

    1. Vegan cookery. I. Title. II. Title: Eat, drink and be vegan.
TX837.B875 2007   641.5'636   C2007-903936-7

Contents

For Bridget and Charlotte, who teach me about compassion every day.

Acknowledgments

To my husband: my culinary work and cookbook writing has often meant long hours in the kitchen or on the computer. Paul, you support my work daily, and share my excitement for my ideas and accomplishments; I truly would not be able to write my books as a stay-at-home mom without your understanding and help. And to our precious daughters: thank you for having patience with your busy mom, and I hope that our healthy food choices will stay with you through all your years.

To Dr Neal Barnard: thank you for contributing the foreword to this book, and for your commitment to clinical research on nutrition. The Physicians Committee for Responsible Medicine has always been a source of credible nutritional information for my family and me, and a resource I recommend for reliable facts on the healthfulness of vegan diets. To Jill Eckart: for your timely assistance and cooperation. Also, to the wondrous vegan chef and cookbook author Bryanna Clark Grogan who aided our communications: your generous spirit shines through in person as well as through your work.

To my mother: for your love and for showing me how kind-hearted and generous one person can be.

To Diane, Vicki, Davin, Trang, and Shyla, my "cover models": even though we changed the cover concept for this book, the photo shoot day was fun and full of energy because of you!

To my darling girlfriends, Vicki, Trish, Tanya, Jen, and my sister Diane: you have always been the most enthusiastic samplers of my recipes, and have always shown interest in and support for all of my projects (and have understood when I haven't been the most "present" friend through busy phases).

To Erik Marcus (*Vegan.com*): for your back cover endorsement, continual support of my work, and for inviting me to regularly contribute to *Vegan.com*. Thank you for the work you do every day to end animal suffering and promote veganism.

To Bob and Jenna Torres (*veganfreak.net*) for your back cover endorsement and for featuring my work on your podcast. Thank you both for the community of support you have created through your Vegan Freak forums, and for connecting thousands of vegans and vegans-in-training.

To all the individuals and groups that have supported my culinary work and cookbooks: specifically, Ryan MacMichael of Veg Blog, Joe Connelly and Colleen Holland of *VegNews*, Wanda Embar of Vegan Peace, Jennifer McCann of Vegan Lunch Box, Erin Pavlina, Stephanie Porter, Melanie Wilson and *Vegetarianbaby.com*, and EarthSave Canada.

Those who graciously offered to test some of my recipes, including Angela, Carrie, Dori, Jess, Julie Farson, Julie Hasson, Leslie, Michelle, and Teresa.

To the Internet community that encouraged and cheered on this project. In particular, to all of you beautiful blogging people (you know who you are) who share your enthusiasm for my recipes on your blogs, as well as by commenting on mine. And, to all of the people who have emailed me through the years with such meaningful comments about how my recipes and cookbooks have positively influenced your lives. Thank you.

To Brian and Robert at Arsenal Pulp Press, for publishing what has now become my vegan trilogy! I appreciate your interest in my projects, and in vegan literature more generally. Thanks to all the staff at Arsenal Pulp Press that brought this project together, including Shyla, Janice, and Bethanne. Also, to photographer Pamela Bethel and her assistant Katie for your stunning photography and creative food image concepts. And finally, to Lisa Eng-Lodge and Diane Yee, for another stellar book design.

Foreword by Dr Neal Barnard

Eat, Drink & Be Vegan is one of a kind. It will delight both beginning and experienced cooks, as author Dreena Burton not only gives tips for making each recipe quick and easy, but also adds special notes and tips to enhance each dish. The creative and flavorful food ideas show just how special it is to dine with Dreena's help—something you'll want to do again and again, savoring each bite and feeling great at the same time.

Vegan diets are growing more popular every year and are endorsed by many experts. Based on our research, we at the Physicians Committee for Responsible Medicine found that a low-fat vegan diet is a winner, whether your goal is trimming your waistline, cutting cholesterol, taming diabetes or high blood pressure, or just feeling better. Additionally, research studies by Dr Dean Ornish and his colleagues at the Preventive Medicine Research Institute showed that diets based on plant foods rather than animal products actually reversed existing heart disease in more than 80 percent of participants without the need for medications or surgery. In fact, many people with diabetes can either reduce their medications or stop them completely as a result of switching to a vegan diet, and the same is true for high blood pressure.

But don't take my word for it. Give this diet a test drive. Take a week or two and try out as many of these delicious recipes as you can. Then, when you have found your favorites, block out a three-week period to eat low-fat, vegan foods exclusively. As you get started, your body will begin to transform, and in all likelihood, you'll feel better than you did when you were a kid. After three weeks, see how great you feel. By then, you'll have all the tools you need for a permanent improvement to your health.

Dreena has done a fabulous job with this cookbook. I hope you enjoy these wonderful meals that will allow you to *Eat, Drink & Be Vegan!*

—*Neal Barnard, MD; President, Physicians Committee for Responsible Medicine*
June 2007

Introduction

Although I thought it would be many years before I wrote another cookbook, I unknowingly started a new one when I created my cooking blog (*vivelevegan.blogspot.com*). It got my creative juices flowing, and as the blog became popular, readers kept asking if I would write a third cookbook. Initially, I thought not, knowing the work and time involved. But soon enough, my commitment to provide new material on a regular basis to the blog made me realize I had many more great-tasting vegan recipes to share.

In *Eat, Drink & Be Vegan*, I hope to give you a little of everything in vegan cooking—everything except cauliflower and cabbage, that is! (Sorry, but I am not overly fond of these cruciferous siblings, so you won't find them anywhere in my recipes!) What you will find are flavor-packed, easy-to-make vegan recipes for special occasions like brunches, dinner gatherings, potlucks, and parties, and for day-to-day meals and snacks. All my recipes are original creations, showcasing whole foods in new and tantalizing ways.

The majority of these recipes are also healthier, lower in fat, and more nutrient-rich than their non-vegan counterparts: meals and snacks featuring legumes, whole-grains, vegetables, nuts and seeds, and tofu and tempeh, and baked goods using whole-grain flours, unrefined sugars, and non-hydrogenated oils. I hope you enjoy these bean, vegetable, and grain-based recipes as much as my own family does. And your palate won't miss the more processed foods. You'll love the full, deep textures and bright, rich flavors in these recipes … and your body will thank you!

Even many of the desserts in this cookbook are healthier than standard desserts because most are made with whole-grain flours, and without refined sugars. For example, the Jam-Print Cookies (page 197) and Sunny Pineapple Yogurt Cake (page 209) both use whole-grain flours but are still fantastically delicious, moist, and will satisfy your sweet tooth. However, there are certainly some dessert recipes that are more indulgent, and these are designed more for special occasions. That rich birthday cake a few times a year won't be a concern when your daily diet is full of wholesome and unprocessed grains, legumes, fruits and vegetables, and nuts and seeds.

Most of these dishes you can make in a flash; I know, because these recipes came out of the kitchen of one hurried, multi-tasking mom, with a five-year-old and a busy toddler underfoot! Moms and dads with full schedules deserve nutritious, fantastically flavoured meals, and are doubly rewarded when we see our children enthusiastically eat these nourishing dishes.

These recipes are also great for singles, couples, and cooks of all levels. Experienced cooks will appreciate my flavor and ingredient combinations while novices will appreciate the ease of preparation and use of common ingredients.

Speaking of ingredients: On the surface, some of my recipes may appear difficult to make, with long ingredient lists and a lot of directions and sidebars. But this doesn't mean the recipe is time-consuming or challenging; I just like to "talk" to you in my recipes! Especially ones that I think are quite flexible and I really love, like Veggie Tempeh Muffuletta (page 112); now that's packed with ingredients and notes, but it's also easy to make, requiring just some veggie chopping and tempeh sautéing—that's it!

In these recipes, I use some ingredients that haven't been showcased in my previous books, including tempeh, polenta, nutritional yeast, and coconut oil. These items are now widely available, so I introduce them to you in a handful of recipes that highlight their unique flavor and textural qualities, showing you ways to use them in this book. If you are new to these foods, approach them with an open mind. I haven't always been a fan of tempeh or nutritional yeast, but I've come to love them in recent years. Give these recipes a try … you just may find yourself loving tempeh, polenta, and nutritional yeast too!

In my second book, *Vive le Vegan!*, I included recipes using hemp foods. I regularly use Manitoba Harvest hemp seeds, hemp nut butter, and hempseed oil, and have created a few new amazing hemp recipes, including "Spicoli" Burgers (page 145). These are unbelievably good, and after making them you'll be excited to try more recipes using hemp foods.

By the size of the desserts chapter, you'll probably guess that it is my favorite section of this cookbook! You'll find cakes, pies, and even truffles—and of course, cookies! After the success of my cookie recipes in *Vive le Vegan!*, I devoted a lot of time to come up with even more cookie and cookie-bar recipes. Since being nicknamed the "Vegan Cookie Queen," I now feel it is my royal duty to offer sensational cookie recipes to suit everyone's preference!

Let's show the world that vegan food is delicious. Make and share these recipes with your friends and family. We can make a difference encouraging people to eat less animal foods. Ideally, we would love folks to not eat any meat, eggs, or dairy, and maybe … just maybe, they will see there is nothing to "miss" on a vegan diet. A fellow vegan (known as "Urban Vegan" in the online world) once said, "When people learn I am vegan and ask, 'What do you eat?' I am actually at the point where I feel sorry for them." I thought this response was so perceptive, because there is such a misconception that vegan food is boring, bland, uninteresting … or too difficult. Let's change that view one recipe at a time … and let's celebrate by sharing delicious vegan meals with loved ones!

Vegan food is indeed something to celebrate. It is about all the spectacular foods we eat, not about what we "cannot" eat (or rather, what we choose not to eat). The vegan diet deserves celebration, not only because it tastes fabulous and is full of variety and exciting choices, but also because it is the best way to eat for the sake of our health, the health of our planet, and all the animals with whom we share it.

So let's celebrate, and let's get cooking! You can always contact me through my blog at *vivelevegan.blogspot. com* or email *dreena@everydayvegan.com*. Until I hear from you, I wish you happy cooking, and please, eat, drink … and be vegan!

I consider myself a "basic cook," as I don't have an over-abundance of gadgets and appliances. Although I enjoy adding these items to my kitchen, I want anyone to be able to make my recipes, whether a young college student or a stay-at-home mom, so I keep it simple. While some of you will have a better equipped kitchen than others, everyone should be able to make these recipes. Still, there are a few "essential" small appliances that I absolutely cannot do without in my own kitchen and which I highly recommend, such as a hand (or immersion) blender and a food processor. With these appliances, you will enjoy more convenience in making smoothies, snacks, and meals for many years to come! But if you don't have these appliances, you can still make many of these recipes.

Here are some other useful tools of the trade:

Baking Pans and Dishes:

Rimmed baking sheets: I have two 18-in (45-cm) rimmed metal baking sheets that I use for everything from baking cookies to roasting vegetables. They are indispensable, and with a lining of parchment paper, a cinch to clean up.

Muffin pans: For muffins as well as cupcakes; be sure to use muffin liners for easy clean-up.

Round metal cake pans (8-in/20-cm): Essential for cake baking.

Square metal baking pans (8-in/20-cm): For brownies, blondies, and cookie bars.

Glass pie plates: I often use prepared crusts for my dessert pies (Wholly Wholesome is my preferred brand). However, I sometimes make pie crusts from scratch and need glass pie plates. Of course, these can be used for savory dishes too, such as casseroles.

Rectangular glass baking dishes (8x12-in/20x25-cm): For casserole and dessert recipes.

Large casserole dishes with glass lid: I use a 4-qt (4-l) dish that I use for one-pot oven meals; a 3-qt (3-l) dish will also do just fine. If you have a large casserole dish with no cover, use aluminium foil.

Chef's knife: Chopping and slicing are efficient and effortless tasks with a good quality chef's knife, an investment that will last for years.

Citrus reamer: I use fresh lemon and lime juices regularly, and this handy and inexpensive kitchen tool makes juicing a snap. (Tip: Place a small fine strainer over a bowl and ream lemons over strainer, which will catch pulp and seeds while bowl catches the juice.)

Colander: Essential for draining pasta and rinsing fresh herbs, berries, and canned foods such as beans. A stainless steel colander is preferred, but plastic is fine.

Cooling rack: Have a few cooling racks of different sizes, including a longer one for batches of cookies.

Cutting boards: It's useful to have a few cutting boards; one for fruits and another one or two for onions, garlic, and vegetables.

Fine strainer: I have two, one smaller and one larger. The smaller strainer fits over small bowls and is perfect for catching seeds when squeezing fresh citrus, and for sifting small amounts of baking powder, baking soda, cocoa powder, and flours. The larger strainer is best for sifting larger amounts of these baking ingredients, and is also useful for quickly cleaning fresh herbs, handfuls of berries, and small vegetables like cherry tomatoes and snow peas.

Food processor (and mini-food processor): What would I do without my food processor? This is a must-have kitchen appliance for making dips, spreads, desserts, pasta sauce, and, let's not forget, hummus! (It is far cheaper and tastier to make your own hummus than to buy store brands.) I use a KitchenAid 12-cup food processor, which is big enough to make double batches of hummus and for chopping, dicing, and slicing large batches of vegetables. It also includes a smaller bowl for lesser quantities.

Hand (immersion) blender: A beloved tool in my kitchen, used daily for shakes and smoothies and weekly for sauces, salad dressings, dessert sauces, and soups. I use a KitchenAid hand blender that has a mini-food processor attachment, which is very handy for making small batches of savory purées for sandwiches, chopping small batches of vegetables, mincing garlic cloves, and pulverizing chocolate chips and nuts. This attachment is also terrific for puréeing small amounts of food for infants.

Heat-resistant spatulas: Many different brands, colors, and sizes of heat-resistant spatulas are available. Have at least one (but preferably two or three) of these spatulas that can withstand temperatures up to 600°F (315°C) (or higher). You can use them for stove-top sauces, sautéing, and melting chocolate. Other flexible spatulas that are not heat-resistant will gradually dissolve into your cooking, and that's something you do not want to eat!

Kitchen rasp: This is one of my favorite inexpensive kitchen tools. A woodworking tool that has been adapted for the culinary world, rasps are excellent for grating nutmeg into a fine powder in seconds, and are the best tool I have used for zesting citrus. They can also be used for grating chocolate, garlic, and ginger.

Kitchen shears: Another favorite item, I use these in place of a knife for cutting parchment paper, snipping chives and other herbs onto finished dishes and salads, and opening food packages and wrappings. They are also handy for cutting tough crusts off bread or cutting pizzas.

Measuring cups & spoons: One set of each is good, but a second set is most useful.

Non-stick frying pans: While most of my cookware does not have non-stick coatings, I keep two non-stick skillets for making a few key items: pancakes, crêpes, and thin strips of marinated tempeh or tofu. I reserve one non-stick pan for sweet items like pancakes, and another for savory items like tempeh bacon.

Parchment paper: Removing finished baking from its pan (including cookies) is a no-stick effort, when you line cake, loaf, and brownie pans with parchment paper. It can also be used for cooking, such as roasting vegetables and baking home fries. Also, parchment paper helps to keep your pans in good condition and makes clean-up a snap.

Pizza stone: Not an essential kitchen item, but pizza stones make prepared or homemade pizza crusts crispier. They aren't expensive, and can be used for baking other items as well.

Pots & pans: I recommend investing in a set of good-quality stainless steel pots and pans, including a skillet; you will have them for many years and will never regret the purchase.

Salad spinner: This is one of the greatest inventions ever! It whisks water away from greens like lettuce, chard, and kale, and from large bunches of herbs like parsley and basil.

Storage containers: Lots of them! Whether you prefer inexpensive storage containers, reused soy yogurt tubs, or Tupperware, you will need containers to store your leftovers of soups, dips, and cookies.

Timer: If you don't have a timer on your oven, then purchase a small manual timer with a bell; having a second manual timer is also useful for cooking two or more dishes.

Toaster oven: I don't use a microwave oven, so my toaster oven is essential for quickly reheating leftovers and sauces. I also use it for toasting nuts, roasting and broiling small amounts of vegetables, and reheating leftovers. A toaster oven will heat much more quickly than your regular oven for small portions of food. If large enough, you can even use it to bake small entrées like personal pizzas. I use a KitchenAid 6-slice countertop toaster oven.

Whisk: Very useful for incorporating ingredients into sauces, especially when using thickeners such as arrowroot and for quickly and effectively mixing pancake and other batters.

COOKING AND FOOD PREPARATION NOTES

Now that you have the basic tools of the trade, here are some ideas that will help you to plan, shop for, prepare, and cook your chosen recipes.

Often, I'm asked: "Isn't it hard or time-consuming to cook vegan?" Unfortunately, our culture has become so accustomed to eating processed and pre-packaged foods, using microwaves and ordering takeout, that a homecooked meal (vegan or otherwise) seems laborious and time-consuming.

Vegans generally eat more unprocessed, whole foods. We buy fresh produce, bring it home, wash it, and prepare it with legumes, whole grains, and/or nuts, tofu, tempeh, or seitan to create a meal. We sometimes make our own baked goods from scratch, as well as sauces and salad dressings.

Cooking and baking does not have to be an elaborate undertaking. In fact, many recipes in this book can be created within thirty minutes. Sure, some chopping and prep are involved, but you will have a choice between recipes that require shorter or longer times. Whichever you choose, the reward is fresh, homecooked, nourishing food for you and your loved ones.

Vegan cooking can be enjoyable and rewarding, even for those with little or no cooking experience. Plus, food prepared at home usually tastes better, and is better for you. I love the experience of bringing a homecooked meal to the table and sharing dinner with my family—every night. There is value in sitting with your loved ones while eating and sharing your day's delights and challenges. I remember my mother making meals from scratch. She had six of us girls, so of course there were nights when our dinners came from cans and were paired with bread to fill us up. But I have fond memories of her homecooked meals, and I want to do the same for my own family and friends … and hopefully for yours as well.

Meal Planning:

Any given week I make mental notes for general meal planning. But if writing out detailed meal plans works better for you, then do it. (Even jotting down two or three recipe ideas that you'd liked to make within a week can get you better organized for regular meal-making.) Make sure you have essential ingredients in your pantry needed for a dozen or so recipes (visit my blog *vivelevegan.blogspot.com* for an extensive pantry list). Once you have your pantry in order, make a meal plan for the week. Write a grocery list of produce and other fresh items required, and select a day of the week to do all your grocery shopping. You should have everything you need for the week, so no extra trips to the store will be necessary.

For days that are hectic, always have the basic vegan staples on hand for quick meals, such as pastas and pasta sauces, veggie burgers or falafel mixes, chilis, seasoned tofu, quinoa, and frozen burritos and other vegan entrées. There are many other ready-made vegan foods available to carry you through busy days, these are just a few suggestions to get a meal on your table with little prep from you.

Read the recipes: Before beginning any cooking or baking, first read the recipe to give yourself an idea of how it will "flow," the timing between steps, and overall preparation and cooking time. This is key. Cooking and baking will be more enjoyable—and successful—when you first read through the entire recipe (even read it twice to be sure!). Also, consider what accompaniments you will want to serve with the dish. For example, you may want to serve Cashew-Ginger Tofu (page 124) with quinoa and a fresh salad. If so, be sure you have quinoa in your pantry. Then all you need to do is quickly rinse and cook the quinoa and prepare a salad while the tofu dish is baking.

Mise en place: When preparing to cook a recipe, particularly a new one, it helps to follow the principle of "mise en place." A French expression that literally translates to "setting in place," it simply means to get your ingredients prepared and "in place" before you begin cooking. Working from a recipe is easier, smoother, and faster when your utensils and kitchen appliances are in place and ready to use, and when your ingredients are pre-measured and assembled. Once you have read the recipe, visualize the cooking process and the steps required. Consider the tools and equipment needed, and get those in place—measuring cups and spoons, bowls and plates, pots or pans, and equipment such as a food processor. Then prep and measure your ingredients and preheat your oven, if needed. You don't need to place individual ingredients in attractive small bowls as you see on cooking shows; setting them out on one or two large plates is good enough. Clearing away any ingredients like bottles and spices, and washing used dishes between steps, will also improve your cooking experience by keeping your cooking space clean and uncluttered. These methods streamline the process and eliminate any stressful moments where you have to omit or substitute a missing ingredient halfway through cooking or have miscalculated the timing of steps.

Produce Tips:

When you buy your produce, make a habit of washing it all as soon as you return home (except for lettuces and delicate berries like raspberries and strawberries). It takes just five or ten minutes to wash a large amount of produce, and it truly saves time later in the week. Whenever you want to grab a piece of fruit or veg for snacking or to use in a recipe, it will be clean and ready to go.

Here is a simple method: Fill your sink with warm water and a squeeze of fruit and veggie wash, or a smidgen of natural dish liquid. I usually start with the heavier, bigger items like bananas, melons, and celery. Give a quick wash, then rinse, and place them all on the dish draining rack. Finish with smaller, lighter items like kiwi fruit, and grapes. Even sturdy greens like kale or collards can be washed and rinsed, then left to partially dry on top of the other veggies.

After washing, let air dry for a couple of hours, or dry with some towels. Items that need to be refrigerated can then be transferred to large unzipped Ziploc bags. Certain vegetables like cucumber, fennel, and bell peppers can be grouped together. Dry the leafy greens as much as possible and transfer the entire bunch to a large Ziploc bag. Zucchini and summer squash benefit from a paper towel tucked in the bag to absorb some of the moisture they naturally release. I keep the bags unzipped and in the produce drawers in the refrigerator to keep the produce fresh for a number of days. Place other produce, like bananas, kiwi, mangoes, and tomatoes in baskets on the counter. Remember not to leave temperature-sensitive veggies sitting overnight in your dish drainer; items like cucumber, celery, and carrots get soft if not chilled.

Should you buy organic?: To reduce your exposure to pesticides, eat organic produce whenever possible. If buying all organic food is too expensive, make informed choices on which items you should buy organic.

At *foodnews.org*, the Environmental Work Group (a non-profit environmental research organization based in Washington, DC), lists their "dirty dozen." These are the fruits and vegetables most heavily treated with pesticides: peaches, apples, sweet bell peppers, celery, nectarines, strawberries, cherries, pears, grapes, spinach, lettuce, and potatoes. Fruits and vegetables that are low in pesticides include avocado, sweet corn (frozen), pineapple, mango, asparagus, sweet peas (frozen), kiwi, and bananas—and onions are the lowest.

Since pesticides are toxic to our bodies, and particularly dangerous to babies, children, and pregnant women, it is wise to avoid buying these produce items if conventionally grown. There are many other reasons to buy organic, and you will likely find the quality and taste of your organic food far superior. For more details, visit the websites *foodnews.org* or *ewg.org*.

One final note about pesticides. Vegans too often hear: "You must be concerned about pesticides in all the produce you eat." In actual fact, the higher on the food chain you eat, the more exposure to toxins and pesticides you have. Pesticides, synthetic hormones, and other chemicals accumulate in animals and thereby in meat and dairy products. Pesticides are sprayed on grains that are fed to cows, chickens, pigs, and other livestock, and these chemicals become concentrated in the animals' tissues (see pcrm. org). Even if you don't eat organic, you are exposed to fewer contaminants eating produce than if you are on a meat and dairy-based diet. Plus, fruits and vegetables provide countless protective substances, antioxidants, and nutrients whereas meat and dairy products contain cholesterol, saturated fat, and these bio-accumulated toxins. Nevertheless, reduce your exposure to pesticides and eat organic produce whenever possible.

What's in season?: Seasonal produce has the best flavor and texture since it is fresh from the fields. It is usually quite affordable too, and you'll often know what items are in season from what's on special at your grocery store. Here is a quick look at when certain produce items are in season (in North America). Some items may spill over from one season to another, but for the most part these are your picks for each season:

SPRING (MARCH, APRIL, MAY)
Vegetables: artichokes, asparagus, carrots, chives, new potatoes, spinach, spring greens/baby lettuce mixes, spring onions.
Fruit: rhubarb, Valencia oranges.

SUMMER (JUNE, JULY, AUGUST)
Vegetables: basil, bell peppers, beets, carrots, cucumber, corn, eggplant, green beans, lettuces, potatoes, summer squash, tomatoes, zucchini.
Fruit: apricots, blackberries, blueberries, cantaloupe, cherries, honeydew melons, mangoes, peaches, plums, raspberries, strawberries, watermelon.

FALL (SEPTEMBER, OCTOBER, NOVEMBER)
Vegetables: broccoli, carrots, celery, celeriac (celery root), parsnips, turnips, wild mushrooms, winter squash.
Fruit: apples, figs, grapes, pears, plums.

WINTER (DECEMBER, JANUARY, FEBRUARY)
Vegetables: Brussels sprouts, cauliflower, cabbage, kale, leeks, rutabaga, spinach, sprouts, Swiss chard.
Fruit: clementines, grapefruit, Mandarin oranges, oranges, pomegranates.

TWENTY (OR SO) RANDOM COOKING TIPS

See page 173 for additional tips related to baking and desserts.

Tastier grains!: To give instant flavor to whole grains, add a vegetable bouillon cube to the cooking water. Use ½–1 cube for every cup of grain (and 2 cups of water). You can experiment with different flavored bouillon, such as mushroom and onion varieties. See page 93 for my preferred brands of bouillon cubes. Adding a sprig of fresh rosemary, several sprigs of fresh thyme, or a bay leaf will also infuse herbaceous deliciousness!

Chop—don't squish—tomatoes: Use a serrated knife for slicing tomatoes. It will cut the flesh without squishing them. Roma tomatoes are my favorite because they are "meaty" with less seeds and juice than other varieties.

Hot stuff!: Hot chili peppers have most of their heat concentrated in the seeds and the white membranes, so you can avoid or include them depending on your heat preference. Always wash your hands after handling hot peppers, and avoid touching your nose or eyes; it is even a good idea to wear rubber gloves when handling.

Avoid chopping clutter: When doing lots of chopping, keep a small bag nearby to quickly clear away and dispose the garbage. If composting or using a garburator, keep a larger bowl on your countertop to collect the scraps.

Wilted greens?: To revive wilted lettuce or limp celery or carrots, soak them in a large bowl or sink full of very cold water for about 20 minutes.

Decaf your tea at home: If you're a tea drinker (like me), you can naturally "decaffeinate" your caffeinated teas in minutes. Pour boiling water over your green or black tea bag or loose teas and let steep for about 30–45 seconds. Then pour off the liquid, keeping the tea bag or leaves in the teapot or cup; about 90% of the caffeine will be removed in that first steeping. Add boiling water to your teapot or cup, and this second brew will still have still have flavor and health benefits, but only a very small amount of caffeine!

Cooked pasta saver: Never rinse cooked pasta, unless you plan to use it cold in a dish such as pasta salad. Rinsing it washes away the starches that help your delicious sauce cling to the pasta. Also, before draining your pasta, reserve a cup of the pasta cooking water. You may want to add a few tablespoons of it to your pasta to help distribute the sauce.

Easiest puréed soups: For puréed soups, using a hand blender is best. It is quicker, easier, and cleaner to use than a blender or food processor. See page 13 for more information on hand blenders.

Cleaning mushrooms: Do not wash mushrooms as they will soak up too much water. Wipe clean with a damp towel or cloth; or peel them: first remove stem, grasp peel from underside of mushroom cap, and pull it upward to remove outside layer, repeating until cap is fully peeled.

Freshly squeezed!: Roll lemons and limes (and other citrus) with the palm of your hand on your countertop before juicing. Apply some pressure as you roll to extract more juice from them (especially limes).

Freshest asparagus: Store asparagus standing up in a cup with a few inches of water. Loosely cover the exposed spears with plastic wrap and refrigerate. Before cooking, remove the fibrous ends of asparagus by holding the end of each stalk and bending until the asparagus snaps. Where it naturally breaks is where the spear begins to become fibrous. Discard the fibrous end or use for vegetable stocks.

Garlic grating magic: A sprinkle of salt added to garlic cloves when mincing will help to keep the garlic from sticking to your knife. You can also use a kitchen rasp (see page 14) to grate garlic cloves, or a mini-food processor to mince five or more cloves.

Blending vinaigrettes: Reuse larger glass jars of nut butters for making sauces and salad dressings. They are the perfect size that your hand blender will fit inside and instantly whiz your vinaigrette or sauce. Simply remove label, and the jar and lid can be washed in the dishwasher and are ready to use. If the lids become old or rusty, they should then be recycled.

Earth Balance makeover: If you like Earth Balance Buttery Spread, then you can use it to make your own homemade seasoned vegan butters. In a mini-food processor, blend Earth Balance spread with fresh herbs like parsley, basil, tarragon, dill, or chives, or with seasonings like ground black pepper, lemon zest, or dried spices. It can be stored in the refrigerator for about a week, or in the freezer for about six months (wrap in small portions in plastic wrap). Spread it on breads or bagels, or dollop on baked potatoes or steamed greens, or toss into pasta or legumes.

Don't cry!: If you need only a small amount of onion for a recipe, use a shallot or the whitish portion of green onions rather than cut into a large onion.

Sneak in that flax or DHA oil!: A good way to sneak flax oil and/or vegetarian DHA oil into food is to mix it into sauces and dips. My children love Annie's Goddess Dressing, so I stir DHA oil into a small container with this dressing for dipping sandwiches or veggies. You can also stir the oils into ketchup, non-dairy yogurt or pudding, or guacamole. Vegetarian DHA oil blends are now available, such as Udo's Oil Blend with DHA (which is algae-derived).

Gone bananas!: When bananas are on sale (especially organic ones), buy a couple of bunches. When the extras become overripe, peel, slice and store them in the freezer in Ziploc (or other) containers or bags. You can use them later for smoothies (see the beverages chapter) or to make banana ice cream (see page 183). The slices may freeze together into chunks, but you can usually pry them apart with a butter knife. You may want to measure out the slices and label your containers, with 1-, 2- or 3-cup portions.

Pear sauce?: If your pears are too ripe, turn them into raw pear sauce. Simply peel and core the pears, then mash. Use straight away (since mashed pears quickly oxidize), such as spooned onto hot cereal or over waffles. You can also steam overripe pears until cooked through and then purée the mixture into a sauce much like bottled applesauce. Cool and refrigerate or freeze extra portions.

Nut-butter cereal boost: Stir nut butters like almond, cashew, or macadamia into hot oatmeal and other hot cereals. Mix it through and then add non-dairy milk, cinnamon, chopped fruits, a drizzle of agave nectar, and anything else you like. This is especially good for children who don't like the stickiness of nut butters, because it dissolves throughout the oatmeal.

Garlic fingers?: No need to buy fancy soaps to remove garlic and onion odors from your hands! Simply wash your hands and rub them over a stainless steel item, such as your kitchen faucet, the side of a cooking pot or a spoon.

No gummy colanders: When draining pasta, after returning it to your cooking pot or serving bowl, quickly rinse your colander in very hot water. It will remove some of the starches and the colander will be easier to wash later, without much scrubbing.

Cooking with canned tomatoes: Canned tomatoes are an essential pantry item, and different varieties are available, including those with seasonings like basil and garlic, and organic varieties. Note that some brands include salt and others do not. If using canned tomatoes that are labeled "no salt added," you will need to adjust the salt used in any given recipe, adding extra to taste. This is particularly important in recipes where one or two full cans of tomatoes are used.

Top o' the Mornin'!

Breakfasts

FOR MOST OF US, weekday breakfasts are very routine. They need to be fast and easy, not requiring us to pull out a cookbook or measuring spoons. Most mornings we rely on fruits and juices, store-bought cold or hot cereals, toast with nut butters, smoothies, or energy bars.

It doesn't always have to be this way. Many recipes in this chapter accommodate the rushed morning mayhem, but there are also others that are appropriate for more leisurely mornings and brunches. For a quick breakfast, try Hemp-anola (page 32); you can make a batch of it on the weekend to enjoy during the week. Polenta Pancakes (page 34) are far easier to make than they sound … and are so fun to eat! Also, don't forget to make a couple of batches of muffins or scones so you can toss one in your bag on those especially harried mornings.

When you have a chance to slow down, even just a little, you can have a more fun with your morning meal. Next time you're feeling inspired, try your hand at Raspberry Corn-meal Pancakes (page 36), Banana Pecan Rice Pudding Pie (page 25), Breakfast Crêpes with Fresh Fruit (page 28) and Celestial Cream (page 29), or Tempeh Hashbrown Casserole (page 37).

Many of these breakfasts and brunches are on the sweeter side, but there are recipes else-where in this book that make terrific savory additions for a more elaborate late-morning meal, including:

Hummus and Dips (served with whole-grain bagels or breads, crisp breads, English muffins, or raw or steamed veggies):

- Roasted Red Pepper & Almond Hummus (page 52)
- White Bean Hummus with Fresh Thyme & Basil (page 53)
- Warm & Cheesy White Bean Dip (page 69)
- White Bean Spread (page 115)

Finger Foods and Nibblers:

- Pan-Fried Tempt-eh! (page 62)
- Softly Spiced Nuts (page 67)
- Tamari-Roasted Chickpeas (page 68)
- Potato Squashers (page 162)
- Rosemary Cornmeal Polenta Fries (page 164)

Also, check out the Ginger Immunity Tea (page 223) for an incredible, immune-boosting way to start your day. For instant, nutritious breakfasts on-the-go, try "But Where Do You Get Your Protein?" Smoothie (page 221), Açai Antioxidant Smoothie (page 219), and Drink Your Greens Smoothie (page 222).

Once you try some of these breakfast ideas, and experiment with other recipes mentioned, you'll see just how easy they are to prepare and how great they taste. You'll be eager to invite friends over for an all-out dynamite vegan brunch!

With the addition of light coconut milk, these pancakes are just a little creamier than others, and the bananas offer a taste of the tropics to brighten your morning. Serve with pure maple syrup or Warm Raspberry Sauce (page 39).

Banana Cream Pancakes

MAKES 12–15 SMALL–MEDIUM PANCAKES | **WHEAT-FREE**

1⅓ cup	**spelt flour**
1 tbsp + ¼ tsp	**baking powder**
½ tsp	**nutmeg**
⅛ tsp	(rounded) **sea salt**
1½ cups	**light coconut milk**
1 cup	**overripe banana** (about 1 large banana), sliced
1 tsp	**pure vanilla extract**
	coconut or canola oil (to coat pan)

In a large bowl, add flour and sift in baking powder. Add nutmeg and salt and stir to combine well. In a blender or with a hand blender, combine coconut milk, banana, and vanilla and blend until very smooth. Transfer wet mixture to dry mixture and stir until well combined. Lightly oil a frying pan (using the edge of a paper towel). On medium-high, heat pan for a few minutes until hot, then reduce heat to medium/medium-low and let it rest for a minute. Using a ladle, scoop batter into pan to form pancakes. Let cook on one side for several minutes, until small bubbles start to form on the outer edge and into the center. Flip pancakes to lightly brown other side, for 1–2 minutes. Repeat until batter is all used.

If you like rice pudding, you will delight in this dish! It is so creamy, sweet, and comforting, you'll be surprised that whole-grain brown rice is used instead of white. The sliced bananas add natural sweetness to the pudding, and the sugar-pecan topping makes it even more ridiculously delicious!

Banana Pecan Rice Pudding Pie

MAKES 4–6 SERVINGS | **WHEAT-FREE**

PUDDING:

1 tbsp	**arrowroot powder**
⅔ cup	**coconut milk** (regular or light)
¼ cup	**brown rice syrup**
2 tsp	**pure vanilla extract**
½ tsp	**cinnamon**
¼–½ tsp	**fresh nutmeg,** grated (optional)
¼ tsp	(rounded) **sea salt**
3 cups	**cooked short-grain brown rice** (see note)
1 cup	**ripe** (but not overripe) **banana,** sliced

TOPPING:

¼ cup	**pecans,** crushed
3 tbsp	**unrefined sugar**
¼–½ tsp	**cinnamon**
1–2 pinches	**sea salt**
½–1 tsp	**canola oil** (for coating pie plate)

Cook your brown rice in advance. When preparing brown rice at dinnertime, make an extra 3 cups. Then store in the refrigerator, and the next morning you can put this recipe together in a snap!

Coconut milk, whether light or regular, gives a buttery richness to this pudding, though you can use any non-dairy milk you like, including rice, soy, almond, or oat. If using vanilla non-dairy milk, you may not need as much brown rice syrup to sweeten the mixture.

Preheat oven to 400°F (200°C). In a large bowl, combine arrowroot powder with 3 tbsp coconut milk and whisk until arrowroot is fully dissolved. Add remaining coconut milk and stir until well combined. Whisk in syrup until well combined. Stir in vanilla, cinnamon, nutmeg, and salt, and then stir in rice and banana. Lightly oil bottom and sides of a 9½-in glass pie plate. Transfer pudding into pie plate. In a small bowl, combine topping ingredients, working mixture with your fingers until crumbly. Sprinkle topping over pudding. Bake for 17–20 minutes, until pudding is bubbly and has thickened. Remove from oven and let cool for about 20 minutes or longer. (The pudding will thicken more as it cools.) Spoon pudding into bowls and serve, topping with a little vanilla non-dairy milk if you like.

I like to use fresh organic strawberries in these muffins, but when they aren't in season, fresh or frozen blueberries are an excellent substitute.

Berry Goodness **Muffins**

MAKES 8–12 MUFFINS | **WHEAT-FREE**

Chickpea flour (also known as "gram" or "chana" flour) tastes unpleasant in uncooked batter, so don't taste test the batter! Wait until the muffins are finished baking, to enjoy the flavor of all of the ingredients together.

You may use fresh or frozen whole blueberries instead of strawberries. If using frozen blueberries, keep in freezer until ready to use. This will prevent the berries from thawing and their juices from seeping into the batter.

1½ cups	oat flour
1 cup	spelt flour
½ cup	chickpea flour (see note)
½ cup	unrefined sugar
¼ tsp	sea salt
½ – ¾ tsp	nutmeg
2 tsp	baking powder
½ tsp	baking soda
¾ cup + 1–2 tbsp	plain or vanilla non-dairy milk
¼ cup	unsweetened applesauce
¼ cup	pure maple syrup
1½ tsp	pure vanilla extract
1 tsp	lemon zest
3 tbsp	canola oil
1 cup	fresh strawberries, cut into small pieces (see note)

Preheat oven to 375°F (180°C). In a large bowl, combine flours, sugar, salt, and nutmeg. Sift in baking powder and baking soda, and mix well. In another bowl, combine milk, applesauce, maple syrup, vanilla, lemon zest, and oil. Gently stir in berries. Add wet mixture to dry, gently folding until combined. Fit a muffin pan with muffin liners. Spoon batter into liners. Bake for 23–28 minutes (less time for smaller muffins, longer for larger), until a toothpick inserted in center comes out clean.

Most of us love blueberry pancakes, and you can give them even more flavor and nutrition by adding carob powder. Tasty and healthy, you can enjoy these fluffy pancakes anytime of the year using fresh or frozen blueberries. Serve with pure maple syrup or Macadamia Maple Butter Cream (page 201).

Blueberry Carob **Pancakes**

MAKES 9–11 MEDIUM PANCAKES | **WHEAT-FREE**

1 cup	**spelt flour** (may substitute with barley flour)
¾ tsp	**cinnamon**
⅛ tsp	**sea salt**
3 tbsp	**carob powder**
2 tsp	**baking powder**
1¼–1⅓ cups	**vanilla non-dairy milk**
1 tbsp	**canola oil**
1 cup	**blueberries,** fresh or frozen (see note)
	canola oil (to coat pan)

Carob is high in calcium, potassium, and magnesium, and does not contain any caffeine.

If using frozen berries, keep in freezer until ready to use. This will prevent the berries from thawing and their juices from seeping into the batter.

In a large bowl, combine flour, cinnamon, and salt. Sift in carob and baking powders and mix well. In a small bowl, combine non-dairy milk and 1 tbsp canola oil and mix. Add wet mixture to dry, stirring until just combined. Gently stir in blueberries just before you are ready to cook pancakes. Lightly oil a non-stick frying pan (using the edge of a paper towel). On medium-high, heat pan for a few minutes until hot, then reduce heat to medium/medium-low and let it rest for a minute. Using a ladle, scoop batter into pan to form pancakes. Cook for several minutes, until small bubbles form on outer edge and into the center. Flip pancakes to lightly brown other side, for 1–2 minutes. Repeat until batter is all used.

Crêpe-making can be tedious, and disappointing if the delicate pancakes fall apart. But these crêpes are quick to make, and easy to cook and flip. You may tear one or two, but overall they should be no fuss! And you don't need a crêpe pan; a non-stick frying pan works just fine. Also, since this batter does not have sweetener, these crêpes can be used for savory fillings (see note) and for entrées or appetizers.

Breakfast **Crêpes** with Fresh Fruit

MAKES 11–14 CRÊPES | **WHEAT-FREE**

Use plain, unsweetened soy milk to prevent sticking. I use 1½ cups soy milk to first mix batter. After cooking half of the batter, the flax meal and flour continue to absorb liquid, so I add another 1–2 tbsp soy milk to thin the batter.

If using fruit that turns brown when cut, such as bananas, apples, or pears, toss with fresh lemon or orange juice to prevent discoloration. Orange juice may be preferable for little ones since it is sweeter.

As an alternative to slicing the fruit, purée it all in a blender or food processor, adding maple syrup or agave nectar to sweeten if desired. Then roll the crêpes and pour the fruit sauce over top.

To use these crêpes for savory fillings, omit vanilla extract and add 2–3 pinches salt. Dried seasonings or herbs can also be added to the batter.

BATTER:

1½ tbsp	**flax meal**
1½ cups + 1–3 tbsp	**plain soy milk** (see note)
½ tsp	**pure vanilla extract**
3 tbsp	**canola oil**
1 cup	**spelt flour**
⅛ tsp	**sea salt**
½–1 tsp	**canola oil** (for coating pan)

FRUIT FILLING:

1–2 cups	**fresh fruit of choice** (e.g, strawberries, blueberries, bananas, mangoes), thinly sliced or chopped in small pieces (see note)

TOPPING:

1 batch	**Celestial Cream** (opposite page)

In a bowl, add flax meal. Whisk in 1½ cups soy milk (see note). Add vanilla and 3 tbsp canola oil and whisk again to combine. In another large bowl, combine flour and salt and stir to combine. Then, add wet mixture to dry and whisk to fully combine. Lightly oil a non-stick frying pan and heat on medium-high for a few minutes until hot. Reduce heat to medium and let it rest for a minute. Scoop ¼ cup of batter onto pan and immediately lift pan away from heat to tilt pan back and forth, spreading out batter into a circle (5–6-in/12–15-cm diameter). Return pan to heat. Cook for a couple of minutes until crêpe is dry on top and you can easily lift it with a wide spatula. If it is still sticky and difficult to lift, it needs more time to cook, another 30 seconds or so. With a wide spatula, carefully lift and flip crêpe, and cook for about 1 minute. Remove, place on a plate, and repeat until the batter is all used. To serve, fill half of each crêpe with fruit, then fold over. Spoon on the Celestial Cream, and enjoy!

You know that glorious taste of pancakes with a pat of butter melting under a pool of pure maple syrup? This recipe replicates that luscious butter and syrup pairing with a cream topping that is heavenly on the Breakfast Crêpes (opposite page) or other pancakes. But don't stop there—it works equally well as a sauce for pies, cakes, and other desserts. And, as an added bonus, it is ridiculously simple to make!

Celestial **Cream**

MAKES 4–6 SERVINGS (2¼–2⅓ CUPS) | **WHEAT-FREE**

½–¾ cup	**pure maple syrup** (see note)
½ cup	**Earth Balance Buttery Spread** (or other non-hydrogenated vegan margarine)
1–1½ tsp	**pure vanilla extract**
12 oz	**(340 g) silken firm tofu**
¼ tsp	(little scant) **sea salt**

In a saucepan on low heat, combine syrup and margarine, and stir until margarine melts. Add vanilla, silken tofu, and salt, and with a hand blender or in a blender, purée until very smooth. Taste, and stir in additional maple syrup if desired.

When using this recipe as a dessert topping, I prefer to use the full ¾ cup maple syrup. However, for crêpes, I use ½–⅔ cup maple syrup so the sauce is not as sweet. You can also reduce the margarine if desired, to ⅓ cup (or less, but taste and texture will not be as rich).

No need to deny yourself chocolate with these muffins. Cocoa contains healthy antioxidants, and paired with wholesome flours, banana, and flax meal, these muffins are delightful and good for you.

Cocoa Banana Muffins

MAKES 8–12 MUFFINS | **WHEAT-FREE**

½ cup + 2 tbsp	plain or vanilla non-dairy milk
2 tbsp	flax meal
1 cup	barley flour
1 cup	oat flour (or ground oats)
¼ cup	unrefined sugar
¼ tsp	sea salt
½ tsp	nutmeg
¼ tsp	cinnamon (optional)
¼ cup	cocoa powder
2 tsp	baking powder
¾ tsp	baking soda
1 cup	banana, mashed (about 2½ medium bananas)
¼ cup	pure maple syrup
1½ tsp	pure vanilla extract
2 tbsp	canola oil

Preheat oven to 375°F (190°C). In a bowl, combine milk and flax meal. Stir, then set aside. In a separate large bowl, combine flours, sugar, salt, nutmeg, cinnamon, and sift in cocoa powder, baking powder, and baking soda. Stir until well combined. In flax meal/milk mixture, add banana, syrup, vanilla, and oil, stirring until well combined. Add wet mixture to dry, gently folding until combined. Fit a muffin pan with muffin liners. Spoon mixture into liners. Bake for 23–26 minutes, until a toothpick inserted in center comes out clean.

The hazelnut-pear combination in these pancakes is unique and memorable, and worth keeping a small jar of hazelnut butter in your fridge. Serve with pure maple syrup.

Hazelnut-Pear **Pancakes**

MAKES 10–13 MEDIUM–LARGE PANCAKES | **WHEAT-FREE**

1⅛ cup	spelt flour
2½ tsp	baking powder
½ tsp	freshly grated nutmeg
⅛ tsp	sea salt
¼ cup	hazelnut butter
1½ cup	vanilla non-dairy milk
1 tsp	canola oil
1	**ripe pear,** peeled, cut in half lengthwise, and sliced (about ¾–1 cup)
	canola oil (for coating pan)
½ cup	**crushed hazelnuts,** skins removed (for garnish)

In a large bowl, add flour and sift in baking powder. Add nutmeg and salt and stir to combine well. In a separate bowl, mix hazelnut butter with 3 tbsp non-dairy milk. Continually stir as you slowly add remainder of milk. Once mixture is smooth, stir in 1 tsp oil. Add wet mixture to dry, stirring until well combined. Gently fold in pears. Lightly oil a non-stick frying pan (using edge of paper towel) and place on medium-high heat for a few minutes until hot, then reduce heat to medium/medium-low and let it rest for a minute. Using a ladle, scoop batter into pan to form pancakes. Allow pancakes to cook for several minutes, until small bubbles form on the outer edge and into center. Flip pancakes to lightly brown other side, for 1–2 minutes. Repeat until batter is all used. Sprinkle with hazelnuts.

This recipe uses less oil than many granola recipes, for a lighter breakfast. Plus, hemp seeds add extra protein to this already nutritious cereal. Serve with cold non-dairy milk of choice.

Hemp-anola

MAKES ABOUT 6½ CUPS | **WHEAT-FREE**

You may use whole almonds, chopped, or other chopped nuts such as pecans, walnuts, or hazelnuts (skins removed).

For a lower fat version, you can reduce oil to 3 tbsp.

If desired, store the larger clumps of this cereal in bags or small containers for snacking on the go.

2 cups	**barley flakes**
1 cup	**oat flakes** (rolled oats; may use quick oats)
1 cup	**hemp seed nuts** (I use Manitoba Harvest brand)
½ cup	**unsweetened shredded coconut**
½ cup	**almond shavings or slivers** (see note)
1 tsp	**cinnamon**
¼ tsp	**freshly grated nutmeg** (or ground cardamom)
¼ tsp + ⅛ tsp	**sea salt**
1 tsp	**pure vanilla extract**
½ tsp	**blackstrap molasses**
⅔ cup	**brown rice syrup**
¼ cup	**canola oil** (see note)
¾–1 cup	**raisins or chopped apricots** (or other dried fruit)

Preheat oven to 300°F (150°C). In a large bowl, combine barley and oat flakes, hemp seeds, coconut, almonds, cinnamon, nutmeg, and salt, and stir until well combined. In another bowl, mix vanilla and molasses to thin out, then stir in brown rice syrup and oil. Add wet mixture to dry, stirring to combine well. Line a large-rimmed baking sheet with parchment paper. Transfer to baking sheet and spread out evenly. Bake for 28–33 minutes, stirring occasionally to ensure granola browns evenly. Remove from oven, stir in dried fruit, and let cool completely.

These cornmeal muffins combine puréed and whole corn kernels for a batter that's moist and not too crumbly. Since they aren't particularly sweet, these muffins are perfect to pair with a savory stew. Spread with non-hydrogenated margarine and serve with a savory dish like Sweet Potato Lentil Chili (page 101), or spread with jam or Traditional Cranberry Sauce (page 89) to enjoy as a sweeter treat.

Kinda Corny Muffins

MAKES 8–10 MUFFINS | **WHEAT-FREE**

1 tbsp	**flax meal**
1 cup	**plain soy milk**
1 cup	**frozen corn kernels**
3 tbsp	**unsweetened applesauce**
2½–3 tbsp	**canola oil** (or light olive oil)
1 cup	**cornmeal** (fine grain, not corn grits)
1 cup	**spelt flour**
3 tbsp	**unrefined sugar**
¼ tsp + ⅛ tsp	**sea salt**
¼ tsp	**ground turmeric** (for color, optional)
2 tsp	**baking powder**
¼ tsp	**baking soda**

To make these muffins a little sweeter without extra sugar, add 1 tsp cinnamon. For a savory twist, add a few dashes of chili powder or cumin, or a few pinches of chopped rosemary.

Preheat oven to 375°F (190°C). Using a mini-food processor or hand blender, combine flax meal, soy milk, and ½ cup corn kernels and purée until smooth. Transfer to a bowl and stir in remaining corn kernels, applesauce, and oil. In a separate large bowl, combine remaining ingredients, sift in baking powder and baking soda, and stir until well combined. Add wet mixture to dry, gently folding until just combined. Fit a muffin pan with muffin liners. Spoon batter into liners. Bake for 22–25 minutes, until a toothpick inserted in center comes out clean.

These are absolutely the simplest pancakes you can make! All you need is a tube of prepared polenta. We sometimes call these "baby pancakes" in our house, because they are so playfully small. Serve drizzled with maple syrup or Warm Raspberry Syrup (page 39) and topped with chopped nuts and fresh fruit, if desired.

Polenta **Pancakes**

MAKES 3–4 SERVINGS | **WHEAT-FREE**

Packaged polenta has a smooth outer coating that I like to trim off with a vegetable peeler.

You may substitute with polenta made from scratch, cutting the cooled, set polenta into thin slices or squares.

1 tube	**(18 oz/510 g) prepared polenta** (plain, not seasoned), "peeled" (see note)
1½–2 tbsp	**cinnamon**
1½–2 tbsp	**unrefined sugar**
3–4 tsp	**canola oil**
1	**medium–large banana,** sliced in thin rounds (optional)

After peeling the polenta, slice into thin "mini-pancakes," about ¼-in (5-mm) thick (to make 26–30 pancakes). On a large plate, mix 1½ tbsp cinnamon and 1½ tbsp sugar. Coat both sides of each pancake in cinnamon-sugar mixture. Repeat until finished, using more sugar and/or cinnamon if needed. In a non-stick frying pan on medium-high, heat 1½–2 tsp oil. Place pancakes on pan (you will probably need to cook in 2 batches, using remaining oil for second batch). Cook first side for 4–5 minutes, then flip to cook for another 2–3 minutes. To serve as "sandwiches," place 4 pancakes on each plate, top each with a banana slice, then sandwich with another pancake. Otherwise, simply serve 8–10 pancakes on each plate.

Raspberries and chocolate are a sublime combination, and with this simple recipe you can enjoy them in the morning, or anytime of day. With your ingredients, bowl, and spoon at hand, you'll be sinking your teeth into a tender, delicious hot scone in just about a half-hour!

Raspberry Chocolate Chip Scones

MAKES 6 SCONES | **WHEAT-FREE**

1 cup	spelt flour
1 cup	oat flour (see note)
¼ cup	unrefined sugar
½ tsp	(scant) sea salt
2 tsp	baking powder
½ tsp	baking soda
¼ cup	canola oil
¼ cup	non-dairy chocolate chips
¼ cup	vanilla or berry flavor soy yogurt
2½–4 tbsp	vanilla or plain soy milk (see note)
1 tsp	pure vanilla extract
⅔ cup	frozen raspberries (keep in freezer until ready to use)
1–2 tsp	spelt flour (for dusting counter)
1–2 tsp	soy yogurt or soy milk (for brushing scones)
1–2 tsp	unrefined sugar (for garnish)

Preheat oven to 375°F (190°C). In a large bowl, combine flours, ¼ cup sugar, and salt. Sift in baking powder and baking soda, and stir until well combined. Add oil, and mix with a spoon or your hands until crumbly, then stir in chocolate chips. In a separate bowl, combine soy yogurt, soy milk, and vanilla and whisk to incorporate yogurt. Add wet mixture to dry, then remove raspberries from freezer and immediately add to mixture. Stir until dough is thick and sticky (try not to break up raspberries, and work swiftly so they don't thaw much). On a lightly floured counter, turn out dough and shape into a circle about 7-in (18-cm) diameter and ¾-in (12-cm) thick. Cut circle into 6 wedges. Line a baking sheet with parchment paper. Use a spatula to transfer wedges to baking sheet, spacing scones. Lightly brush tops of scones with soy yogurt or milk, and sprinkle with sugar if desired. Bake for 19–22 minutes, until tops are lightly golden and scones are firm to touch. Remove and transfer to a cooling rack.

You can use extra spelt flour in place of the oat flour if you prefer, though I do like the nutty, sweet flavor that the oat flour lends these scones.

I use 2½–3 tbsp soy milk in this recipe, but depending on the brand of spelt flour you may need a little more. If batter is thick and dry, add an extra tbsp milk. If making the date and walnut version (see below), you'll likely need 4 tbsp soy milk since the raspberries add extra moisture.

My children love to dip these scones in Warm Raspberry Sauce (page 39) for a double dose of raspberry delight! Or, pair with Celestial Cream (page 29).

Another delicious version of this scone uses dates and walnuts: Replace chocolate chips and raspberries with ½ cup chopped dates and ½ cup crushed or lightly chopped walnuts, adding them after mixing in canola oil. Also add ¼–½ tsp ground cardamom, cinnamon, or nutmeg (or combination) to the dry mixture. You will likely need the full 4 tbsp soy milk.

These pancakes are thick and fluffy and bring the taste of summer to your table any month of the year. Fresh, fragrant, and delightful! Serve with Celestial Cream (page 29) or pure maple syrup.

Raspberry Cornmeal Pancakes

MAKES 9–10 MEDIUM PANCAKES | **WHEAT-FREE**

These are not completely gluten-free pancakes—while some gluten-sensitive people can eat oats, others cannot. To make these pancakes truly gluten free, substitute oat flour with ⅓ cup white or brown rice flour, or ⅓ cup amaranth flour, and add 2 tbsp tapioca starch flour to dry mixture (you will likely need the full 1 cup + 2 tbsp milk).

This small amount of almond extract gives a very slight cherry-like flavor, which works well with the raspberries. If you don't have almond extract, you can certainly make these pancakes without it.

If using frozen raspberries, the pancakes will take longer to cook (use a lower heat if they are taking a while to set).

1 tbsp	**flax meal**
1 cup + 1–2 tbsp	**vanilla non-dairy milk** (see note)
¾ cup + 2 tbsp	**oat flour** (see note)
½ cup	**fine cornmeal**
⅛ tsp	**sea salt**
1 tbsp	**baking powder**
⅛ – ¼ tsp	**pure almond extract** (see note)
1½ tbsp	**canola oil**
1 cup	**raspberries,** fresh or frozen (see note)
	canola oil (for coating pan)

In a small bowl, combine flax meal and non-dairy milk, then set aside. In a large bowl, combine flour, cornmeal, and salt. Sift in baking powder and stir to combine well. To flax-milk mixture, add almond extract and oil and stir to combine. Add wet mixture to dry, stirring until just combined. Stir in raspberries just before you are ready to cook the pancakes. Lightly oil a non-stick frying pan (using the edge of a paper towel) and place pan on medium-high heat for a few minutes until hot, then reduce heat to medium/medium-low and let it rest for a minute. Using a ladle, scoop batter into pan to form pancakes. Cook for several minutes, until small bubbles form on the outer edge and into the center. Flip and cook other side for 2–3 minutes, until golden. Repeat until batter is all used.

This savory casserole makes a sensational brunch dish. It's easy, and can be made in advance by baking the potatoes ahead of time or preparing the entire casserole the day before. Pair it with salad or steamed veggies and another side dish to make an incredible dinner meal as well. Try serving it with Guacamole con Alga Marina (page 61) or Traditional Cranberry Sauce (page 89).

Tempeh Hashbrown **Casserole**

MAKES 5–7 SERVINGS | **WHEAT-FREE**

2 lb	**(1 kg) red or Yukon Gold Potatoes** (about 7–9 small–medium potatoes), skins on
6–8 oz	**(170–230 g) tempeh,** chopped (see note)
½ tbsp	**tamari**
1½–2 tbsp	**apple cider vinegar**
½ tsp	**sea salt**
1 cup	**green onions** (white and green portions), sliced
½ tsp	**fresh rosemary,** chopped (or 1 tsp fresh thyme, chopped)
¼–½ tsp	**paprika**
2 tbsp	**olive oil**
	canola oil (for coating pan)
1 tbsp	**olive oil**
	fresh parsley, chopped (for garnish)

Preheat oven to 400°F (205°C). With a sharp knife or skewer, pierce potatoes a few times and place in oven. Bake for 45–60 minutes, until tender when pierced. While potatoes are baking, chop tempeh (or pulse briefly in a food processor). In a bowl, add tempeh and toss with tamari and vinegar, then set aside to marinate. Remove potatoes from oven when done, then increase oven temperature to 425°F (220°C). Once potatoes are cool enough to handle, cut into chunks, place in a large bowl, and mash a little, keeping some chunks. Add tempeh, salt, green onions, rosemary, paprika, and 2 tbsp olive oil and toss. Lightly oil an 8x12-in (20x30-cm) baking dish. Transfer mixture to baking dish and press down evenly with a spatula. Drizzle 1 tbsp olive oil on top of casserole and spread with a spatula. Bake for 18–20 minutes. Remove, sprinkle with parsley, and serve.

In this recipe, I prefer to use Green Cuisine's tempeh burgers, which are premarinated and precooked. If you want to use standard frozen tempeh, simmer it in broth to draw out any bitterness. To do so, slice frozen tempeh and simmer for 15–20 minutes in 2 cups vegetable broth and a bay leaf. Then remove, drain, and chop for recipe, increasing the tamari to 1 tbsp and using the full 2 tbsp vinegar for the marinade. (The Green Cuisine tempeh burgers do not have any bitterness, which is one of the reasons I love to use them.)

Tomatoes and basil add freshness to this quesadilla, while the bean spread (instead of cheese) helps to hold the layers together. This savory breakfast quesadilla also makes a marvelous lunch or mighty fine party nibblers! Serve on its own or paired with Smoky Avocado Sauce (page 87), Guacamole con Alga Marina (page 61), a splash of oil and vinegar, or a dollop of non-dairy sour cream.

Tomato Basil Breakfast **Quesadilla**

MAKES 1–2 SERVINGS.

Be sure to buy tortillas that do not contain hydrogenated oils. Look for whole-wheat tortillas or seasoned varieties.

You can use other bean spreads or hummus of choice. I really like the Roasted Red Pepper Almond Hummus in this quesadilla, but White Bean Spread (page 115) and White Bean Hummus with Fresh Thyme & Basil (page 53), for example, are also very nice.

Tempeh bacon adds a smoky flavor, and additional protein and substance. If you don't have tempeh bacon, use thinly sliced pieces of smoked or seasoned tofu (about $^1/_8$–$^1/_4$ cup), or leave the quesadilla as is with the bean spread, tomatoes, and basil—still delicious.

2	**(10-in/25-cm) whole wheat tortillas** (or other tortillas of choice)
⅓ cup	**Roasted Red Pepper & Almond Hummus** (page 52) (see note)
½ cup	**tomato,** thinly sliced, lightly blotted with towel (about 1 medium tomato)
2–3 pinches	**sea salt**
2–3 pinches	**freshly ground black pepper**
6–10	**large basil leaves** (more for smaller ones)
2 strips	**cooked Lightlife tempeh bacon,** crumbled or chopped (see note)
1 tsp	**olive oil** (for coating pan)

With a spatula or spreading knife, evenly spread hummus on each tortilla. On one tortilla, place tomatoes on hummus and sprinkle with salt and pepper. Place basil over tomatoes and evenly distribute tempeh bacon on top. Cover with other tortilla (hummus side down), lining up edges as evenly as possible. In a non-stick frying pan on medium-high, heat oil, tilting pan to coat. Place quesadilla on pan and cook for about 3 minutes, until lightly browned. With a wide spatula, flip and cook for 2–3 minutes, until lightly browned. (For perfect quesadillas, tortillas should be crisp, and tomatoes and basil warmed, but not cooked). Transfer to a rack (so the underside doesn't soften) to cool slightly, then transfer to a plate and cut into wedges. Serve warm.

This warm, slightly tart syrup is a delightful alternative to pure maple syrup for pancakes, crêpes, and waffles, or as a dessert sauce for pies, cakes, and ice cream.

Warm Raspberry Sauce

MAKES 1 CUP (3–4 SERVINGS) | **WHEAT-FREE**

¼ cup	**pure berry juice** (may use apple or other juice)
2 tsp	**arrowroot powder**
1 cup	**frozen or fresh raspberries** (see note)
¼–⅓ cup	**agave nectar**
⅛ tsp	**sea salt**

In a bowl, whisk together juice and arrowroot until fully mixed. In a saucepan over medium heat, combine the juice-arrowroot mixture, raspberries, ¼ cup agave nectar (adding more to sweeten taste, if desired), and salt and let cook a few minutes until raspberries dissolve. Increase heat to bring mixture to a boil for about 30 seconds. Remove from heat and cool just enough to serve.

Other berries can be substituted for the raspberries, including strawberries, blackberries, or a blend of these with some blueberries. Adjust sweetener as desired.

This syrup can also be enjoyed cooled, and makes a fabulous, not-too-sweet raspberry jam. My daughter loves a PB&J sandwich with this sauce, since it oozes out of her sandwich and she can dip it … because all kids love to dip their foods!

It's summer, bananas are overripe, and you have a bounty of zucchini: What to do? Whip up a batch or two of these delicious, lightly sweet muffins for guests! (Oh, and don't let the über-healthy name discourage you— these are tender, moist, and marvelous muffins.)

Zucchini Spelt **Muffins**

MAKES 9–12 MUFFINS | **WHEAT-FREE**

If you don't have overripe bananas, unsweetened applesauce is a great substitute. Applesauce is less sweet than bananas, so you may want to add extra cinnamon and/or another tbsp sugar.

Yellow squash is a good substitute if children do not like the green flecks of zucchini.

Add 1/3 cup walnuts or pecans to this mixture for a delicious crunch, or some raisins for a chewy bite.

2 tbsp	flax meal
½ cup + 2 tbsp	plain or vanilla non-dairy milk
1 cup	overripe banana (see note)
1 cup	zucchini (or yellow squash) (see note)
¼ cup	maple syrup
1 tsp	pure vanilla extract
3 tbsp	canola oil
2 cups	spelt flour
¼ cup	unrefined sugar
¼ tsp	sea salt
½–¾ tsp	cinnamon
½ tsp	nutmeg
2½ tsp	baking powder
½ tsp	baking soda

Preheat oven to 375°F (190°C). In a bowl, combine flax meal and non-dairy milk and set aside. Mash bananas and grate zucchini, and combine with the milk-flax meal mixture. Add syrup, vanilla, and oil and stir to combine. In a separate large bowl, combine remaining dry ingredients, sift in baking powder and baking soda, and stir until well combined. Add wet mixture to dry, gently folding until just combined (do not overmix). Fit a muffin pan with muffin liners. Spoon batter into liners. Bake for 21–25 minutes, until a toothpick inserted in center comes out clean.

Hummus, Hummus . . .

and More Hummus

MY HOME IS "the house of hummus"; at any given time, you can find a couple varieties of this Middle Eastern dip in my fridge. My kids devour it with tortilla chips or straight off a spoon! For a long while, the Creamy Hummus, found in *Vive le Vegan!*, was the one I made most often at home. This mild, traditional version won over my family (and many of you) with its delicate taste and a hint of toasted sesame oil. But, it was time to mix things up, and soon I had more ideas than I could test! This section includes my favorite flavor combinations that will appeal to every palate: Olive & Sun-Dried Tomato Hummus (page 50) for olive lovers; Kids' Dynamo Hummus (page 49), boosted with raw cashews, nutritional yeast, and flax oil; White Bean Hummus with Fresh Thyme & Basil (page 53), one of my personal favorites; and exotic twists like Curry Chickpea Hummus with Pappadums (page 48), and Peanut Sesame Hummus (page 51).

Surely, with these varieties you will not tire of hummus anytime soon! And remember, hummus is not just for dipping. Try it as a base for pizzas, instead of tomato sauce, using either a traditional pizza crust or a flour tortilla, and choose toppings that will complement the flavors in your hummus. Some ideas for using hummus for pizzas include:

- Peanut Sesame Hummus: Choose Asian-inspired toppings, such as sliced snow peas, sliced red bell peppers, and/or diced pineapple. Bake, then top with mung bean sprouts and peanuts when done.

- Chipotle Lime Two-Bean Hummus: Top pizza with sliced green or red bell peppers, sun-dried tomatoes, and/or corn kernels. Sprinkle cooked pizza with chopped fresh cilantro leaves and julienned jicama.

- Kids' Dynamo Hummus: Choose vegetables that your kids like, perhaps sliced zucchini, corn kernels, and/or green peas (warmed in boiled water and then drained and patted dry). Sprinkle with grated vegan cheese and bake.

- Olive and Sun-Dried Tomato Hummus: Top with fresh sliced tomatoes, marinated artichokes, spinach, and/or sliced green onions. Garnish cooked pizza with chopped fresh herbs such as basil or parsley.

Hummus can also be incorporated into wraps and sandwiches. For dinner parties, it can be served elegantly, piped into mini-bell peppers, grape tomatoes, or endive leaves, or served with artisan crackers and breads.

Enough talk, now get out your food processor!

This is one of those recipes that you taste and before you know it, you've eaten half the batch! The black beans and orange are an irresistible combination of flavors. Serve cool, alongside veggies, crackers, or flatbreads, or warm with a selection of breads or as a sandwich spread. Also, don't forget to try this hummus on a pizza crust (or toasted flour tortilla).

Black Bean & Orange Hummus

MAKES 6–7 SERVINGS (ABOUT 2¼ CUPS). | **WHEAT-FREE**

Before juicing oranges, zest to collect the rind. I find a kitchen rasp (also called a microplane grater) is the best tool for zesting citrus.

2½ cups	**cooked black beans**
¼ cup	**freshly squeezed orange juice** (see note)
2½ tbsp	**almond butter**
1	**large clove garlic,** sliced
1 tbsp	**extra virgin olive oil**
3 tbsp	**red wine vinegar**
¾ tsp	**sea salt**
½ tsp	**ground cumin**
1 tsp	**ground coriander**
¼ cup	**fresh parsley**
1 tsp	**orange zest,** grated (see note)
	freshly ground black pepper to taste
1–2 tbsp	**fresh parsley,** chopped (for garnish)

In a food processor, combine all ingredients (except parsley for garnish) and purée until smooth, scraping down sides of bowl several times. Transfer to a serving bowl and garnish with parsley.

Lime juice and zest give this dip a bold tangy element while the chipotle sauce adds a smoky, slightly spicy tone. The cilantro perfectly suits these flavors, but if you aren't partial to it you can leave it out. Serve with tortilla chips and fresh vegetables such as jicama sticks and sliced bell peppers.

Chipotle Lime Two-Bean Hummus

MAKES 5–6 SERVINGS (ABOUT 2 CUPS). | **WHEAT-FREE**

1 cup	**cooked kidney beans**
1 cup	**cooked chickpeas (garbanzo beans)**
4–4½ tbsp	**freshly squeezed lime juice** (see note)
1½–2 tbsp	**tahini**
1	**medium clove garlic,** sliced (see note)
2–2½ tbsp	**extra virgin olive oil**
½ tsp	**sea salt**
1½ tsp	**chipotle hot sauce** (I use Tabasco)
1 tsp	**agave nectar**
¹⁄₁₆–¹⁄₈ tsp	**allspice**
1–2 tbsp	**water** (to thin dip as desired)
1 tsp	**lime zest,** grated (see note)
¼ cup	(not packed) **fresh cilantro leaves**

In a food processor, combine all ingredients except water, lime zest, and cilantro. Purée until smooth, gradually adding water as desired to thin dip and scraping down sides of bowl as needed. Add lime zest and cilantro and purée briefly to incorporate cilantro.

I prefer this dip with just a hint of garlic, so I use a very small clove. If you are a garlic lover, feel free to use more.

Before juicing limes, zest one or two to collect about 1 tsp of the rind; be careful to avoid the bitter white pith. I find a kitchen rasp (also called a microplane grater) is the best tool for zesting citrus.

For a burrito filling: Spread this hummus onto whole-wheat (or your favorite) tortillas and top with sautéed veggies seasoned with cumin, chili powder, or other seasonings. Roll, bake until golden, and enjoy!

This hummus is terrific served with pappadums—Indian lentil-based crackers. If pappadums are not available, you can substitute pita breads. Also, fresh bite-sized veggies like broccoli florets, strips of bell pepper, and cherry tomatoes are great accompaniments; consider including Cucumber Mint Raita (page 79) and chutney for more of an Indian flavor experience.

Curry Chickpea **Hummus** with Pappadums

MAKES 5–6 SERVINGS (ABOUT 2 CUPS) | **WHEAT-FREE**

One tsp curry powder imparts a mild curry taste that doesn't over-power the other flavors in the dip. Use more curry powder if you like it stronger.

I love the Taj Mahal brand (by Everland Natural Foods) of tamarind or mango chutney. It's delicious, and made with all-natural ingredients.

2 cups	**cooked chickpeas (garbanzo beans)**
2–2½ tbsp	**freshly squeezed lemon juice**
2 tbsp	**cashew butter**
1	**medium clove garlic** (or to taste), sliced
2 tbsp	**extra virgin olive oil**
1 tsp	**curry powder** (see note)
½ tsp	**sea salt**
⅛ tsp	**ground turmeric**
¼ tsp	**agave nectar**
	freshly ground black pepper to taste
4–5 tbsp	**water** (to thin dip as desired)
2–3 tbsp	**raisins or currants**
1 pkg	**pappadums** (I use Patak's 100-g/ 3½-oz plain pappadums)

In a food processor, combine all ingredients (starting with 2 tbsp lemon juice) except water, raisins or currants, and pappadums. Purée until smooth, gradually adding water as desired to thin dip and scraping down sides of bowl as needed. Once smooth, add raisins, and purée briefly to lightly incorporate raisins. Season with salt and additional pepper and/ or lemon juice if desired. Cook pappadums according to package directions, and serve with dip.

Hemp-anola (page 32) with
Açai Antioxidant Smoothie (page 219)

Raspberry Cornmeal Pancakes (page 36)
with Celestial Cream (page 29)

White Bean Hummus with Fresh Thyme & Basil
(page 53) and Peanut Sesame Hummus (page 51)

Creamy Cashew Dip (page 60), Cinnamon Sweet Tortilla Strips (page 59),
Tamari-Roasted Chickpeas (page 68), fresh fruit, and Softly Spiced Nuts (page 67)

Kids love this very mellow hummus, and you will love giving it to them because it is chock-full of nutritious ingredients like cashews, chickpeas, tahini, and flax oil! Serve with breads, tortilla chips, or raw veggies, or as a spread in sandwiches.

Kids' Dynamo Hummus

MAKES 5–6 SERVINGS (ABOUT 2–2¼ CUPS). | **WHEAT-FREE**

¾ cup	raw cashews
3–3½ tbsp	freshly squeezed lemon juice
1½ cups	cooked chickpeas (garbanzo beans)
1	very small clove garlic (or larger clove if making for adults)
1 tbsp	tahini
1 tbsp	extra virgin olive oil
1½–2 tbsp	flax oil (see note)
½ tsp	sea salt
2 tbsp	nutritional yeast
5–6 tbsp	water (to thin dip as desired)

In a food processor, combine cashews with 3 tbsp lemon juice and purée until almost smooth. Add remaining ingredients except water and purée again until smooth, gradually adding water as desired to thin dip and scraping down sides of bowl as needed. Season to taste with additional salt, remaining lemon juice, and/or nutritional yeast.

In my experience, some brands of flax oil are better than others. Select a flax oil that has a clean, almost sweet flavor with no bitter aftertaste, and be sure to keep it refrigerated. One of my favorite brands is Spectrum. Also, you can substitute more olive oil in place of the flax oil if you prefer.

For even more omega-3's, add 1–2 tbsp flax meal (ground flax seeds). I purchase flax meal that is refrigerated in-store and keep it in my freezer at home because flax meal can go rancid quickly.

Add some vitamin power and vibrant color to this hummus: Add 1–2 handfuls fresh spinach and/or green peas and purée until smooth for a "Dinosaur Hummus." Or, add a little grated beet or 2–3 tbsp fresh beet juice for a "Radical Pink Hummus." Or, add cooked sweet potato, carrots, or dark winter squash for a "Halloween Hummus."

This is my husband's favorite hummus. He says, "Normally I'll eat a little, but with this stuff, I eat the entire batch!"

Olive & Sun-Dried Tomato **Hummus**

MAKES 5–6 SERVINGS (ABOUT 2¼ CUPS). | **WHEAT-FREE**

Garlic can easily overpower the flavor of hummus. If you love raw garlic use a medium or large clove; for a more delicate garlic flavor, use a small clove.

Try to purchase olives that are already pitted, as it will save you time and patience. Most grocery delis have a variety of pitted olives.

2 cups	cooked chickpeas (garbanzo beans)
3–3½ tbsp	freshly squeezed lemon juice
1 tbsp	tahini
2 tbsp	extra virgin olive oil
1	medium clove garlic, sliced (see note)
½ tsp	sea salt
	freshly ground black pepper to taste
3–5 tbsp	water (to thin dip as desired)
¼ cup	pitted Kalamata olives
¼ cup	pitted green olives
2 tbsp	sun-dried tomatoes (packed in oil), drained, patted dry, and sliced

In a food processor, combine chickpeas, 3 tbsp lemon juice, tahini, garlic, salt, pepper, and 1 tbsp water. Purée until smooth, gradually adding remaining water and lemon juice to thin dip as desired, scraping down sides of the bowl as needed. Once smooth, add olives and tomatoes, and purée briefly, keeping olives and tomatoes a little chunky. Season to taste with additional salt, pepper, and/or remaining lemon juice. Serve in a large bowl and drizzle with extra virgin olive oil.

This dip combines chickpeas with Asian-inspired ingredients like peanut butter, lime juice, ginger, and toasted sesame oil for a truly distinct and delicious take on hummus. Serve with raw snow peas, baby carrots, red bell pepper slices, endive leaves, fresh pineapple wedges, rice crackers, and/or tortilla chips.

Peanut Sesame Hummus

MAKES 4–5 SERVINGS (ABOUT 2 CUPS). | **WHEAT-FREE**

2 cups	cooked chickpeas (garbanzo beans)
¼ cup	freshly squeezed lime juice
3 tbsp	natural peanut butter
1 tbsp	extra virgin olive oil
1 tbsp	toasted sesame oil
1	medium clove garlic, sliced
1–1½ tsp	fresh ginger, peeled and chopped (see note)
1 tsp	tamari
½ tsp	agave nectar
½ tsp	sea salt
⅛ tsp	crushed red pepper flakes (see note)
1–3 tbsp	water (to thin dip as desired)
3 tbsp	raw or roasted peanuts, chopped or crushed (for garnish)
	toasted sesame oil (for finishing)
	fresh parsley or cilantro leaves, chopped (for garnish)

If you like the heat, add more red pepper flakes to taste.

Fresh ginger will impart flavor and also "heat" the hummus, so adjust measurement to your preference.

In a food processor, combine chickpeas, lime juice, peanut butter, olive oil, 1 tbsp sesame oil, garlic, ginger, tamari, agave nectar, salt, and red pepper flakes. Purée until smooth, gradually adding water as desired to thin dip and scraping down sides of bowl as needed. Serve in a large bowl, sprinkle with peanuts, a few dashes of toasted sesame oil, and parsley or cilantro.

This variation will taste different from any roasted red pepper hummus you may have tried. The almonds add a mellow, rich flavor and a denser texture.

Roasted Red Pepper & Almond Hummus

MAKES 6–7 SERVINGS (ABOUT 2½ CUPS). | **WHEAT-FREE**

This hummus makes a dynamite sandwich spread, and if you make it quite thick, it will help to hold the veggies between the slices of bread.

Try this hummus as a base on pizza, using a regular pizza crust or a tortilla lightly baked for an ultra-thin pizza crust.

½ cup	**raw almonds** (with skins on)
2 tbsp	**red wine vinegar**
2–2½ tbsp	**extra virgin olive oil**
2 cups	**cooked chickpeas (garbanzo beans)**
½ cup	**roasted red peppers** (from jar), excess liquid drained or patted off
1	**medium clove garlic** (or to taste), sliced
½ tsp	**Dijon mustard**
½ tsp	**sea salt**
	freshly ground black pepper to taste
2–4 tbsp	**water** (to thin dip as desired)
¼–⅓ cup	**fresh parsley,** chopped **(for garnish)**
1–2 tbsp	**almonds,** chopped (for garnish)

In a food processor, add ½ cup almonds and pulse until very fine. Add vinegar, oil, chickpeas, roasted red peppers, garlic, mustard, salt, and pepper. Purée until smooth, gradually adding water as desired to thin dip and scraping down sides of bowl several times. Once smooth, add parsley and purée briefly to lightly incorporate ingredients. Season with additional salt and pepper if desired. Serve in a large bowl, garnish with parsley and 1–2 tbsp almonds. Drizzle with additional oil to finish, if desired.

The fresh thyme and basil adds a bright color and vibrant taste to this hummus. The puréed cannellini beans are creamy white, which together with the green flecks from the fresh herbs make this pretty to look at, and scrumptious to eat!

White Bean **Hummus** with Fresh Thyme & Basil

MAKES 6–7 SERVINGS (ABOUT 2½ CUPS). | **WHEAT-FREE**

2 cups	cooked cannellini (white kidney) beans
1 tbsp	freshly squeezed lemon juice
2 tbsp	tahini
1	medium clove garlic (or to taste), sliced
1–2 tbsp	extra virgin olive oil (see note)
2 tbsp	red wine vinegar (see note)
½ tsp	Dijon mustard
½ tsp	sea salt
	freshly ground black pepper to taste
2–3 tbsp	water (to thin dip as desired)
2½–3 tsp	fresh thyme, chopped (not dried)
¼ cup	fresh basil, torn or chopped (not dried)

In a food processor, combine all ingredients except water, thyme, and basil. Purée until smooth, gradually adding water as desired to thin dip and scraping down sides of bowl as needed. Add thyme and basil and purée briefly to incorporate ingredients.

This dip tastes lovely even with just 1 tbsp extra virgin olive oil. For a richer flavor, use 2 tbsp extra virgin olive oil, or more.

I have used a raspberry-flavored red wine vinegar in place of the lemon juice in this dip, and it adds a beautiful flavor.

You can make this dip look very elegant. As described in the chapter introduction, pipe the dip into mini-bell peppers (cut in half), halved grape tomatoes, or endive leaves. Alternatively, spread it thinly on slices of bread with a layer of "shaved" cucumber (using a vegetable peeler to remove thin strips lengthwise off cucumber, before reaching the seedy portion). Cut crusts off bread and slice in strips or cut in shapes with cookie cutters.

Bits & Bites

Other Dips & Nibblers

AT YOUR NEXT PARTY, in addition to different kinds of hummus (see previous chapter), serve a selection of these dips and nibblers that will not disappoint. You can choose from a mix of savory dips like Artichoke Dip with Olive & Potato (page 58) or Warm & Cheesy White Bean Dip (page 69), which you can serve with Pizza Focaccia (page 63) or Simplest Garlic Bread (page 66). Creamy Cashew Dip (page 60) and Cinnamon Sweet Tortilla Strips (page 59) offers sweeter alternatives for your guests as well as day-to-day snacking. And don't forget to tempt your guests (and yourself) with several hot bites of Pan-Fried Tempt-eh! (page 62) finished with fresh lemon juice. These few finger foods can also be snacks that carry you through the day; Tamari-Roasted Chickpeas (page 68) and Softly Spiced Nuts (page 67) satiate midday cravings just perfectly.

Additionally, there are other recipes found elsewhere in this book you can prepare for party nibblers, including:

- Beats a BLT Sandwich! (page 109): use the avocado-tempeh mixture as an alternative to standard guacamole (see note in recipe).

- Veggie Tempeh Muffuletta (page 112): use the filling to stuff mini-pitas or serve on crackers.

- Peanut Butter Tortilla Turnovers (page 111): make these for kids at parties, using almond butter or other nut butters (if needed for peanut allergies); cut into small wedges.

- Cashew-Ginger Tofu (page 124) or Cumin Lime Tofu (page 126): for elegant finger food, simply cool tofu (and cut in smaller pieces if needed) and wrap in rice paper rolls with raw shredded veggies such as carrots and lettuce. Serve with a dipping sauce if you like.

- Moroccan-Infused Vegetable Phyllo Rolls (page 134) or Walnut, White Bean & Spinach Phyllo Rolls (page 150): instead of making large rolls, cut phyllo in strips and make small rolls or fold phyllo over filling in a triangular shape. Bake until golden (this requires less time for the smaller pockets). Serve the Moroccan rolls as an appetizer drizzled with Balsamic Maple Sauce (page 76) and serve the walnut rolls to dip in the Traditional Cranberry Sauce (page 89).

- Lemon-Broiled Green Beans (page 160), Rosemary Cornmeal Polenta Fries (page 164), and Seared Portobello Mushrooms (page 165) will also dazzle your guests.

This artichoke dip steps away from traditional recipes because it uses cooked potato—yes, potato—instead of cream cheese or mayonnaise to thicken the dip and add a creamy texture. The recipe also includes olives and fresh basil instead of the more traditional spinach. Serve hot with sliced breads or pita breads.

Artichoke **Dip** with Olive & Potato

MAKES 5–6 SERVINGS.

To cook the potatoes, I prefer to bake them whole, in advance. Compared to boiling, baked potatoes have more flavor and do not absorb any water. Plus, there is no fuss or clean up! I usually bake more potatoes than I need for a meal and refrigerate leftovers to use in this or other recipes.

WHEAT-FREE OPTION: Use kamut, spelt, or another wheat-free bread and process into crumbs using a food processor.

Before baking, the dip may appear somewhat loose, but it thickens as it cooks and will be just right for spreading on pitas or other breads.

½ cup	(packed) **cooked red or Yukon gold potatoes,** broken or chopped (see note)
2 tbsp	**freshly squeezed lemon juice**
1 tbsp	**apple cider vinegar**
1	**medium–large clove garlic** (to your taste), quartered
¾ tsp	**dry mustard**
¾ tsp	**sea salt**
2 tbsp	**nutritional yeast**
2–3 pinches	**freshly ground black pepper,** to taste
1 cup	**plain non-dairy milk** (soy milk is best for creamy, thick texture)
3–3½ tbsp	**olive oil**
3 tbsp	**fresh parsley leaves**
1 can	**(14-oz/398-ml) artichoke hearts**, drained, rinsed, and liquid lightly squeezed out
¼ cup	(packed) **fresh basil leaves**
¼–⅓ cup	**pitted Kalamata or black olives, or combination of both** (Kalamatas impart a stronger flavor)
½ cup	**breadcrumbs** (see note)
½ tbsp	**olive oil**
1–2 pinches	**sea salt,** to taste

Preheat oven to 375°F (190°C). In a food processor, combine potato, lemon juice, vinegar, garlic, mustard, ¾ tsp salt, nutritional yeast, and pepper, and briefly pulse. Add about ¼ cup milk and purée until very smooth. Then add remaining milk, 3–3½ tbsp oil, and parsley, and purée until smooth, scraping down sides of bowl as needed. Once dip is very smooth, add artichokes, basil, and olives, and pulse to lightly incorporate ingredients (retaining some chunky consistency). Transfer to a medium-sized baking dish (I use a round 24-oz/710-ml dish). In a small bowl, combine breadcrumbs, ½ tbsp oil, and salt, then sprinkle evenly over dip. Bake uncovered for 25–30 minutes. Remove from oven and let cool for 5 minutes before serving.

Do you have fond memories of cinnamon-sugar toast as a kid? I sure do, and this recipe brings those memories back with a new twist that kids and adults alike will love. Eat these sweet tortilla strips on their own, or dip in non-dairy yogurt, Creamy Cashew Dip (page 60), or Molassa-Sauce (page 111).

Cinnamon Sweet Tortilla Strips

MAKES 3–4 SERVINGS.

2	**(10-in/25-cm) whole wheat tortillas** (see note)
1–1 ½ tbsp	**canola oil**
3 tbsp	**unrefined sugar**
1½ tsp	**cinnamon**
1/16 tsp	**sea salt,** to taste

Preheat oven to 375°F (190°C). Line a baking sheet with parchment paper. Using a pastry brush, lightly coat both sides of tortillas with oil. Cut tortillas into 1–1¼-in thick strips. On a plate, combine sugar, cinnamon, and salt. Take each strip and press both sides into sugar mixture then place on baking sheet, ensuring they do not overlap. Sprinkle any remaining sugar mixture over strips, lightly pressing on. Bake for 4–5 minutes, then flip over and bake for an additional 4–5 minutes until strips are fragrant and just becoming crispy (be sure not to overcook). Lift the parchment paper with strips still on it and transfer to a rack to cool before serving.

I like to use whole wheat tortillas, but you can use plain white tortillas if you prefer. Be sure to choose a brand without hydrogenated oils.

Kids and adults will enjoy this slightly sweet dip. It can be used as a spread on bagels, muffins, or waffles in the morning, or as a dip for fresh sliced fruit (such as pineapple, melon, banana, apple, pear, or orange segments) at parties.

Creamy Cashew Dip

MAKES 3–4 SERVINGS (ABOUT 1⅛ CUPS). | **WHEAT-FREE**

I like to keep this dip on the thicker side, so I use ⅔ cup soy yogurt. Feel free to use more soy yogurt for a thinner dip or sauce.

The unsweetened applesauce gives a lovely tartness to the dip; if you prefer a sweeter (and thicker) dip, you can omit it.

If serving with fruits that oxidize (turn brown), like apples and pears, toss them in a little lemon juice diluted with water or in some orange juice.

Double the recipe to use as a topping for cakes and cupcakes; just omit the applesauce to thicken, and sweeten with soy yogurt or powdered sugar if desired.

½ cup	**cashew butter** (may substitute almond butter or peanut butter)
⅔ cup	**vanilla soy yogurt** (see note)
2–3 tbsp	**unsweetened applesauce** (see note)
2 tsp	**agave nectar**
⅛ tsp	**sea salt**
⅛ tsp	(rounded) **cinnamon**

In a blender or mini-food processor, combine all ingredients and purée until very smooth. (You can also mix by hand, whisking until very smooth, but using a processor is much faster and easier.)

Guacamole does not have to be complicated. In fact, it's one of the easiest, fastest—and most delicious—dips you can make. This basic recipe uses kelp granules to add a salty flavor along with extra nutrition. A visitor to my blog suggested the name for this recipe, which literally translates as "guacamole with seaweed." Serve with tortilla chips, Cocoa Coconut Chili (page 94), Gimme Chimis (page 128), Polenta Casserole (page 138), Tempeh Hashbrown Casserole (page 37), or Veggie Sizzle Burritos (page 149).

Guacamole con Alga Marina

MAKES 4–5 SERVINGS (ABOUT 1¼ CUPS). | **WHEAT-FREE**

1¾ cups	**avocado,** cut in chunks (about 2 medium-large avocados)
1–1½ tbsp	**freshly squeezed lemon juice** (or lime juice)
¼ tsp	**sea salt**
1 tsp	**kelp granules** (I use Maine Coast Sea Seasonings brand)

In a bowl, combine avocado, 1 tbsp lemon juice, salt, and kelp granules. Mash to desired consistency. Season to taste with additional salt and remaining lemon juice.

To jazz up this guacamole, incorporate ½ cup chopped fresh tomatoes, finely chopped green onions and garlic to taste, 1/3 cup finely chopped cilantro, and/or a few pinches of cumin.

Use the filling from Beats a BLT Sandwich! (page 109) for a smoky tempeh variation on this guacamole.

Since avocado oxidizes quickly, it's best to serve immediately. If you need to store it for an hour or more, put it in a very deep, narrow container and place plastic wrap directly on guacamole to cover (leaving no space between guacamole and plastic wrap). When you are ready to serve, simply use a spoon to scrape off and discard oxidized top layer.

This is so good, even my normally "tempeh averse" husband loves it. I originally created the recipe using tofu, which is an excellent variation. Either way, this Tempt-eh! is a little crispy, a little tender, and a whole lot delicious. This appetizer can also be served in an entrée with noodles or a whole grain.

Pan-Fried **Tempt-eh!**

MAKES 5–6 SERVINGS AS A SIDE DISH OR NIBBLER, OR 3–4 SERVINGS AS AN ENTRÉE. | **WHEAT-FREE**

I sometimes use the Green Cuisine brand of tempeh burgers in this recipe, which are thick patties of marinated tempeh that are sold refrigerated. If you use these burgers, you can skip the marinating step (although marinating them will infuse more flavor). If you use unmarinated, frozen tempeh, thaw it slightly before marinating.

You can substitute tempeh with tofu in this recipe: use 1 pkg (12-oz/350-g) fresh extra-firm tofu, cut into 1/4–1/2-in thick squares and press between paper towels to remove excess moisture, then marinate it as you would the tempeh (using 2 tbsp tamari).

If tempeh cools while nibbling, simply place in an oven preheated to 425–450°F (220–230°C) for several minutes until they are hot once again.

1½ tbsp	**rice vinegar** (may use apple cider vinegar)
1½ tbsp	**tamari**
1 pkg	**(8-oz/227-g) tempeh** (see note)
3–4 tbsp	**arrowroot powder** (may use cornstarch)
3 tbsp	**coconut or olive oil**
	lemon wedges (for serving)

In a large shallow dish, mix rice vinegar and tamari. On a cutting board, cut tempeh into about ½x3½-in (1x9-cm) slices. Add tempeh to vinegar-tamari mixture to marinate, turning slices to absorb marinade on both sides. If possible, allow tempeh to marinate for 20 minutes or more in the refrigerator.

In a large dish, spread arrowroot powder. Dip each tempeh slice in arrowroot, gently tapping to remove any clumps (some areas will have a thicker layer of arrowroot, this is okay). In a non-stick frying pan on high, heat oil. Add tempeh slices and fry on one side for 3–5 minutes until golden brown and crispy. Flip over and cook for 3–4 minutes until crispy, adding more oil if needed. Flip again if needed. Remove and serve immediately with a squeeze of lemon wedge or with a favorite dipping sauce … be sure to eat them while still hot (see note).

I'm not one for making my own bread, but I did find a way to mimic focaccia bread using a pre-made pizza shell. I know it's not exactly authentic, but it's darn tasty (not to mention quick) and healthier because of its whole wheat base.

Pizza **Focaccia**

MAKES 6–7 SERVINGS AS A NIBBLER, 4–5 AS A SIDE BREAD FOR A MEAL.

1	**(10-in/25-cm) whole wheat pizza shell**
1 tbsp	**extra virgin olive oil**
1¼–1½ tsp	**fresh rosemary,** chopped (see note)
⅓–¼ tsp	**sea salt,** to taste
	freshly ground black pepper to taste
½–1 tbsp	**extra virgin olive oil**
¼ cup	**fresh basil,** julienned (see note) or chopped (optional)

Fresh rosemary really gives this pizza a wonderful taste and aroma. If fresh rosemary is not available, you can substitute with ¾–1 tsp dried rosemary leaves, crushed between your fingers or lightly chopped.

Preheat oven to 425°F (220°C). Line a baking sheet with parchment paper. Using a pastry brush, spread 1 tbsp oil over top of pizza shell, then sprinkle on rosemary, salt, and pepper. Bake for 9–12 minutes, until edges are golden. (If using a frozen pizza shell, you will need to bake for another 3–5 minutes.) Remove from oven and drizzle ½–1 tbsp oil over the hot bread, then sprinkle on basil. Cut into slices or wedges.

This dip made entirely with raw ingredients will knock your socks off! The mix of nuts can be altered to taste (see notes), and the dip can be enjoyed any time of year for snacks, sandwiches, parties, or in entrées.

Rawesome Nut Dip

MAKES 1¾ CUPS. | **WHEAT-FREE**

You may change the proportions of nuts in this recipe or substitute with other nuts or seeds. Note that nuts differ in natural sweetness and bitterness: cashews, almonds, and pistachios have sweeter flavors, whereas walnuts and pine nuts have more savory and bitter tones. Since substitutions will affect the overall flavor, you may want to adjust lemon juice or salt to taste.

This dip has a slight "cheesy" taste, and is a good cheese replacement, such as a layer for lasagna, filling for ravioli, or sandwich spread. For a cheesier flavor, you can add 1–2 tbsp nutritional yeast, although nutritional yeast may not be considered "raw."

½ cup	**raw almonds** (see note)
½ cup	**raw pistachios**
¼ cup	**raw walnuts**
¼ cup	**raw pine nuts** (or more walnuts or other nuts, see note)
½ cup	**red or orange bell pepper,** chopped
3–3½ tbsp	**freshly squeezed lemon juice**
1	**very small clove garlic,** sliced (may use a larger clove if desired)
½ tsp	**sea salt**
	freshly ground black pepper to taste
4½–6 tbsp	**water** (or more to thin as desired)
½ cup	**fresh basil leaves**
1–1½ tsp	**fresh thyme leaves**

In a food processor, combine nuts, bell pepper, lemon juice (starting with 3 tbsp), garlic, salt, and pepper, and water (starting with 4½ tbsp), and purée until fairly smooth, scraping down sides of bowl several times. Add basil and thyme, and purée again until well combined and to desired smoothness. Add more lemon juice to taste and/or water to thin dip if desired.

This is the easiest, fastest artichoke spread you can possibly make—and it may also be the tastiest. The simplicity of artichokes, combined with fresh garlic, high-quality olive oil, and fresh herbs that are all roasted until they melt together—what's not to love? Serve with Pizza Focaccia (page 63), whole-grain breads or crackers, and a big ol' spoon!

Roasted Garlic Artichoke **Spread** with Fresh Oregano

MAKES 5–6 SERVINGS (ABOUT 2 CUPS). | **WHEAT-FREE**

2 cans	**(14-oz/398-ml each) artichoke hearts,** drained, rinsed, and water lightly squeezed out
10–11	**cloves garlic,** roughly chopped
3 tbsp	**fresh oregano,** chopped (see note)
¼–⅓ cup	**olive oil** (see note)
1 tbsp	**lemon juice**
½ tsp	**sea salt**
	freshly ground black pepper to taste
	lemon wedge (for serving)

If you don't have fresh oregano, use 1½–2 tsp dried oregano. You may also substitute with other fresh herbs, such as 1 tbsp fresh thyme or ¼ cup fresh basil or parsley (or combination of both), adding them about halfway through baking time.

If you want to lower the fat content in this recipe, reduce the oil to 3–4 tbsp.

Preheat oven to 400°F (205°C). Chop artichokes into small chunks and pieces. In a baking dish, combine artichokes with remaining ingredients (except lemon wedge) and mix until well combined. Cover with aluminum foil and bake for 45–50 minutes, stirring once or twice, until garlic is softened. Remove from oven and let cool a little before serving. Season to taste with additional salt and pepper if desired, and a squeeze of lemon.

This tasty garlic bread is a cinch to make. Just remember to slice the bread before freezing.

Simplest Garlic Bread

MAKES 2–4 SERVINGS (SEE NOTE).

This recipe is flexible. If serving more people, simply use more garlic, oil, and salt as needed.

WHEAT-FREE OPTION: Use kamut, spelt or other wheat-free bread.

4–5 slices	**bread (or small baguette**, sliced), frozen (see note)
1	**large clove garlic**
1½–2 tbsp	**olive oil or Earth Balance Buttery Spread**
3–4 pinches	**sea salt,** to taste
2–3 tsp	**nutritional yeast** (optional)

Preheat oven to 400°F (205°C). Line a baking sheet with parchment paper. Remove bread from freezer, and while still frozen, firmly rub garlic clove over one side of each slice so bread (which is rough and acts like a grater) is lightly coated with garlic juice and pulp. (If bread has softened and it is not easy to wear down garlic, place bread on a baking sheet and return it to the freezer for about 10 minutes.) Drizzle on oil, or spread on margarine, using as little or as much as you like. Sprinkle on salt and nutritional yeast. Bake for 8–9 minutes, until lightly golden and fragrant.

This recipe is festive and makes a perfect party nibbler. Unlike some spiced nuts, which can be heavy on the seasonings, these are just lightly flavored.

Softly Spiced **Nuts**

MAKES 4–6 SERVINGS (ABOUT 2 CUPS).

2 cups	**mixed unsalted raw nuts** (e.g., almonds, pecans, walnuts, and cashews)
1½ tbsp	**unrefined sugar**
¼ tsp	**sea salt**
¾ tsp	**cinnamon**
⅛ tsp	(scant) **ground cardamom** (optional)
⅛ tsp	**freshly ground nutmeg**
1/16 tsp	**ground allspice or cloves** (optional)
⅛ tsp	**mild chili powder** (see note)
2 tsp	**tamari**
½ tsp	**vegan Worcestershire sauce** (see note)
1 tsp	**canola oil**

Preheat oven to 300°F (150°C) (see note). In a bowl, combine nuts, sugar, salt, cinnamon, cardamom, nutmeg, allspice or cloves, and chili powder and stir to combine well. Stir in tamari, Worcestershire sauce, and oil and toss for 1–2 minutes to thoroughly coat nuts with spices. Line a baking sheet with parchment paper. Transfer nuts to baking sheet, spreading out evenly (use a spatula to scrape all seasonings from the bowl). Bake for 15–17 minutes, tossing once or twice. Remove before spices and nuts become too toasted, otherwise they will taste bitter. Watch carefully toward the end of baking to ensure nuts do not overcook or burn. Remove from oven. Lift parchment paper with nuts and transfer to a cooling rack to cool completely. Store in an airtight container and refrigerate until ready to serve.

Chili powder is optional in this recipe, but if you want extra heat in these spiced nuts, add 1–2 additional pinches chili powder or cayenne pepper to spice mixture.

WHEAT-FREE OPTION: Substitute vegan Worcestershire sauce with additional tamari for a wheat-free recipe.

If you know that your oven's temperature is higher than its setting, then set temperature lower, perhaps to 275°F (135°C), to prevent overcooking nuts and burning seasonings. Bake at that temperature for 18–20 minutes.

These chickpeas absorb the lemon juice and tamari as they bake, making them irresistible. This is a fantastic, simple recipe for parties, and ideal for snacking and packing in lunches.

Tamari-Roasted Chickpeas

MAKES 4–6 SERVINGS (ABOUT 1¾ CUPS). | **WHEAT-FREE**

To lower fat content in this recipe, use 1–2 tsp oil.

These chickpeas make a sensational topper for salads, pasta dishes, soups, and stir-fries. Also, leftovers can be lightly mashed with condiments for a sandwich spread.

1 can	**(14-oz/398-ml) chickpeas (garbanzo beans)** (about 1¾ cups)
1 tbsp	**olive oil or coconut oil** (see note)
2–2½ tsp	**freshly squeezed lemon juice**
2–2½ tsp	**tamari**
½ tsp	**fresh rosemary,** chopped (or 1 tsp fresh thyme or oregano) (optional)
⅛ tsp	**sea salt**
⅛–¼ tsp	**agave nectar**

Preheat oven to 400°F (205°C). Line a baking sheet with parchment paper. On the baking sheet, add all ingredients and toss to combine. (If using coconut oil, warm it first to melt it, or stir it through after first few minutes of baking.) Bake for about 25 minutes, tossing chickpeas once or twice during baking, until tamari and lemon juice are absorbed. Serve warm for appetizers or at room temperature for snacks.

Cannellini beans and cashews provide the creamy base to this tasty cheesy dip that is made without any soy products. Eat this dip warm as a spread on crackers or breads, cool for sandwiches, or hot as a dip with steamed veggies or tortilla chips!

Warm & Cheesy White Bean Dip

MAKES 5–6 SERVINGS (ABOUT 1¾ CUPS). | **WHEAT-FREE**

1 cup	**cooked cannellini (white kidney) beans or navy beans**
½ cup	**raw cashews**
2 tbsp	**freshly squeezed lemon juice**
2 tsp	**red wine vinegar**
⅓ cup	**nutritional yeast**
1	**medium clove garlic,** sliced
½ tsp	**onion powder**
½ tsp	**dry mustard**
¼ tsp	**ground turmeric** (for color)
¾ tsp	**sea salt**
½ tsp	**fresh rosemary,** minced (optional)
½ cup + 2 tbsp	**plain rice milk**
1½–2 tbsp	**olive oil**
1–3 tbsp	**plain rice milk** (to thin dip as desired)

Try this dip as a sauce tossed into pasta, drizzled over pizza, or added to veggies and grains in a baked tortilla wrap. Alternatively, instead of heating on the stovetop, bake this dip in a small dish and top with breadcrumbs tossed with olive oil for a crunchy contrast!

In a food processor, combine beans, cashews, lemon juice, and vinegar and purée to break down cashews, scraping down sides of bowl as needed. Add nutritional yeast, garlic, onion powder, dry mustard, turmeric, salt, rosemary, ½ cup + 2 tbsp rice milk, and 1½ tbsp olive oil and purée again until very smooth (this may take 2–3 minutes), scraping down sides of bowl as needed. Transfer mixture to a saucepan on medium-low heat and cook to thicken mixture and heat through, stirring frequently and adding extra rice milk to thin dip as desired. Taste, and stir in additional olive oil for a richer taste if desired.

I love the combination of white beans and walnuts, and along with the herbs and seasonings in this bruschetta, this pairing is even more delicious—and healthful!

White Bean & Walnut **Bruschetta**

MAKES 4–6 SERVINGS.

A baguette or Italian loaf is best for this recipe, but you can use a whole-wheat loaf, or even whole-wheat pitas or pizza crust!

WHEAT-FREE OPTION: Use kamut, spelt or other wheat-free bread.

	crusty bread, sliced (see notes)
1 cup	**cooked cannellini (white kidney) beans,** (may use navy beans)
2 tsp	**red wine vinegar**
¾ cup	**tomatoes,** minced
⅓ cup	**walnuts,** chopped
1	**medium–large clove garlic** (to your taste), minced
1½ tbsp	**extra virgin olive oil**
¼ tsp	(rounded) **sea salt**
	freshly ground black pepper to taste
1 tbsp	**fresh oregano** (or fresh thyme), chopped
¼–⅓ cup	**fresh basil,** chopped or julienned (may use fresh parsley)
	extra virgin olive oil (for finishing)

Preheat oven to 425°F (220°C). Line a baking sheet with parchment paper. Place bread slices on baking sheet and bake for 3–4 minutes to slightly toast. Remove from oven, but keep temperature at 425°F (220°C), and let bread cool while preparing bean mixture. In a bowl, mash ½ cup beans with vinegar. Add remaining ingredients and mix to combine well. Once bread is cool, spoon mixture onto bread slices, portioning mixture as desired. Bake for 6–8 minutes, until the topping is warmed through. Do not overbake, since the beans can dry out. Remove from oven, and serve drizzled with extra virgin olive oil if desired.

Pour It On!

Sauces, Dressings, & Toppers

I'VE SAID IT MORE than once—I'm a saucy girl! I'm talking sauces and dressings and vinaigrettes and slurries. They can enhance just about any dish. Here you'll find ways to easily sauce, top, or dress up your meals, as well as a quick guide to making your own vinaigrettes.

I am often unimpressed by store-bought dressings, with a few exceptions (Annie's Goddess Dressing, and both Brianna's Rich Poppy Seed and Zesty French Dressings). In general, store-bought dressings are too heavy in texture and lack the fresh flavor and acidic quality of a homemade vinaigrette. They can also be expensive, which isn't necessary considering that the primary components are oil and vinegar. For these reasons, I regularly make my own vinaigrettes and dressings. All you need is a hand blender (see page 13) or whisk, and a few key ingredients.

- *Good quality oils:* Olive oil is an obvious choice, but other options include walnut, hemp, canola, sunflower, flax, sesame, and safflower. Extra virgin olive oil has a lot of flavor, as well as infused oils and toasted sesame oil. For neutral flavouring, use walnut, canola, or safflower oils. Nutritionally, walnut, flax, and hemp oils are sources of omega-3 fatty acids.

- *Acids:* Vinegar, lemon, lime, grapefruit, or (sometimes) orange juice. Use vinegars with low acidity, such as balsamic, apple cider, red wine, ume plum, or rice, and store them in your pantry. For citrus, always use freshly squeezed; it only takes a minute to ream the juices, and the flavor far surpasses that of bottled. If using orange juice, it may be a little too sweet (depending on the variety and quality of the orange) so you may wish to combine it with a little vinegar as well.

- *Seasonings:* Sea salt and pepper are two key ingredients. Other seasonings include fresh garlic and ginger, and various herbs and spices.

- *Emulsifiers:* Emulsifying is the process of combining two liquids that normally do not combine well, such as oil and vinegar. Salad dressings can be enjoyed when the oil and vinegar are naturally separated, but, to unify the two, an emulsifying agent is needed. Dijon mustard is the most common choice, but others include roasted garlic, avocado, and thick vegetable purées like tomato paste.

- *Sweeteners:* Maple syrup and agave nectar work nicely in vinaigrettes, and barley malt or brown rice syrup are also good options. Although sweeteners are not essential in dressings, they do help cut the acidity of vinegar or citrus, and can help reduce the amount of oil you use, if this is important to you.

Once you have the ingredients at hand, you can prepare a vinaigrette quickly. First combine the acid with the salt, pepper, and seasonings. The salt will dissolve best when first combined with the vinegar. Then, using a hand blender or whisk, mix in Dijon mustard (or other emulsifier) and sweetener. If whisking by hand, drizzle oil in gradually, starting slowly to help it to emulsify; if using a hand blender, adding oil gradually is not as important.

I like to use large, recycled nut butter jars when making dressings (as well as sauces); they're large enough that I can place my hand blender right in the jar when blending ingredients. The jar can then be covered with its lid and refrigerated until ready to use.

For ingredient proportions, here is a quick rule of thumb:

For every ¼ cup acid, add:
½ tsp sea salt; 1–2 pinches freshly ground black pepper; additional seasonings, to taste
½–1 tsp Dijon mustard
2–4 tbsp sweetener
3–5 tbsp oil

This is merely a rough guideline; with each dressing, I adjust seasonings to taste. Also, depending on the type of acid, oil, and sweetener, I adjust quantities to taste. Most vinaigrette recipes will call for two to three times the amount of oil to acid. However, you can significantly reduce the amount of oil you use by adding some sweetener, and also by choosing a good quality vinegar that's not too acidic.

Of course, if you want to take the guesswork out of the equation, there's plenty of vinaigrette recipes in this chapter, or in my other books, to choose from. Don't forget to try the sauces too—for me, a meal isn't quite "dressed" without them!

This tangy, sweet sauce will perk up any vegetable or grain … and it's a breeze to make! Serve warm over sautéed greens, baked sweet potatoes, steamed or grilled vegetables, or cooked grains, or use for dipping tofu, tempeh, potstickers, spring rolls, or with Moroccan-Infused Vegetable Rolls (page 134).

Balsamic Maple Sauce

MAKES 4–5 SERVINGS (ABOUT ½ CUP). | **WHEAT-FREE**

Leftovers can be refrigerated. This sauce is delicious chilled and drizzled over sandwich ingredients or on green, grain, or noodle salads.

¼ cup	**pure maple syrup**
¼ cup	**balsamic vinegar**
2 tsp	**Earth Balance Buttery Spread**
1	**medium clove garlic,** minced
⅛ tsp	(rounded) **sea salt**
1 tsp	**arrowroot powder**
3 tbsp	**tamari**

In a saucepan on low heat, combine syrup, vinegar, Earth Balance spread, garlic, and salt, and heat for several minutes. Meanwhile, in a bowl, combine arrowroot and tamari, stirring through until well incorporated. Add tamari mixture to saucepan, whisk to combine, and increase heat to bring mixture to a boil, stirring continually. Let boil gently for 1 minute, then remove from heat and let cool slightly (the mixture will thicken more as it cools down).

This is such a simple, quick dressing that even the busiest of us can make it in just minutes!

Back-to-Basics Balsamic Vinaigrette

MAKES ⅔ CUP. | **WHEAT-FREE**

¼ cup	**balsamic vinegar** (see note)
3 tbsp	**pure maple syrup or agave nectar**
1 tsp	**Dijon mustard**
½ tsp	(rounded) **sea salt**
	freshly ground black pepper to taste
1	**small clove garlic** (optional)
3½–4 tbsp	**walnut oil** (see note)

With a hand blender or in a blender, combine all ingredients except oil and purée. Continue blending while slowly adding oil until emulsified. Season to taste with additional salt and pepper if desired.

Other flavorful vinegars can be substituted for the balsamic, including white balsamic, red wine, or sherry vinegar.

Instead of walnut oil, try olive oil or a combination of both, with a touch of toasted sesame oil.

This dressing gets its creaminess from the non-dairy milk combined with raw almonds; it can also be made soy-free using rice, oat, or another non-dairy, non-soy milk. Try it generously drizzled over a spinach salad with tomatoes, green onions, sliced bell peppers, and avocado, or with Lemon Garlic Pasta (page 130), or any simple vegan pizza.

Creamy Basil Dressing

MAKES ¾–1 CUP. | **WHEAT-FREE**

This dressing can be made thicker or thinner to taste. Start with ¼ cup milk, and then thin with extra milk if desired, using the full 1/3 cup or more to taste. Also, it will thicken considerably after refrigeration, and may need 1–2 tbsp of non-dairy milk stirred through.

For a raw version of this recipe, replace non-dairy milk with raw nut milk or water, and omit Dijon mustard if you like.

¼–1/3 cup	**plain non-dairy milk** (see note)
¼ cup	**raw almonds** (or cashews)
1½–2 tbsp	**freshly squeezed lemon juice**
1½ tsp	**Dijon mustard**
½ tsp	**sea salt**
1	**very small clove garlic**
	freshly ground black pepper to taste
½ cup	(packed) **fresh basil leaves**
2 tsp	**agave nectar**
2 tbsp	**walnut oil or olive oil**
1–2 tbsp	**plain non-dairy milk** (to thin dressing if desired)

With a hand blender or in a blender, combine all ingredients and purée until smooth. If a thinner consistency is preferred, add an additional 1–2 tbsp milk. Season with additional salt and pepper if desired.

Raita is a yogurt mixture used in Indian cuisine to balance hot, spicy foods. It is very simple to prepare and the perfect complement to spicy samosas and Zucchini Chickpea Tomato Curry (page 151).

Cucumber Mint Raita

MAKES 3–4 SERVINGS (ABOUT 1½ CUPS). | **WHEAT-FREE**

1 cup	**plain soy yogurt,** strained overnight and puréed (see note)
⅓–½ cup	**grated cucumber** (seeds removed, peeling optional) (see note)
1 tbsp	**fresh mint,** chopped (or fresh cilantro)
2 tbsp	**fresh parsley,** chopped (or fresh cilantro)
1 tbsp	**green onion,** chopped (optional)
2–3 tsp	**freshly squeezed lemon juice**
¼ tsp	**sea salt** (or more to taste)
⅛ tsp	**ground cumin** (optional)

Combine all ingredients in a bowl and stir until well combined.

This raita will be thicker and creamier if you have time to strain your yogurt. To strain, line a fine sieve with a paper towel and place over a bowl. Pour yogurt slowly into sieve, then cover sieve and bowl with plastic wrap. Place in refrigerator overnight or for at least several hours, then carefully remove sieve from bowl, and scrape thickened yogurt into another bowl.

If yogurt (strained or not) is not very smooth, purée it in a mini-food processor or with a hand blender before mixing with other ingredients.

Instead of cucumber, grated zucchini or jicama are great substitutes.

I really enjoy the sour punch in this vinaigrette, and the slight taste of cinnamon lightens the smokier cumin. Serve with salads that accompany starchy and spicy meals.

Cumin-Cinnamon **Vinaigrette**

MAKES ¾ CUP. | **WHEAT-FREE**

Use this vinaigrette in a Baby Spinach & Fennel Salad:

5–6 cups fresh baby spinach
½ cup fennel bulb, thinly sliced
¼ cup green onions, thinly sliced
2 tbsp dried cranberries
¼ cup walnuts (preferably toasted)
*2–2½ tbsp Cumin-Cinnamon
  Vinaigrette (or more to taste)*
1 ripe avocado, thinly sliced.

In a large bowl, combine salad ingredients except vinaigrette and avocado. Toss with vinaigrette, and top with the sliced avocado.

Makes 4 servings as a side salad.

2 tbsp	apple cider vinegar
2 tbsp	freshly squeezed lemon juice (or additional apple cider vinegar)
3½–4 tbsp	agave nectar
1 tsp	Dijon mustard
¼ tsp	ground cumin
⅛ tsp	cinnamon
1 pinch	allspice
½ tsp	(rounded) sea salt
¼–⅓ cup	walnut oil (or olive oil)

With a hand blender or in a blender, combine all ingredients, slowly adding oil (start with 3½ tbsp agave nectar and ¼ cup oil, then adjust to taste), and purée until emulsified.

This dressing is incredibly simple, and nicely mimics the flavor of honey mustard … without the honey!

"Honey" Mustard **Vinaigrette**

MAKES 1 CUP. | **WHEAT-FREE**

3½ tbsp	**freshly squeezed lemon juice**
1 tbsp	**red wine vinegar**
⅓ cup	**agave nectar** (see note)
2 ½ tbsp	**prepared yellow mustard**
½ tsp	(rounded) **sea salt**
1	**small clove garlic**
	freshly ground black pepper to taste
⅓ cup	**extra virgin olive oil** (see note)

With a hand blender or in a blender, combine all ingredients except oil and purée. Continue blending while slowly adding oil until emulsified. Season to taste with additional salt and pepper if desired.

For a creamy version of this dressing, substitute oil with 3½–4 tbsp Nayonaise and ½ cup soft tofu. You may need a little less agave as well—start with ¼ cup and add more if desired. Makes 1¹/₃ cups dressing.

You can use the vegan product "Just Like Honey" instead of agave nectar.

These homemade extra-large croutons are an absolute "must" to accompany my White Bean Rosemary Soup (page 104). You can also serve them on top of any other soup or chili, or to dunk in dips/spreads or toss into salads.

Jumbo Croutons

MAKES 3–4 SERVINGS.

WHEAT-FREE OPTION: Use a kamut, spelt or other wheat-free bread for croutons.

I prefer croutons simple with olive oil and salt, but you can add paprika, chili powder, fresh chopped herbs, or other spices or herbs to taste.

5–6 slices	**bread** (see note)
1 ½–2 tbsp	**olive oil**
⅛ tsp	**sea salt**

Preheat oven to 400°F (200°C). Cut bread slices into 1-in (2½-cm) squares. In a large bowl, gently toss bread with oil. Line a baking sheet with parchment paper. Transfer bread to baking sheet and sprinkle with salt. Bake for 9–12 minutes, tossing once or twice, until lightly browned. For crunchier croutons, bake 2–3 minutes longer.

When I concocted this entirely "raw" Caesar dressing, it quickly became a sensation! The creaminess is derived from the blended raw nuts, and the taste is absolutely marvelous—almost unbelievable, in fact, that it tastes so authentic. Drizzled this dressing on raw salad garnished with raw pumpkin seeds, pine nuts, and/or sliced tomatoes, or use as a raw veggie dip.

Living Caesar Dressing

MAKES ABOUT ¾ CUP. | **WHEAT-FREE**

¼ cup	**raw cashews** (or raw sunflower seeds) (see note)
⅛ cup	**raw pine nuts** (or raw sesame seeds) (see note)
3 tbsp	**freshly squeezed lemon juice**
1 tbsp	**cold-pressed extra virgin olive oil** (or other cold-pressed oil of choice)
1	**medium clove garlic,** chopped
1 tsp	**mild miso**
½ tsp	**sea salt**
½ tsp	**kelp granules** (I use Maine Coast Sea Seasonings brand)
	freshly ground black pepper to taste
½–1 tsp	**raw agave nectar**
¼ cup	**water** (or more to thin as desired)

This dressing will thicken after refrigeration; you can thin it by stirring in 2–3 tsp water if desired. When thick, this dressing can be used as a veggie dip.

If nut allergies are a concern, substitute raw sunflower and sesame seeds in place of cashews and pine nuts, respectively. The dressing will be just as delicious, though you may need additional agave nectar to sweeten to taste.

Using a hand blender or in a blender, combine all ingredients (starting with ½ tsp agave nectar) and purée until very smooth. Add additional water to thin dressing if desired. Taste test, adding additional agave nectar if desired.

Most of us love a peanut sauce. A must in your recipe repertoire, it is nutritious, delicious, easy to make, and can be used in so many ways. The fresh kiss of lime zest and juice brings a vibrant tang to this sauce and heightens the flavors of the other ingredients.

Peanut Passion Sauce

MAKES ABOUT 1 CUP.

You can substitute almond or cashew butter in place of peanut butter for variety, or if peanut allergies are a concern.

If using this sauce as a dip for raw veggies, you can reduce the garlic and ginger to taste so the heat won't be as intense.

For soba noodles: Using an 8-oz (230-g) package of noodles, toss ¾ cup Peanut Passion Sauce and ¼–⅓ cup plain non-dairy milk or a combination of milk and water with cooked noodles. After noodles sit, you may need to add more milk or water, since they will absorb sauce. Add steamed broccoli or other veggies, top with cilantro, and serve with lime wedges for squeezing.

To make an instant bean dip: Purée ¾–1 cup white beans or chickpeas with ¼–⅓ cup Peanut Passion Sauce. Add 1–2 tsp lime juice to taste, and 2–3 tsp water to thin, and 1 extra tsp sesame oil if desired. Sprinkle with cilantro and serve.

½ cup	**natural smooth peanut butter** (see note)
3 tbsp	**tamari**
1 tbsp	**ginger,** peeled and cut in small chunks (see note)
2	**medium cloves garlic,** halved (see note)
⅛ tsp	**sea salt**
⅛ tsp	**crushed red pepper flakes** (see note)
3½ tbsp	**freshly squeezed lime juice** (zest lime before juicing, see below)
2½ tbsp	**agave nectar**
2 tsp	**lime zest** (see note)
1 tbsp	**toasted sesame oil**
¼ cup	**fresh cilantro,** chopped (optional)
	warm or hot water, plain non-dairy milk, or light coconut milk (to thin sauce as desired) see note)

In a food processor, combine all ingredients except cilantro and water or milk and purée until smooth, scraping down sides of bowl as needed. (If not using a processor, first grate garlic and ginger, then whisk all ingredients together in a large bowl.) If serving as a dip, keep sauce thick. Stir in cilantro, or use as a garnish. If using sauce to toss with soba noodles, steamed vegetables, or to drizzle on grains or greens, add water or plain non-dairy milk to thin as desired, and use fresh cilantro as garnish (see notes).

Serve these instead of regular croutons with the Living Caesar Dressing (page 83), or with any salad and dressing that you enjoy.

Polenta Croutons

MAKES 3–5 SERVINGS (ABOUT 3 CUPS). | **WHEAT-FREE**

1 tube	**(18 oz/510 g) prepared polenta,** "peeled" (see note)
½–1 tbsp	**olive oil**
⅛ tsp	**sea salt**
	freshly ground black pepper to taste
	sea salt to taste

Preheat oven to 450°F (230°C). If you have a pizza stone, place it in oven to get hot. If you don't have one, line a baking sheet with parchment paper and set aside. After peeling polenta, trim edges to make a rectangular shape. Cut polenta into ½-in (1-cm) cubes. Transfer to a bowl and drizzle with oil (to taste) and sprinkle with ⅛ tsp salt and pepper. Gently toss to coat, then transfer to pizza stone or baking sheet. Bake for 30–35 minutes (see note), tossing once or twice, until golden and crispy on some of the edges. (Note that polenta croutons will crisp more as they cool. Also, if squares are cut larger, they will require longer baking time.) Remove, season with additional salt if desired, and let cool.

Packaged polenta has a smooth outer coating that I like to trim off with a vegetable peeler.

The croutons will crisp a little quicker using a pizza stone. If using a baking sheet, bake for a little longer, 35–40 minutes, until just golden around some of the edges. The croutons will continue to crisp as they cool.

Polenta Croutons are also terrific toppers for soups and stews. Try a handful on Cocoa-Coconut Chili (page 94) or Monkey Minestrone (page 97).

This rich aioli is made without vegan mayonnaise or other soy products, and is completely raw. It is very rich and luscious, and made with nutritious nuts, seeds, and olive oil. It's also reasonably thick, and can be made even thicker to become a sumptuous dip for veggies or other accompaniments.

Raw Red Pepper Aioli

MAKES ABOUT ¾ CUP. | **WHEAT-FREE**

If you prefer a tangier flavor, add another ½ tsp or more lemon juice to taste.

For a dip with veggies or other accompaniments: Blend all ingredients, but start with just 3 tbsp water and 2 tbsp oil, and add more water and oil as desired to thin to preferred consistency. Or, you can blend in an additional 1 tbsp cashews. Also note that this sauce will thicken considerably with refrigeration.

Be sure to blend this sauce until it is creamy. I use my hand blender, which takes several minutes at high-speed to achieve a smooth texture.

¼ cup	**raw cashews**
¼ cup	**raw sesame seeds**
½ cup	**red bell pepper,** skin removed with peeler and chopped
3–3½ tsp	**freshly squeezed lemon juice** (see note)
1	**medium clove garlic,** quartered
½ tsp	(scant) **sea salt**
	freshly ground black pepper to taste
3½–4 tbsp	**water** (more or less as needed) (see note)
2½ tbsp	**olive oil** (more or less as needed) (see note)

In a blender or with a hand blender, combine all ingredients and purée until very smooth, adding more water and/or oil to smooth out and thin as desired. Taste test, and add additional salt, pepper, and lemon juice if desired.

Avocados are always on hand in our house. Not only are they delicious and chock full of healthy fats, they can be very versatile, such as in this recipe. This sauce is great with burritos or spring rolls, and is also spectacular topped on hot pizzas! Serve with Tomato Basil Breakfast Quesadilla (page 38), Sweet Potato Lentil Chili (page 101), Lentil Veggie Chimichangas (page 132), or Veggie-Sizzle Burritos (page 149).

Smoky Avocado **Sauce**

MAKES 3–4 SERVINGS (ABOUT ¾ CUP). | **WHEAT-FREE**

½ cup	(packed) **ripe avocado** (about 1 small avocado)
⅛ tsp	**sea salt**
1 tsp	**tamari**
3 tbsp	**freshly squeezed orange juice**
3–4 tsp	**freshly squeezed lime juice**
⅛–¼ tsp	**natural liquid smoke** (see note)
¼ cup	**water**
¼ tsp	**agave nectar** (optional)

Liquid smoke has a very intense flavor, so use it sparingly. You can always add a few drops extra if you want a smokier flavor, but add it conservatively to begin with so it does not overwhelm the sauce.

With a hand blender or in a blender or mini-food processor, combine all ingredients and purée until smooth. Season to taste if desired, and thin with extra water if desired.

This thick, cheesy gravy has a comforting quality that will keep you wanting to ladle on a little bit more! Serve paired with mashed potatoes (or sweet potatoes), Popcorn Fries (page 161), or Potato Squashers (page 162). Also serve tossed into cooked pasta with raw or steamed chopped veggies for a quick and delicious meal.

Thick 'n' Rich Gravy

MAKES ABOUT 1⅓ CUPS. | **WHEAT-FREE**

For a "cheesier" gravy, add an additional 1–2 tbsp nutritional yeast (the gravy will also get thicker); for a milder cheese flavor, reduce nutritional yeast to 3 tbsp.

Adjust the sweetness depending on whether you use tahini or cashew butter. Tahini is more bitter, so you may want extra agave nectar, whereas cashew butter is naturally sweeter.

1 cup	**vegetable broth**
¼ cup	**nutritional yeast** (see note)
1 tbsp	**mild miso** (I use Genmai brown rice miso)
1 tbsp	**tamari**
1	**large clove garlic,** sliced
2 tsp	**onion powder**
1 tbsp	**arrowroot powder**
2 tbsp	**tahini** (or combination of tahini and cashew butter)
1½–2½ tbsp	**red wine vinegar**
1 ½ tsp	**blackstrap molasses**
½–¾ tsp	**agave nectar** (see note)
2 tbsp	**olive oil**
3 tbsp	**water** (optional; to thin gravy as desired)

With a hand blender or in a blender or food processor, combine all ingredients (starting with 1½ tbsp vinegar) except water and purée until smooth. In a pot on medium-high heat, transfer mixture and bring to a boil, stirring occasionally. Once boiling, reduce heat to medium, allowing it to bubble gently for 2–3 minutes until thickened. Taste test, and add additional vinegar and/or thin with water if desired.

You'll never buy another store-bought cranberry sauce after you've tasted this one. Serve with holiday dinners, and also to dollop on the White Bean Rosemary Soup (page 104), Blackened Tofu (page 121), or Walnut, White Bean & Spinach Phyllo Rolls (page 150). This sauce also pairs well with savory and sweet muffins and scones, and also with Tempeh Hashbrown Casserole (page 37).

Traditional Cranberry Sauce

MAKES 4–5 SERVINGS (ABOUT 1 CUP). | **WHEAT-FREE**

1½ cups	**fresh cranberries,** rinsed (see note)
½ cup	**pure maple syrup**
¼ tsp	**sea salt**
1 tsp	**balsamic vinegar** (optional)

In a pot on medium-high heat, combine ingredients and bring mixture to a boil, stirring occasionally. Once boiling, reduce heat to simmer for 10–15 minutes, stirring occasionally, until cranberries have broken down. (Reduce heat is sauce is sticking or is simmering too rapidly.) Once sauce has thickened, taste test, and add balsamic vinegar for a touch of sourness if desired. Serve warm or chilled.

Frozen cranberries can also be used; just continue simmering until cranberries break down into sauce and entire mixture thickens and becomes deeper in color.

Soup's On!
Soups & Stews

HERE YOU'LL FIND WONDERFULLY satisfying soups that can also be meals in a bowl. I love creating soups that are a rich purée of vegetables or full of beans or grains. Because soups and stews are so easy to prepare, so very nourishing, and also yield leftovers that taste even better after refrigerating or freezing, we eat soup any time of the year.

Pair soups with whole-grain breads, or serve whole grains like brown rice or barley side-by-side in the same bowl (spoon in grain first, push it to one half of the bowl, and fill remaining half with soup … elegant-looking, but simple). Round out that meal with a fresh salad, or some lightly sautéed, steamed, or grilled veggies.

Soups also provide *the* perfect vehicle to "hide" certain ingredients from children. My good friend Vicki makes the Mellow Lentil ("Sniffle") Soup (page 96), and adds minced broccoli. You can do the same, and even purée the final soup with a hand blender. A lot of children don't like onions either, but when you mince them and serve them in soup, your kids will never know the difference.

A couple of notes about ingredients:

1) Where fresh herbs are specified, try to use them as much as possible. Keep small pots of fresh herbs like thyme and rosemary in your home or garden. I have a bay tree in my backyard that produces fragrant bay leaves that far surpass the dried variety.

2) For vegetable stock, I prefer to use organic vegetable bouillon cubes combined with water over pre-made liquid stocks for several reasons. First, they take up no storage space. A small box of bouillon cubes can stored in a spice drawer. Second, they can be used economically, 1 cube per 2 cups water, and if you want less, simply cut the cube in half or quarters. With Tetra-Pak packaged liquid broths, I either end up freezing portions of it which I later forget about, or I have to throw it out after refrigerating for too long. Third, bouillon cubes are cheaper than store-bought pre-made stock. Finally, although some people say bouillon cubes are too salty, I do not find this to be the case with the organic vegetable stocks, and in fact, I prefer the taste to the liquid vegetable stocks. There are two brands I like: Rapunzel Organic Vegan Vegetable Bouillon and Harvest Sun Organic Vegetable Bouillon Cubes. Regardless of which brand you use, a box or two of organic vegetable bouillon cubes is definitely a pantry essential for soup recipes.

This is truly a change of pace from that old vegan chili recipe, and this one is packed with healthful ingredients—including cocoa powder, which is rich in antioxidants. Serve chili with a salad of romaine lettuce, chopped jicama, and fresh tomatoes tossed with Cumin-Cinnamon Vinaigrette (page 80), and tortilla chips with Guacamole con Alga Marina (page 61).

Cocoa-Coconut Chili

MAKES 7–9 SERVINGS. | **WHEAT-FREE**

You can use regular cocoa powder; however, Dutch-processed cocoa powder will give this chili a very dark chocolate color and a deeper, richer taste than regular cocoa.

I like this combination of beans, but you can use whatever canned beans you have on hand.

Coconut milk adds a creamy quality and light coconut flavor. If you use it, you likely won't need to add any agave nectar since coconut milk adds a subtle sweetness to the chili. You may omit coconut milk if desired.

Have leftovers? Make "Ta-quinos": Cook quinoa and let cool until just warm. Lightly toast or warm corn taco shells. Layer warm quinoa on bottom of the shells and cover with leftover chili, a few spoonfuls of guacamole, and any additional toppings you like, such as chopped tomatoes, shredded lettuce, grated jicama, chopped cilantro, or grated vegan cheese. Don't forget lime wedges for serving!

1–1½ tbsp	**coconut oil** (may use olive oil)
2 cups	**onion,** diced
1¼–1½ cups	**celery,** diced
½ cup	**red or yellow bell peppers,** diced (optional)
4–6	**medium cloves garlic,** minced
1 tsp	**sea salt**
	freshly ground black pepper to taste
2 tbsp	**mild chili powder**
½ tsp	**cinnamon**
⅛ tsp	**allspice**
2½–3 tbsp	**Dutch-processed cocoa powder** (see note)
2 cans	**(28-oz/796-ml) diced tomatoes**
1 can	**(14-oz/398-ml) black beans,** rinsed and drained (see note)
1 can	**(14-oz /398-ml) kidney beans,** rinsed and drained (see note)
1 can	**(14-oz/398-ml) pinto beans,** rinsed and drained (see note)
1 can	**(14-oz/398-ml) light coconut milk** (see note)
½ cup	**unsweetened shredded coconut**
2 tsp	**chipotle hot sauce** (I use Tabasco brand)
1 cup	**frozen corn kernels**
1–1½ tsp	**agave nectar** (optional) (see note)
1–2	**fresh limes,** cut in wedges (for garnish)

In a large pot on medium heat, add oil, onion, celery, bell pepper, garlic, salt, pepper, chili powder, cinnamon, and allspice and stir to combine. Cover and cook for 7–9 minutes, stirring occasionally; reduce heat if onions or garlic starts to burn. When onions start to soften, add cocoa and stir for 1–2 minutes, then add tomatoes, beans, coconut milk, and coconut, and stir to combine. Increase heat to bring to a boil. Once boiling, reduce heat to low, cover, and simmer for 20–25 minutes, stirring occasionally. Stir in corn kernels and agave nectar, and cook another 5 minutes to heat through. Remove cover to let liquid reduce if desired. Season to taste with additional salt, pepper, or hot sauce. Serve with lime wedges and squeeze on generous amounts of juice.

This soup has warm, earthy tones of cumin and thyme. It's easy to make, and yields extra portions for leftovers or freezing. Pair this smooth-yet-rustic soup with a whole-grain bread or brown rice and a light salad drizzled with "Honey" Mustard Vinaigrette (page 81), Simplest Garlic Bread (page 66), and Simple Swiss Chard (page 166).

Lemon Chickpea Lentil **Soup**

MAKES 6–8 SERVINGS. | **WHEAT-FREE**

1–1½ tbsp	**olive oil**
2 cups	**onion,** diced
1½ cups	**celery,** diced
3	**large cloves garlic,** minced
¾ tsp	**sea salt**
	freshly ground black pepper to taste
1 tsp	**mustard seeds**
1 tsp	**cumin seeds**
1½ tsp	**paprika**
½ tsp	**dried oregano**
1–1½ tsp	**dried thyme**
1 cup	**dry red lentils**
3½ cups	**cooked chickpeas (garbanzo beans)**
2 cups	**zucchini or tomatoes,** chopped
3 cups	**vegetable stock**
2 cups	**water**
2 dried	**bay leaves**
¼–⅓ cup	**fresh lemon juice**

In a large soup pot on medium heat, add oil, onion, celery, garlic, salt, pepper, mustard seed, cumin seeds, paprika, oregano, and thyme and stir to combine. Cover and cook for 6–7 minutes, stirring occasionally. Rinse lentils. Add lentils and 2½ cups chickpeas (reserve remaining 1 cup), zucchini or tomatoes, stock, water, and bay leaves and stir to combine. Increase heat to bring mixture to a boil. Once boiling, reduce heat to low, cover, and simmer for 20–25 minutes until lentils are completely softened. Remove bay leaves. Stir in ¼ cup lemon juice, then using a hand blender, purée the soup, keeping some texture. Stir in remaining 1 cup chickpeas. Season with additional sea salt, pepper, and lemon juice if desired, and serve.

I created this soup one evening when our older daughter had a cold. I told her that this soup helps the sniffles go away. She loved it, and even when she was feeling better, she still asked for "sniffle" soup (and does to this day)! Serve with Pizza Focaccia (page 63) and a generous salad for a complete meal.

Mellow Lentil "Sniffle" Soup

MAKES 5–6 SERVINGS. | **WHEAT-FREE**

If you don't have fresh rosemary, you can use dried. However, add it at the beginning of the cooking process, along with the other dried spices, and use less—about 1 tsp.

1–1½ tbsp	**olive oil**
1½ cups	**onion,** diced
1 cup	**celery,** diced
¾ cup	**carrots,** diced
3	**large cloves garlic,** minced
½ tsp	**sea salt**
	freshly ground black pepper to taste
¾–1 tsp	**curry powder**
1 tsp	**paprika**
¼ tsp	**dried thyme**
2 cups	**dry red lentils**
3 cups	**vegetable stock**
4–4½	**cups water**
2½–3 tsp	**fresh rosemary,** chopped (see note)
2½ tbsp	**apple cider vinegar**

In a large pot on medium heat, add oil, onion, celery, carrots, garlic, salt, pepper, curry powder, paprika, and dried thyme and stir to combine. Cover and cook for 7–8 minutes, stirring occasionally. Rinse lentils. Add lentils, stock, and water and stir to combine. Increase heat to bring mixture to a boil. Once boiling, reduce heat to low, cover, and simmer for 12–15 minutes. Add rosemary and simmer for another 8–10 minutes or more, until lentils are completely softened. Stir in vinegar, season to taste with additional salt and black pepper if desired.

Salad with Living Caesar Dressing (page 83) and Polenta Croutons
(page 85); Lemon Rooibos Iced Tea (page 225)

White Bean Rosemary Soup with Jumbo Croutons & Fresh Basil (page 104)
and Puréed Spicy Sweet Potato & Peanut Stew with Chickpeas (page 99)

Gimme Chimis (page 128) with Guacamole con Alga Marina (page 61) and
a cucumber salad with Cumin-Cinnamon Vinaigrette (page 80)

Veggie Tempeh Muffuletta (page 112)

When your kids are acting like monkeys, give them a soup filled with fun pasta shapes to suit their silly mood! But don't pass up on this soup yourself, as it's full of flavor and fabulous textures. Top soup with Polenta Croutons (page 85).

Monkey Minestrone

MAKES 7–8 SERVINGS. | **WHEAT-FREE**

1 tbsp	**olive oil**
1 ½–1¾ cup	**onion,** diced
1 cup	**celery,** diced
1 cup	**carrots,** diced
2 large	**cloves garlic,** minced
1 tsp	**dried thyme**
1 tsp	**dried marjoram**
¾ tsp	**sea salt**
	freshly ground black pepper to taste
⅛–¼ tsp	**allspice**
1 can	**(28-oz/796-ml) crushed tomatoes** (see note)
2 cans	**(14-oz/398-ml) beans** (e.g., chickpeas and kidney beans), rinsed and drained
2	**bay leaves**
1 tbsp	**fresh rosemary,** chopped (or 1 tsp dried)
4 cups	**vegetable stock**
1½ cups	**water**
1 cup	**frozen corn kernels**
¾–1 cup	**fresh green beans,** trimmed and chopped (may use frozen)
¾–1 cup	**dry wheat-free pasta** (see note)
1–1½ tbsp	**fresh thyme,** chopped (see note)
1 tbsp	**fresh sage or oregano,** chopped (see note)

In a large pot on medium heat, add oil, onion, celery, carrots, garlic, thyme, marjoram, salt, pepper, and allspice and stir to combine. Cover and cook for 4–6 minutes, stirring occasionally. Add tomatoes, beans, bay leaves, rosemary, stock, and water. Increase heat to bring to a boil. Once boiling, reduce heat to medium-low, cover, and simmer for 5–10 minutes. Add corn kernels, green beans, and pasta, and continue to cook for another 6-10 minutes, or until pasta is almost fully cooked (see note). Stir in fresh thyme and sage, heat through for 1–2 minutes, season to taste with additional salt and pepper if desired, and serve.

If you only have whole or diced canned tomatoes, use a hand blender to crush them: pour off some liquid from can into pot first, then use a hand blender to purée tomatoes directly in can.

You can use any pasta you like for this soup, such as macaroni, penne, or rotini. One of my favorites is Tinkyada Brown Rice Little Dreams, which includes trains, teddy bears, dinosaurs, boats, bunny rabbits, and airplanes. Keep in mind that the pasta continues to cook after you have turned off the heat, so if you aren't serving the soup right away, undercook the pasta and let it sit in the hot soup to continue to cook through. You could also use leftover pasta instead of dry; just add 1–2 cups a few minutes before finishing the soup.

If fresh herbs are not available, add an additional ½–1 tsp dried thyme and ½–1 tsp dried sage earlier with other dried herbs.

Wild rice combined with chickpeas and home-cookin' seasonings make this a comfort soup to curl up with. Serve with a salad of romaine lettuce tossed with Living Caesar Dressing (page 83) and cherry tomatoes for a fresh, juicy bite.

One Wild Chick Soup!

MAKES 6–7 SERVINGS. | **WHEAT-FREE**

If you don't have fresh sage or thyme, you can add an additional ¼–½ tsp dried sage and about ½ tsp more dried thyme along with the other dried herbs.

1 tbsp	**olive oil**
1¼–1½ cups	**red onion,** diced
1½ cups	**celery,** diced
¾ cup	**carrots,** diced
2	**large cloves garlic,** minced
½ cup	**uncooked wild rice,** rinsed
¼ tsp	**sea salt**
	freshly ground black pepper to taste
1 tsp	**dry mustard**
1 tsp	**dried thyme**
1 tsp	**dried oregano**
½ tsp	**dried marjoram**
3½ cups	**cooked chickpeas (garbanzo beans)**
4 cups	**vegetable stock**
3 cups	**water**
2	**bay leaves**
2 tbsp	**nutritional yeast**
1 tbsp	**fresh sage,** minced (see note)
1 tbsp	**fresh thyme,** minced (see note)

In a large pot on medium heat, add oil, onions, celery, carrots, garlic, wild rice, salt, pepper, dry mustard, dried thyme, oregano, and marjoram and stir to combine. Cover and let cook for 5–6 minutes, stirring once or twice. Add 2½ cup chickpeas (reserving 1 cup), stock, water, and bay leaves and stir to combine. Increase heat to bring mixture to a boil. Once boiling, reduce heat to low, cover, and simmer for 45–55 minutes, until rice is fully cooked and inner white of grain is exposed. With a hand blender, briefly pulse soup to add some body and creaminess if desired. Stir in the reserved 1 cup chickpeas, nutritional yeast, sage, and fresh thyme, and cook for 2–3 minutes. Season to taste with additional salt and pepper, and serve.

This soup combines sweet potatoes with earthy spices, a good dose of fresh ginger, and just a small amount of peanut butter. It is puréed and then whole chickpeas are added for more texture and protein. Serve with brown basmati rice or quinoa, and a salad drizzled with Cumin-Cinnamon Vinaigrette (page 80).

Puréed Spicy Sweet Potato & Peanut Stew with Chickpeas

MAKES 6–8 SERVINGS. | **WHEAT-FREE**

1–1½ tbsp	**olive oil**
5½–6 cups	**sweet potatoes,** peeled and chopped (see note)
2 cups	**onions,** diced
1 cup	**celery,** diced
3–4	**large cloves garlic,** minced
1 tsp	**sea salt**
2 tsp	**cumin seeds**
3–3½ tsp	**ground coriander**
1 tsp	**paprika**
¼–½ tsp	**crushed red pepper flakes** (or to taste)
2 cups	**vegetable stock**
3 cups	**water**
5 tbsp	**fresh ginger,** grated
2 tbsp	**natural peanut butter**
2 cups	**cooked chickpeas (garbanzo beans)**
3–4 tbsp	**freshly squeezed lime juice**
	lime wedges (for garnish)
	fresh cilantro leaves, chopped (for garnish)

This soup uses the orange-flesh tubers that many people know as sweet potatoes. In some countries, like Canada, they are commonly referred to as yams. You can use garnet or jewel yams ... or sweet potatoes; just be sure the flesh is orange.

In a large pot on medium heat, add oil, sweet potatoes, onion, celery, garlic, salt, cumin seeds, ground coriander, paprika, and red pepper flakes and stir to combine. Cover and cook for 5–7 minutes, stirring once or twice. Add stock, water, and 2½ tbsp ginger (reserve remaining 2½ tbsp). Stir to combine and increase heat to bring mixture to a boil. Once boiling, reduce heat to medium-low, cover, and simmer for 15–18 minutes or longer, until sweet potatoes have completely softened. Stir in remaining ginger and peanut butter. With a hand blender, briefly purée soup until it is just smooth but keeping some texture. Stir in chickpeas and lime juice, and serve with additional lime wedges and fresh cilantro.

This is a traditional split pea soup that uses smoked tofu to give it nuance. Serve with crusty whole-grain bread and a simple salad with crunchy vegetables like cucumber, grated beet, and chopped fresh parsley, drizzled with Back-to Basics Balsamic Vinaigrette (page 77), and topped with toasted seeds or nuts.

Smoky Green Split Pea **Soup**

MAKES 7–9 SERVINGS. | **WHEAT-FREE**

I use Soya Nova Tofu Shop brand of tofu for this recipe, but if you don't want a smoky flavor in your soup, then simply omit it. Also, the longer the smoked tofu cooks, the smokier the soup gets. If desired, wait to add tofu until the last 5–10 minutes of cooking.

Instead of smoked tofu, try sprinkling on crumbled cooked tempeh bacon after the soup is cooked. I use 6-oz (17-g) Lightlife's "Fakin' Bacon" Tempeh Bacon Strips.

1–1½ tbsp	olive oil
2 cups	**onions**, diced
1 cup	**celery**, diced
1 cup	**carrot**, diced
1½–2 cups	**sweet potatoes** (yellow-fleshed), or parsnip or white potato, chopped
3	**large cloves garlic**, minced
½ tsp	(rounded) **sea salt**
	freshly ground black pepper to taste
1½ tsp	**dried oregano**
½ tsp	**dried thyme**
1 tsp	**paprika**
2½ cups	**dried green split peas**, rinsed
4 cups	**vegetable stock**
6 cups	**water**
2 bay	**leaves**
1 pkg	**(8-oz/225-g) smoked tofu**, cubed (see notes)
2 tbsp	**freshly squeezed lemon juice** (optional)

In a large pot on medium heat, add oil, onion, celery, carrot, sweet potatoes, garlic, salt, pepper, oregano, thyme, and paprika, and stir to combine. Cover and cook for 5–6 minutes, stirring once or twice. Add split peas, stirring for 1–2 minutes. Add stock, water, and bay leaves and increase heat to bring to a boil. Once boiling, reduce heat to medium-low, cover, and simmer for 30 minutes. Add tofu, stir to combine, cover, and cook for another 18–20 minutes, until peas have fully cooked and soup has thickened. If you like, you can remove cover and let soup continue to simmer for another 8–10 minutes to thicken more. Stir in lemon juice, season to taste with additional salt and pepper if desired, and serve.

Red lentils work nicely to thicken this chili, while the sweet potato gives a mellow, sweet contrast to the spices. Serve with a big dollop of Guacamole con Alga Marina (page 61) and tortilla chips or artisan breads for dipping, or topped with slices of Cornmeal-Crusted Plantains (page 158).

Sweet Potato Lentil Chili

MAKES 5–6 SERVINGS. | **WHEAT-FREE**

1 tbsp	**coconut oil or olive oil**
1 ¾ cups	**onions,** diced
1 cup	**celery,** diced
2–2½ cups	**sweet potatoes,** peeled and cubed about 1-in (2½-cm) thick
3	**large cloves garlic,** minced (see note)
1 tsp	**sea salt**
	freshly ground black pepper to taste
2 tsp	**chili powder**
1 tsp	**paprika**
½ tsp	**freshly grated nutmeg**
½ tsp	**cumin**
¼ tsp	**cinnamon**
½ tsp	**crushed red pepper flakes** (or to taste)
1¼ cups	**dry red lentils**
2½ cups	**water**
1 can	**(28-oz/796-ml) crushed tomatoes** (see note)
1 can	**(14-oz/398-ml) black beans or kidney beans,** rinsed and drained
1	**bay leaf**
3 tbsp	**freshly squeezed lime juice**
	lime wedges (for garnish)

If you only have whole or diced canned tomatoes, use a hand blender to crush them: pour off some liquid from can into pot first, then use a hand blender to purée tomatoes directly in can.

In a large pot on medium heat, add oil, onions, celery, sweet potatoes, garlic, salt, pepper, chili powder, paprika, nutmeg, cumin, cinnamon, and red pepper flakes and stir to combine. Cover and cook for 6–8 minutes, stirring occasionally; reduce heat if onions are sticking to bottom of pot. Rinse lentils. Add lentils, water, tomatoes, beans, and bay leaf. Stir to combine and increase heat to bring to a boil. Once boiling, reduce heat to low, cover, and simmer for 25 minutes or longer until sweet potatoes are softened, stirring occasionally. Stir in lime juice, season to taste with additional salt, pepper. Serve with lime wedges and generously squeeze on juice!

This stew is fragrant with Thai flavors of coconut, lime, coriander, and lemongrass. This stew is delicious served in a bowl side-by-side with brown basmati rice. It can also be served as a smaller portion, with spring rolls, and a tofu dish such as Cumin Lime Tofu (page 126).

Thai Coconut Corn Stew

MAKES 4–5 SERVINGS. | **WHEAT-FREE**

Lemongrass adds a distinctive lemony aroma. It is available in produce sections or Asian markets, and can be stored in the refrigerator for 2–3 weeks.

½ tbsp	**coconut oil**
1 cup	**onion,** diced
1 cup	**celery,** diced
3	**medium cloves garlic,** minced
1 tbsp	**fresh ginger,** grated
½–¾ tsp	**coriander seeds**
¾–1 tsp	**sea salt**
¼ tsp	**crushed red pepper flakes** (or to taste)
1 stalk	**lemongrass** (see note)
4 cups	**frozen corn kernels**
2 cups	**vegetable stock**
1 can	**(14-oz/400-ml) light coconut milk** (may use regular)
1 cup	**red bell pepper,** diced
1½–2 tsp	**lime zest** (zest limes before juicing, see below)
2–3 tbsp	**freshly squeezed lime juice**
⅓–½ cup	**fresh cilantro or Thai basil,** chopped
	lime wedges (for garnish)

In a large pot on medium heat, add oil, onions, celery, garlic, ginger, coriander seeds, salt (start with ¾ tsp), and red pepper flakes and stir to combine. Cover and cook for 5–7 minutes, stirring occasionally. Meanwhile, cut off lower yellow bulbous portion of lemongrass, and remove and discard tough outer leaves along with upper portion of stalk. Using a chef's knife, "bruise" bulbous portion to release flavor: cut a few slits and using pressure of knife, open and bruise stalk. Add it to the pot, along with 3 cups corn kernels, stock, and coconut milk, and increase heat to bring to a boil. Once boiling, reduce heat to medium-low, cover and cook for 10 minutes. Remove lemongrass, and with a hand blender, briefly purée soup to make it a little creamier. Return lemongrass to pot, and stir in remaining 1 cup corn kernels and red pepper flakes. Cover and cook for another 5–6 minutes on medium-low heat. Stir in lime zest and lime juice (adjust to taste). Season with additional salt if desired. Just before serving, stir in cilantro or basil. Serve with lime wedges.

This thick, robust soup uses dill seeds to impart an earthy dill taste that doesn't overpower the soup. I especially enjoy this soup as leftovers … the flavors are even better! Serve with Jumbo Croutons (page 82), alongside a mixed field greens salad dressed simply with a drizzle of Back-to-Basics Balsamic Vinaigrette (page 77).

Tomato Dill Lentil Soup

MAKES 6–8 SERVINGS. | **WHEAT-FREE**

1½ tbsp	olive oil
2 cups	**onions,** diced
1½ cups	**celery,** diced
2	**large cloves garlic,** minced
2½ tsp	**dill seeds**
½ tsp	**cumin seeds**
2½ tsp	**ground mustard**
1–1¼ tsp	**sea salt**
	freshly ground black pepper to taste
1 can	**(28-oz/796-ml) crushed tomatoes** (see note)
2 cups	**brown (or green) lentils,** rinsed
2 cups	**vegetable stock**
5½–6 cups	**water**
1½ tbsp	**tamari**
1 tbsp	**blackstrap molasses**
2 dried	**bay leaves**
2–3 tbsp	**fresh dill,** chopped (for garnish)

If you only have whole or diced canned tomatoes, use a hand blender to crush them: pour off some liquid from can into pot first, then use a hand blender to purée tomatoes directly in can.

In a large pot on medium heat, add oil, onions, celery, garlic, dill seeds, cumin seeds, ground mustard, salt (start with 1 tsp), and pepper and stir to combine. Cover and cook for 4–5 minutes, stirring occasionally. Add tomatoes, lentils, vegetable stock, water (starting with 5½ cups), tamari, molasses, and bay leaves and stir to combine. Increase heat to bring to a boil, then reduce heat to medium-low, cover and cook for 50–60 minutes, until lentils are very soft. Add remaining water (or more if desired) to thin soup. Season to taste with the additional salt and pepper if desired, and garnish with fresh dill to serve.

This soup will captivate your tastebuds. The olive oil-drizzled croutons slowly soften into this mellow, rosemary-infused concoction. A dollop of Traditional Cranberry Sauce (page 89) may also suit your taste!

White Bean Rosemary **Soup** with Jumbo Croutons & Fresh Basil

MAKES 5–6 SERVINGS.

Since this soup uses a lot of beans, I prefer cooking the white beans from dried rather than canned because it imparts a fresher taste. For tips on cooking beans, see page 229.

WHEAT-FREE OPTION: Use the Polenta Croutons (page 85).

1–1½ tbsp	**olive oil**
1 cup	**onions,** diced
1½ cups	**celery,** diced
4	**large cloves garlic,** minced
2 tsp	**dry mustard**
¾–1 tsp	**sea salt**
	freshly ground black pepper to taste
6 cups	**cooked white kidney (cannellini) beans** (see note)
3 cups	**vegetable stock**
1½ cups	**water**
2 tsp	**fresh rosemary,** chopped
2–2½ tbsp	**freshly squeezed lemon juice**
1 batch	**Jumbo Croutons** (page 82) (see note)
¼ cup	**fresh basil,** sliced in thin strips or chopped
1–2 tbsp	**olive oil** (for finishing)

In a large pot on medium heat, add oil, onion, celery, garlic, dry mustard, salt, and pepper, and stir to combine. Cover and cook for 6–8 minutes, stirring occasionally. Add 4 cups beans, stock, water, and 1½ tsp rosemary, and increase heat to bring to a boil. Once boiling, reduce heat to medium-low, cover, and cook for 15 minutes. With a hand blender, purée soup until smooth. Stir in remaining 2 cups beans, remaining ½ tsp rosemary, and lemon juice. Season with additional salt and pepper if desired. Serve in individual bowls, topped with a handful of Jumbo Croutons, sprinkle of fresh basil, and drizzle of olive oil, if desired.

The Best Things Since Sliced Bread

Sandwiches & Spreads

LONG GONE ARE THE days of white bread sandwiching a slice of cold bologna. At least, those days are long gone for us vegans (thank goodness)! To build delicious sandwiches for guests, use whole-grain breads full of texture and flavor, and then layer on some spreads, crunchy veggies, and tasty condiments.

This section provides recipes that can be made any day of the week that will dazzle your palate and fill your belly. Some are very simple and kid-friendly, like Goddess Garbanzos (page 110) and Peanut Butter Tortilla Turnovers (page 111). Others, like Beats a BLT Sandwich! (page 109) and Veggie Tempeh Muffuletta (page 112), will be hits with adults at brunches, picnics, or everyday lunches and munches.

Keep in mind that leftovers of other recipes make great sandwich fillings, such as:

- Any hummus, pages 46–53: spread between sliced bread, in pitas and wraps, and fill with fresh veggies of choice.

- Roasted Garlic Artichoke Spread with Fresh Oregano (page 65): spread on warm or chilled, and add sliced fresh tomatoes and lettuce.

- Tamari-Roasted Chickpeas (page 68): mash with condiments, including vegan mayonnaise, mustard, vegan BBQ sauce, or hot sauce. Layer with sliced bell peppers and cukes.

- Veggie patties or tofu dishes, such as Blackened Tofu (page 121), Cashew-Ginger Tofu (page 124), Chickpea Sensation Patties (page 125), and Cumin Lime Tofu (page 126): mash patties or lightly purée tofu pieces, and mix with condiments to suit the flavorings in each recipe. Spread mixture on bread and top with sliced fresh vegetables or lettuce leaves.

- Roasted Winter Squash Rings (page 163) and Seared Portobello Mushrooms (page 165): reheat them in a toaster oven and add to a sandwich along with other veggies and/or spreads.

This sandwich rivals any BLT out there! Lightlife Tempeh Bacon is not chewy or fatty like "real" bacon and offers a delightful whole-foods tempeh texture with a smoky seasoned flavor—perfect with the cool creaminess of avocado. These two ingredients combined with lettuce, tomato, and seasonings between two slices of fresh bread make a top-notch sandwich!

Beats a BLT **Sandwich!**

MAKES FILLING FOR 2–4 SANDWICHES, OR AS A DIP TO SERVE 4–6 PEOPLE (SEE NOTE).

1 pkg	**(6-oz/170-g) Lightlife "Fakin' Bacon" Tempeh Bacon** (about 1–1¼ cups)
1 cup	**tomatoes,** chopped, seeds and juices lightly squeezed out
1¼–1½ cups	**avocado,** diced small
2 tbsp	**freshly squeezed lemon or lime juice**
¼ tsp	**sea salt**
	freshly ground black pepper to taste
⅛ cup	**green onions,** chopped
⅛ cup	**fresh parsley, cilantro, or basil,** chopped
4–8 slices	**bread of choice**
1–2 tbsp	**vegan mayonnaise** (optional)
4–6	**leaves of lettuce** (preferably crisp lettuce like romaine)

This filling can double as a smoky, chunky twist on guacamole: add another ½–1 cup avocado to mixture, a few extra squeezes of lemon juice, and salt to taste, and serve with tortilla chips.

Since avocados discolor once cut, it is best to use this filling soon after making it. You can refrigerate it as long as you don't mind the discoloration; it will still be fine to eat.

In a non-stick frying pan, cook tempeh bacon according to package directions. Let cool, then chop. In a large bowl, combine tempeh, tomatoes, avocado, lemon juice, salt, pepper, green onions, and parsley and mix well (squishing some avocado pieces helps to hold ingredients together). Season with additional pepper and/or more fresh herbs if desired. Spread mixture evenly on a slice of bread. On another slice, spread mayonnaise, top with 1–2 lettuce leaves, and sandwich two slices together. Repeat depending on how many sandwiches you are making.

This sandwich filling uses the ever popular Goddess Dressing by Annie's Naturals, and can be whipped together in minutes. With the addition of kelp granules, the seasoning is reminiscent of tuna sandwiches—only much better!

Goddess Garbanzos

MAKES FILLING FOR 3–4 SANDWICHES.

If making this recipe for kids, you can sneak other veggies into the mixture if you mince or grate them. For example, replace celery with grated or minced carrot or cucumber. They may also like additional chopped apples or raisins added to the mixture. Finally, for us big kids, try stirring in a sprinkling of chopped fresh herbs like dill, chives, or parsley.

1 cup	**cooked chickpeas (garbanzo beans)**
3–3½ tbsp	**Annie's Naturals Goddess Dressing**
1 tbsp	**Nayonaise or Vegenaise**
1–1½ tsp	**freshly squeezed lemon juice**
1 tsp	**tahini**
½ tsp	**kelp granules** (optional; I use Maine Coast Sea Seasonings brand)
1/16–1/8 tsp	**sea salt** (to taste)
2 tsp	**capers** (optional)
¼ cup	**celery,** minced
2 tbsp	**apple,** minced (optional)

In a large bowl, mash all ingredients except celery and apples (alternatively, you can use a food processor and pulse until blended but still chunky). Stir in celery and apples, and season with additional salt and pepper and/or more mayonnaise if desired.

Sweet simplicity: toasted tortillas layered with protein-rich peanut butter, a sprinkle of cinnamon and sliced banana. This is a kid favorite, but I'm not imposing any age restrictions here! Serve as is or with soy yogurt for dipping or Molassa-Sauce (below).

Peanut Banana Tortilla **Turnovers**

MAKES 2 SERVINGS.

2	**(10-in /25-cm) whole wheat tortillas** (see note)
¼ cup	**natural peanut butter** (or other nut or seed butter)
¼ tsp	**cinnamon**
1	**medium–large banana,** sliced
½–1 tsp	**canola oil** (for coating pan)

Spread peanut butter evenly on tortillas. Sprinkle with cinnamon and place banana on half of each tortilla (filling a half-moon shape). Fold each tortilla so you have two half-moon shaped sandwiches. Wipe oil (using a corner of a paper towel) on a non-stick frying pan. Heat pan on medium, then add the two folded tortillas. Cook for 3–5 minutes, until lightly browned, then flip to cook other sides until lightly browned. Remove, let cool slightly, and cut into wedges.

Be sure to buy tortillas that do not contain hydrogenated oils.

A magnificent variation on this recipe is strawberry quesadillas. Use almond butter instead of peanut butter, and thinly sliced fresh strawberries instead of banana; cinnamon is optional. Use canola oil or Earth Balance Buttery Spread to cook them. They also make a delicious dessert served with non-dairy ice cream.

Blackstrap molasses is healthy, but it can be very strong-tasting, so here it is mixed into applesauce for a nutrient-boosted dip for dunking veggies, fruit, bread, waffles, or sandwiches like Peanut Banana Tortilla Turnovers (above)

Molassa-**Sauce**

MAKES 4–5 SERVINGS.

¾ cup	**unsweetened applesauce**
1 tbsp	**blackstrap molasses** (see note)
½ tsp	**cinnamon** (see note)
½–1 tsp	**agave nectar** (optional)

In a bowl, combine all ingredients and stir until well combined.

Since blackstrap molasses is slightly bitter, you can try this recipe with 1–2 tbsp at first, and see if you want more next time.

Adding cinnamon helps with the flavor, so you can use more if you like!

Traditionally, the muffuletta is a large Sicilian sandwich made using a round loaf of bread that is cut in half and layered with sliced meats and an olive filling. I've switched it up vegan-style, with a zesty, magnificent filling consisting of olives, veggies, herbs, seasonings, and sautéed marinated tempeh.

Veggie Tempeh **Muffuletta**

MAKES 4–6 SERVINGS.

1 pkg	**(8-oz/225-g) tempeh,** diced small (see note)
½ tbsp	**tamari**
1 tbsp	**vegan Worcestershire sauce**
1 tbsp	**olive oil**

VEGGIE FILLING:

½ cup	**fennel bulb,** cored and diced (see note)
¾ cup	**red** (or orange or yellow) **bell peppers,** diced
¾–1 cup	**roasted red bell peppers,** diced small; or **marinated artichokes,** drained, lightly patted dry, and diced (or combination of both)
3–3½ tbsp	**sun-dried tomatoes** (from jar), drained and minced
1 tbsp	**capers**
¼–⅓ cup	**fresh basil or parsley,** chopped (or combination of both)
¼ cup	**pitted Kalamata olives,** diced
¼ cup	**pitted green olives,** diced
¼ cup	**green onions,** sliced thinly
1	**medium clove garlic,** minced
2–2½ tbsp	**extra virgin olive oil**
2 tbsp	**red wine vinegar**
½ tsp	**dried oregano**
½ tsp	**Dijon mustard**
⅛ tsp	**sea salt**
	freshly ground black pepper to taste
1	**unsliced round loaf bread** (8–10-in/20–25-cm diameter) (see note)
	avocados, tomatoes, lettuce leaves, or other sliced veggies of choice
1 tbsp	**olive oil** (optional)

In a bowl, toss tempeh with tamari and Worcestershire sauce. In a frying pan on medium-high, heat oil. Add tempeh and sauté for 7–9 minutes, until lightly browned. While tempeh is cooking, chop veggie filling ingredients. Remove tempeh from heat and let cool. In a bowl, combine all veggie filling ingredients and stir to combine. Add cooled tempeh to mixture and stir to combine. At this point, you can refrigerate the filling for 1–2 days until ready to use, or use immediately. To serve immediately, slice loaf in half horizontally. Scrape out some of the bread from the top and bottom halves to accommodate the filling. Drizzle 1 tbsp olive oil into the hollowed bread shells. Scoop filling into one half, add slices of avocados, tomatoes and/or lettuce leaves, and top with other half. If you have time, cover and refrigerate for a couple of hours. Cut into wedges and serve.

You can use pre-marinated tempeh, such as Green Cuisine's tempeh burgers, or frozen, unmarinated tempeh. If using the latter, simmer first in 2 cups vegetable broth for 20 minutes (I use a vegetable bouillon cube, 2 cups of water, and 1 bay leaf) to remove some of the bitter taste. After simmering, drain and use in recipe. If you don't want to use tempeh, you can substitute marinated tofu, diced small and pre-marinated in 2 tsp tamari and balsamic or red wine vinegar, or chopped chickpeas; sauté either until lightly browned.

If you don't want to use fennel, feel free to substitute celery, cucumber, carrots, or zucchini.

Muffuletta is usually prepared with a white Italian-style round loaf, but you can use any loaf you like, such as whole wheat; just ensure it's not pre-sliced. If you'd prefer to make individual stuffed sandwiches, use "mini" round loaves such as ciabatta buns (as shown in photograph on page 106). Use same process of slicing in half, hollowing the center, and filling with the mixture. Cut in half and serve, or wrap to tote along on a picnic! Of course, this filling can also be sandwiched in sliced breads or pita.

This tempeh veggie mixture can be used to create one magnificent pizza: use a pizza crust of choice, top with a touch of tomato sauce, and then heap on this filling! Sprinkle with grated vegan cheese if desired.

I made this mixture at lunchtime once when I was out of hummus. Knowing how much my kids love tamari, I blended chickpeas along with tamari and mayo, and the rest is cookbook history. Serve as a sandwich spread; it's especially good with avocado, lettuce, and tomatoes!

Tamari Tease Chickpea **Spread**

MAKES FILLING FOR 3–4 SANDWICHES. | **WHEAT-FREE**

You can substitute the vegan mayo with 1½–2 tbsp olive oil.

1 cup	cooked chickpeas (garbanzo beans)
2 tbsp	Vegenaise or Nayonaise (see note)
1½ tbsp	tamari
1 tsp	unseasoned rice vinegar

In a blender or food processor, combine all ingredients and blend until smooth, scraping down sides of bowl as needed. Season with additional tamari if desired.

This spread combines beans with cashews to give your sandwich some substance (and much flavor)! It can be whipped up in minutes using a food processor. Serve between slices of your favorite bread with veggies of choice.

White Bean **Spread**

MAKES 3–4 SERVINGS. | **WHEAT-FREE**

¾ cup	cooked cannellini (white kidney) beans or navy beans
¼ cup	raw cashews
2 tsp	red wine vinegar
2 tsp	freshly squeezed lemon juice
¼ tsp	sea salt
¼ tsp	prepared mustard
1–1½ tbsp	olive oil
1½ tbsp	nutritional yeast

In a blender or food processor, combine all ingredients and blend until smooth, scraping down sides of bowl as needed. Season with additional salt and pepper if desired.

This smooth spread makes an ideal filling for tortilla roll-ups: spread on whole wheat tortillas, roll them up, and slice into bite-sized rounds for lunches, nibblers, or party fare.

The Main Events

Casseroles, One-Pot Meals, Pastas & More

HERE IS A BOUNTY of recipes that will help you create fantastic weekday dinners and special occasion feasts. Some days, when we're in a rush, we need to be able to be pull a meal together within a half-hour; other days, on weekends and holidays, we have more time to plan and be creative. No matter what day of the week, there are recipes here that will meet your needs.

When it's a busy day and you need a quick meal fix, instead of reaching for that frozen burrito, try Veggie Sizzle Burritos (page 149), they're fast, fun, and fabulous. Or, instead of making your standard spaghetti with tomato sauce, try a unique pasta, like brown rice penne, kamut rotini, or gnocchi, with "Hide the Lentils" Tomato Sauce (page 129). Other fast and easy dishes here include Lemon Garlic Pasta (page 130), Olive Oyl Pasta (page 133), Orange Sesame Tofu (page 136), and Savory French (Puy) Lentils (page 143), to name a few.

When you do have a little more time and pizza's on your mind, turn to Thai Chick-Un Pizza (page 148) for an exotic interpretation on a traditional favorite that will send taste-buds soaring. When Mexican food is on the menu, prepare the Avocado & Pinto Bean Enchiladas (page 119) or Gimme Chimis (page 128). When you want lots of fresh veggies stir-fried with a tasty sauce adorning rice or soba noodles, be sure to check out Broccoli Cashew Teriyaki Tofu Stir-fry (page 122). Want to impress some guests? Definitely make the Moroccan-Infused Veggie Phyllo Rolls (page 134), or Sun-Dried Tomato Pesto with Toasted Almonds & Pine Nuts (page 146). Looking to get more legumes in your diet? Then try the Chickpea Sensation Patties (page 125), Brown Rice 'n' Beans Jumble-aya (page 123), or Polenta Casserole (page 138). Finally, if you're one of those folks building up the nerve to eat tofu, then turn immediately to page 124 for the Cashew-Ginger Tofu—you and tofu will be bosom buddies thereafter!

If you're shy about full-on vegan cooking, try at least one recipe a week; maybe it will become a family favorite. I'm certain you'll find some blow-your-mind, wickedly good, must-make-again dishes that will become part of your meal-making repertoire!

This is spicy comfort food: enchiladas stuffed with beans and veggies, with cashews and lightly mashed avocado, making them utterly delicious. Pair with a generous, crisp salad with Cumin-Cinnamon Vinaigrette (page 80), or send the meal over the top with Cornmeal-Crusted Plantains (page 158) on the side.

Avocado & Pinto Bean Enchiladas

MAKES 4 SERVINGS.

9–10	(6-in/15-cm) corn tortillas (may use whole-wheat)		1 can	(14-oz/398-ml) pinto beans, rinsed and patted dry
½–1 tbsp	olive oil		½ cup	raw cashew pieces (or whole, lightly crushed)
1 cup	onions, thinly sliced (1 small–medium onion)		2 tbsp	freshly squeezed lime juice
1 tsp	mild chili powder		1¼–1½ cups	avocado (2 medium avocados)
½ tsp	cumin powder		¼ tsp	sea salt
¼ tsp	allspice		1 jar	(14½-oz/425-ml) prepared enchilada sauce (about 1¾ cups)
¼ tsp	sea salt			
	freshly ground black pepper to taste		¾–1 cup	prepared chili sauce (see note)
			¾–1 cup	vegan cheese, grated (optional)
2–2½ cups	white button mushrooms, sliced		½ cup	fresh cilantro leaves, chopped (for garnish)

Preheat oven to 400°F (205°C). Place tortillas (frozen or room temperature) in a 8x12-in (20x30-cm) baking dish, cover tightly with aluminium foil, and place in oven to soften for 5–10 minutes while preparing filling. In a frying pan on medium heat, add oil, onions, chili powder, cumin, allspice, salt, and pepper and sauté for 2–3 minutes. Increase heat to medium-high, add mushrooms, beans, and cashews and sauté for 5–6 minutes, tossing once or twice. Immediately toss in lime juice and remove from heat to slightly cool. In a large bowl, mash avocado and salt (can be chunky). Add veggie sauté and lightly mix to incorporate. In a separate bowl, mix enchilada and chili sauces. Remove tortillas from oven, transfer to a plate, and cover with a tea towel to keep warm. In the same baking dish, pour half of sauce evenly over bottom. Place ¼–1/3 cup avocado-veggie mixture in center of each tortilla. Roll tortillas up, tucking in sides as you go, and place seam-side down in baking dish. Pour remaining sauce over top, and cover with aluminium foil. Bake for 16–18 minutes, then uncover and bake for another 4–5 minutes, until bubbling around edges. If adding cheese, sprinkle on after casserole has baked for 15 minutes, then bake uncovered for another 6–7 minutes to melt cheese. Sprinkle with cilantro and serve.

I like adding a mild, sweet chili sauce to the enchilada sauce to boost flavor. You can also make it with regular enchilada sauce, using 1–1½ jars.

If corn tortillas dry out, re-soften them by returning to oven in covered dish (or by coating with some enchilada sauce).

Don't let the long list of ingredients discourage you; this is one tasty, simple casserole that uses basic ingredients and can be assembled in under a half-hour. Pair with a large crispy salad tossed with Cumin-Cinnamon Vinaigrette (page 80).

Bean & Corn Tortilla Lasagna with Avocado

MAKES 4–5 SERVINGS. | **WHEAT-FREE**

1 can	**(14-oz/398-ml) tomato sauce**
1 tsp	**chili powder**
1¼ tsp	**cumin powder**
1 tsp	**dried oregano**
⅛ tsp	**allspice**
¼ tsp	(rounded) **sea salt**
	freshly ground black pepper to taste
½ tsp	**chipotle hot sauce** (I use Tabasco brand)
¼ tsp	**agave nectar**
2	**medium cloves garlic,** finely minced or pressed
⅓ cup	**onion,** diced

1 can	**(14-oz/398-ml) black or pinto beans,** rinsed and drained (about 1¾ cups)
6–7	**(6-in/15-cm) corn tortillas**
1	**large avocado,** thinly sliced (or 2 small)
1 pinch	**sea salt**
¾ cup	**frozen or fresh corn kernels**
1½ tbsp	**fresh lime juice** (about 1 lime)
½ cup	**tortilla chips,** crushed
¾ cup	**vegan cheese, grated** (optional)
¼ cup	**fresh cilantro leaves,** chopped (for finishing)
	fresh lime wedges (for garnish, a must!)

Preheat oven to 400°F (205°C). In a large bowl, combine tomato sauce, chili powder, cumin, oregano, allspice, ¼ tsp salt, pepper, hot sauce, agave nectar, garlic, onion, and beans and stir to mix well. Lightly oil an 8x12-in (20x30-cm) baking dish. Pour half of mixture in baking dish and tip back and forth to distribute evenly. Place half of tortillas on top of mixture (use 2 whole tortillas and cut a third tortilla to cover spots; or cut them all into strips). Place avocado slices on top of tortillas and season with a pinch of salt. Distribute corn kernels over avocado, then drizzle with lime juice. Top this layer with remaining tortillas, spread with remaining sauce, and sprinkle with crushed tortilla chips, then cheese. Cover with aluminium foil and bake for 20 minutes, then uncover and bake for another 7–10 minutes, until the cheese is melted and casserole is bubbling at edges. If cheese hasn't melted, broil for 1–2 minutes. Remove from oven and cut into squares. Sprinkle with cilantro and serve with lime wedges.

Before becoming vegetarian, my husband loved a certain blackened halibut entrée from a local restaurant. He said it was the spicy flavor that he loved, so I came up with a tofu version. Serve with a sweet side such as Autumn Purée (page 155). Brown rice, quinoa, simple mashed potatoes, or a bean dish are also suitable accompaniments, along with a crisp salad drizzled with Back-to-Basics Balsamic Vinaigrette (page 77).

Blackened Tofu

MAKES 3–4 SERVINGS (24–28 SQUARES). | **WHEAT-FREE**

1 pkg	**(12-oz/350-g) firm or extra-firm tofu,** sliced ¼– ½-in (5–10-mm) thick squares and patted to remove excess moisture
2 tbsp	**lime juice** (or lemon juice, or combination)
1 tbsp	**paprika**
2 tsp	**onion powder**
1 tsp	**garlic powder**
½ tsp	**ground black pepper**
¼ tsp	**cayenne pepper**
½ tsp	**ground oregano or marjoram**
½ tsp	**dried thyme**
½ tsp	**ground fennel seeds**
½ tsp	**celery seed**
½ tsp	**sea salt**
1 tbsp	**arrowroot** (or potato starch or cornstarch)
2–2½ tbsp	**olive oil**

In a large dish, drizzle tofu with lime juice and marinate for 20 minutes or longer, turning over halfway through. In a bowl, combine remaining ingredients except oil and mix well. Add each piece of tofu to spice mixture to coat, gently tapping to remove excess clumps, and set aside. In a non-stick frying pan on high, heat oil. Add tofu and brown for 5–6 minutes, then turn over to brown for another 3–5 minutes (avoid turning over too soon as some spices may cling to pan). Once both sides are nicely browned/blackened, remove and serve immediately.

The veggies in this Asian-style stir-fry stay fresh and vibrant when lightly cooked until tender, but retaining some crunch. The salty-sweet sauce comes alive with fresh garlic and ginger. Add tofu and cashews and serve over soba or rice noodles and you have one crowd-pleasing meal!

Broccoli Cashew Teriyaki Tofu Stir-Fry

MAKES 3–4 SERVINGS. | **WHEAT-FREE**

TOFU (SEE NOTE):

1 pkg	**(12-oz/350-g) firm or extra-firm tofu,** cubed ½–¾-in (1–2-cm) thick
1 tbsp	**tamari**
1½ tbsp	**rice wine vinegar or red wine vinegar**

TERIYAKI SAUCE:

⅓ cup	**tamari**
¼ cup	**water**
3½ tbsp	**agave nectar**
1–1½ tbsp	**freshly squeezed lemon juice**
1 tbsp	**toasted sesame oil**
1 tsp	**blackstrap molasses**
5–6	**medium cloves garlic,** minced
2–2½ tsp	**freshly grated ginger**
1 tbsp	**arrowroot powder**

STIR-FRY:

1–2 tbsp	**canola or olive oil**
4½–5 cups	**broccoli (florets and peeled stalks),** chopped (about ½ lb/225 g)
1–2 pinches	**sea salt**
1–2 tsp	**water**
1½ cups	**red, yellow, or orange bell pepper,** sliced (1 medium-large pepper)
½–¾ cup	**raw cashews**
½ cup	**green onions,** sliced

Marinating adds extra flavor to the tofu, but you can skip this step if you are in a hurry.

In a shallow dish, add tofu. Pour tamari and vinegar over tofu and marinate for 10 minutes or longer (flip tofu once while marinating). Meanwhile, in a large bowl, whisk all ingredients for teriyaki sauce until arrowroot is dissolved (or use a hand blender to purée). In a large frying pan or wok on high, heat ½–1 tbsp oil. Add tofu and sauté for 4–5 minutes, then turn over to sauté for another 3–4 minutes, until to lightly brown each side. Remove from pan and set aside. Reduce heat to medium, add another ½–1 tbsp oil to pan or wok, and add broccoli, salt, and water. Toss, cover, and cook for 4–5 minutes, until broccoli turns bright green, then add bell peppers and sauté uncovered for another 1–2 minutes. Add teriyaki sauce and increase heat to high. Toss to coat, and let sauce come to a slow boil. As soon as sauce has reached a slow boil and has thickened, add tofu, cashews, and green onions, and toss to combine. Remove pan from heat and serve immediately.

This is my take on the classic Cajun dish, Jambalaya. It is also reminiscent of a Spanish rice dish my mother made when I was young, so I named it "Jumble-aya." Serve alongside Lemon-Broiled Green Beans (page 160) and a large green salad drizzled with Back-to-Basics Balsamic Vinaigrette (page 77).

Brown Rice 'n' Beans "Jumble-aya"

MAKES 4 SERVINGS.

½ tbsp	olive oil
1½ cups	onion, diced
1 cup	celery, diced
1 cup	green bell pepper, diced
3	large cloves garlic, minced
1 tsp	dried thyme
½ tsp	dried oregano
1 tsp	file powder (optional) (see note)
1 tsp	paprika
¾–1 tsp	sea salt
2–3 pinches	cayenne pepper (optional)
	freshly ground black pepper to taste
1½ tbsp	vegan Worcestershire sauce
1 can	(28-oz/796-ml) diced tomatoes
2 tbsp	tomato paste
1 cup + 1–2 tbsp	vegetable stock
1 cup	uncooked long or short-grain brown rice
2	bay leaves
1 can	(14-oz/398-ml) kidney beans, drained and rinsed
¾–1 cup	green onion stalks, sliced (optional)
⅓–½ cup	fresh parsley leaves, chopped (optional)
	olive oil (for finishing)

File powder is made from dried, ground sassafras leaves. It can be found in specialty shops and some grocery stores. If it is not available, it's okay to omit it.

In a large pot on medium heat, add oil, onion, celery, bell pepper, garlic, thyme, oregano, file powder, paprika, salt, cayenne, and black pepper. Stir to combine, cover, and cook for 5–7 minutes, stirring occasionally. Add Worcestershire sauce, tomatoes, tomato paste, vegetable stock, rice, bay leaves, and beans. Increase heat to bring to a boil, then reduce heat to low, cover, and simmer for 40–45 minutes, until rice is tender. (If more cooking is required, add 1–2 tbsp stock or water and cook for another 5 minutes.) Once rice is cooked, turn off heat and let stand for 5 minutes. Stir in green onions and parsley, season to taste with additional salt and pepper, and serve drizzled with a little olive oil if desired.

This dish is amazing: each piece of tofu is tender and generously coated in a creamy, tangy cashew sauce. Serve over quinoa, wild rice, or millet, and alongside Roasted Winter Squash Rings (page 163), and steamed vegetables or a salad drizzled with Cumin-Cinnamon Vinaigrette (page 80).

Cashew-Ginger Tofu

MAKES 4–5 SERVINGS (ABOUT 24 SQUARES). | **WHEAT-FREE**

Leftovers of this tofu are terrific paired with veggies and rolled into a rice paper wrap, or baked in a tortilla wrap.

⅓ cup	**cashew butter**
3½ tbsp	**tamari**
3 tbsp	**apple cider vinegar**
2	**large cloves garlic,** chopped
1 tbsp	**fresh ginger,** peeled and chopped
2 tbsp	**agave nectar**
¾ cup	**water**
1 pkg	**(12-oz/350-g) firm or extra-firm tofu** (frozen or fresh), sliced ¼–½ -in (5–10-mm) thick squares and patted to remove excess moisture

Preheat oven to 375°F (190°C). Using a hand blender or food processor, combine cashew butter, tamari, vinegar, garlic, ginger, and agave nectar and purée, until cashew butter is incorporated and mixture is smooth. Add water and purée again until smooth, scraping down sides of bowl as needed. Pour a little of mixture into an 8x12-in (20x30-cm) baking dish to cover bottom, then add tofu and pour in remaining sauce to cover evenly. At this point, either cover and refrigerate to marinate for 1 hour or more, or bake immediately. To bake, cover with aluminium foil and bake for 15 minutes. Remove cover, stir well, and bake again uncovered for 5–7 minutes, until sauce has thickened (lightly stir if necessary). Do not overbake, or the sauce will become too thick and pasty.

One of my husband's Top 10 favorite meals, these patties are tender with a lightly crisp coating, and hold together nicely. The capers and thyme impart a subtle, savory flavor. Serve topped with a slurry of balsamic vinegar and flax oil, tucked inside pita breads with all the fixin's, or without sauce or condiments alongside Potato Squashers (page 162), or Popcorn Fries (page 161) with Thick 'n' Rich Gravy (page 88), and a salad.

Chickpea Sensation **Patties**

MAKES 4 SERVINGS.

2 tsp	**olive oil** (for sautéing vegetables)
1½ cups	**onion,** chopped
1 cup	**celery,** chopped
⅛ tsp	**sea salt**
	freshly ground black pepper to taste
2 cups	**cooked chickpeas (garbanzo beans)**
2	**medium–large cloves garlic,** quartered
2 tbsp	**vegan Worcestershire sauce**
2 tbsp	**tamari**
2 tsp	**fresh thyme leaves** (may use ¾ tsp dried)
1 tbsp	**capers**
⅛ tsp	**sea salt**
2 cups	**cooked short-grain brown rice**
¾ cup + 1 tbsp	**quick oats**
1½–2 tbsp	**olive oil** (for frying patties)

If after chilling the mixture is not firm enough to form patties, stir in an additional 2–3 tbsp quick oats, or breadcrumbs.

Have leftover cooked patties? Refrigerate them and re-use another day as a sandwich filling; simply mash and add chopped fresh veggies and condiments of choice.

In a frying pan on medium heat, add oil, onion, celery, salt, and bell pepper and sauté for 7–10 minutes, stirring occasionally, until onions and celery start to soften. Meanwhile, in a blender or food processor, purée chickpeas with garlic, Worcestershire sauce, tamari, thyme, capers, and salt. Add sautéed veggies and purée to incorporate. Add 1 cup brown rice and purée to combine, then add remaining rice and pulse to incorporate but retain some texture. Transfer mixture to a large bowl and stir in oats. Cover and refrigerate for at least 30 minutes to firm up. Remove from refrigerator and form into patties with your hands. In a frying pan on medium-high, heat oil. Add patties in batches, frying for 6–9 minutes each side, until golden.

This is another very simple tofu dish that yields bold, baked-in flavors. The lime juice, cumin, and touch of cayenne are in every bite, and the addition of pumpkin seeds adds just the right amount of crunch. Serve with Autumn Purée (page 155) and with a dressed salad topped with Polenta Croutons (page 85).

Cumin Lime Tofu

MAKES 4–5 SERVINGS (ABOUT 24 SQUARES). | **WHEAT-FREE**

Adjust quantity of agave nectar to suit sweetness of side dishes. For example, use the full 2 tbsp if serving over a whole grain, but just 1 ½ tbsp if serving with the naturally sweet Autumn Purée.

¼ cup	**freshly squeezed lime juice**
1½–2 tbsp	**agave nectar** (see note)
1½ tbsp	**tamari**
¾ tsp	**ground cumin**
¼ tsp	**curry powder**
⅛ tsp	**allspice**
2–3 pinches	**cayenne pepper** (or to taste)
¼ tsp	**sea salt**
1½ tbsp	**olive oil or coconut oil**
1 pkg	**(12-oz/350-g) firm or extra-firm tofu** (frozen or fresh), cut in half lengthwise then sliced ¼–½-in (5–10-mm) thick squares, and patted to remove excess moisture
2–3 tbsp	**raw or pre-roasted pumpkin seeds** (or pistachios), lightly crushed or chopped

Preheat oven to 375°F (190°C). In an 8x12-in (20x30-cm) baking dish, combine lime juice, agave nectar, tamari, cumin, curry powder, allspice, cayenne, and salt and stir to mix well. Stir in oil (if using coconut oil, melt first or stir through early in the baking process). Add tofu and turn to coat each side. Cover with aluminium foil and bake for 15 minutes. Remove from oven to turn tofu over, sprinkle with pumpkin seeds, and return to oven to bake uncovered for another 13–15 minutes, until tofu has soaked up most of marinade. Serve warm, pouring any remaining oil and/or spices over tofu.

I created these one night when I was craving a burrito. I had fresh broccoli in the fridge, so I seasoned the florets and tucked them inside for a tasty treat. Serve with a squeeze of a lime wedge, and a splash of balsamic vinegar and flax oil (or Balsamic-Garlic Flax Oil from *Vive le Vegan!*) or with Smoky Avocado Sauce (page 87).

Garlicky Broccoli, Corn & Bean Burritos

MAKES 4 SERVINGS.

1 can	**(14-oz/398-ml) black beans,** drained and rinsed (see note)		**VEGGIE SAUTÉ:**	
1½ tbsp	**balsamic vinegar**		1 tbsp	**olive oil**
1 tbsp	**tamari**		3–4	**medium cloves garlic,** minced
2½–3 tbsp	**water**		¼ tsp	**sea salt**
1	**medium clove garlic,** quartered			**freshly ground black pepper** to taste
1½ tsp	**curry powder**		2½–3 cups	**broccoli (florets and peeled stalks),** chopped
4	**(10-in/25-cm) flour tortillas** (see note)		2 tbsp	**vegan Worcestershire sauce**
1 cup	**vegan mozzarella cheese,** grated (optional)		2 tsp	**hoisin sauce**
	fresh lime wedges		1 tsp	**tamari**
			¾–1 cup	**frozen corn kernels**

Preheat oven to 400°F (205°C). Lightly oil (or line with parchment paper) a 8x12-in (20x30-cm) baking dish. In a food processor, combine beans, vinegar, tamari, water, garlic, and curry powder and purée until smooth. In a frying pan on medium-low heat, add oil, garlic, salt, and pepper and toss, then cover and cook for 1–2 minutes (reduce heat and/or add a few drops of water if needed to prevent garlic from burning). Add broccoli, then Worcestershire sauce, hoisin sauce, and tamari. Cover and cook for another 2–3 minutes to lightly steam broccoli. Stir in corn, then remove from heat (do not overcook, as ingredients will be heated again in burrito). On a flat surface, spoon ¼ of bean mixture down center of each tortilla, leaving 1-in (2½-cm) space on top and bottom. Top mixture with ¼ of sautéed veggies. Fold bottom edge over filling and roll up, tucking in the sides as you go. Place burritos, seam-side down, in baking dish. Bake for 20–25 minutes, sprinkling on cheese during last 3–5 minutes. Serve with lime wedges to squeeze fresh juice on each portion.

If short on time, skip the first step of puréeing beans and seasonings, substituting with a can of refried beans.

Be sure to buy tortillas that do not contain hydrogenated oils.

After creating the Lentil Veggie Chimichangas (page 132), I created this version with a smokier, spicier tone. Serve with Guacamole Con Alga Marina (page 61) and chopped cucumber, bell peppers or tomatoes, and parsley or cilantro tossed with Cumin-Cinnamon Vinaigrette (page 80). If serving a group, pair with Potato Squashers (page 162) or Cinnamon Lime Quinoa with Apricots & Almonds (page 156).

Gimme **Chimis**

MAKES 4 SERVINGS.

½–1 tbsp	**olive oil**
½ cup	**onion, diced** (1 small onion)
2	**large cloves garlic,** minced
1 tbsp	**chili powder**
2 tsp	**dried oregano leaves**
1–1½ tsp	**chipotle hot sauce** (I use Tabasco brand) (see note)
½ tsp	**cumin**
¼ tsp	**cinnamon**
⅛ tsp	**ground cloves**
½ tsp	**sea salt**

1½ cups	**zucchini,** julienned (or combined with julienned green bell peppers)
½–¾ cup	**tomatoes,** chopped
1 can	**(14-oz/395-ml) pinto beans,** drained and rinsed
½ cup	**tempeh,** chopped (or extra-frim tofu, veggie "chicken," or an additional ½ cup beans of any variety)
1½ tbsp	**balsamic vinegar**
4	**(10-in/25-cm) whole wheat tortillas** (or tortillas of choice) (see note)
2 tbsp	**olive oil** (for frying)
	fresh lime wedges (for garnish—a must!)
	fresh cilantro leaves, chopped (for garnish)

WHEAT-FREE OPTION: Use hemp or rice tortillas. Regardless, use ones that do not contain hydrogenated oils.

You can use the mixture to fill 6 smaller chimis, just use two additional tortillas.

These chimis are spicy and smoky, but without an intense "heat." If you'd like them spicier, add more hot sauce or chopped jalapeño peppers to sauté.

These chimis are crispiest when fried only, but baking heats them thoroughly. If you prefer a crispier chimi (but not as hot), skip the baking step.

In a frying pan on medium heat, add oil, onion, garlic, chili powder, oregano, chipotle sauce, cumin, cinnamon, cloves, and salt and sauté for 2–3 minutes, stirring occasionally. Add zucchini and tomatoes, and sauté for another 5 minutes until veggies soften. Add tempeh (or substitute), stir to combine, and sauté for another 3–5 minutes. Stir in vinegar and transfer mixture to a bowl (scraping out all filling and reserving pan for later). Preheat oven to 425°F (220°C). Line baking sheet with parchment paper. On a flat surface, spoon ¼ of filling down center of each tortilla, leaving 1–2-in (2½–5-cm) space on top and bottom. Fold bottom edge over filling and roll up, tucking in sides as you go. In the same frying pan on medium-high, heat oil for 30 seconds, then place burritos seam-side down on pan. Cook for 2–3 minutes on each side to lightly brown, then transfer to lined baking sheet (or if frying pan is oven-proof, then simply place it in oven) and bake for 12–15 minutes. Remove and serve with lime wedges and a sprinkling of cilantro.

This is a versatile, mellow sauce that is superb with pasta or grains, or even for dunking warm bread. Serve over pasta, quinoa, barley, or polenta with Seared Portobello Mushrooms (page 165) or Lemon-Broiled Green Beans (page 160), and use leftover sauce with Lentil Veggie Chimichangas (page 132).

"Hide the Lentils" Tomato Sauce

MAKES 4–5 SERVINGS. | **WHEAT-FREE**

1 tbsp	olive oil
3	**large cloves garlic,** minced
¾ tsp	(rounded) **sea salt**
	freshly ground black pepper to taste
¾ cup	**dry red lentils**
1 can	**(28-oz/796-ml) crushed tomatoes** (see note)
1½ cup	**water**
2 tsp	**fresh rosemary, chopped** (or 1 tsp dried)
1½ tsp	**dried basil**
½ tsp	**agave nectar**
1	**fresh or dry bay leaf**
1 tbsp	**red wine vinegar or apple cider vinegar**

If you only have whole or diced canned tomatoes: pour some liquid from the can into the pot first, then insert hand blender in can and blend.

You may want to double this recipe if serving a group, and store any leftovers in the fridge or freezer. This sauce freezes well, but if thawing it for Lentil Veggie Chimichangas (page 132), be sure to simmer it first to reduce excess moisture.

In a large pot on medium-low heat, add oil, garlic, salt, and pepper. Cover and cook for 4–5 minutes (reduce heat and/or add a few drops of water if needed to prevent garlic from burning). Rinse lentils. Add lentils, tomatoes, water, rosemary, basil, agave nectar, and bay leaf. Increase heat to high to bring mixture to a boil. Once boiling, reduce heat to medium-low, cover, and cook for 22–25 minutes, stirring occasionally, until lentils are fully softened. Uncover and simmer for 3 minutes to reduce liquid. Stir in vinegar and season with additional salt, pepper, and/or agave nectar if desired. Remove bay leaf, and serve sauce as is (or purée it with a hand blender to hide the lentils from picky eaters!).

I created this dish one night when I craved pasta, but didn't have any sauce on hand. Not in any mood for chopping, I started squeezing lemons and grating garlic, and within a half-hour, this dish was ready! It's tangy and fresh, with a perfect dose of garlic. Serve with White Bean & Walnut Bruschetta (page 70), or with a mixed green salad with Creamy Basil Dressing (page 78).

Lemon Garlic **Pasta**

MAKES 3–4 SERVINGS.

WHEAT-FREE OPTION: Use a brown rice, spelt, or quinoa pasta.

Use a kitchen rasp to grate garlic, or simply quarter garlic cloves if using a hand blender.

I like two cloves of garlic in this sauce, giving the sauce enough kick without overwhelming it. If you are a garlic lover, use an extra clove, but keep in mind that it's raw, so it will taste stronger.

If you like nutritional yeast, sprinkle each serving with 2–3 tsp and toss—very tasty!

¾ lb	**(340 g) dry spaghetti or fettuccine** (or pasta of choice) (see note)
⅓ cup	**freshly squeezed lemon juice**
2	**large cloves garlic,** minced (see note)
½ tsp	**sea salt**
	freshly ground black pepper to taste
1½ tsp	**agave nectar**
½ tsp	**Dijon mustard**
3½–4½ tbsp	**olive oil**
¼–⅓ cup	**toasted pine nuts** (or chopped walnuts or almond slivers)
¼–⅓ cup	**fresh parsley or basil leaves,** chopped

Cook pasta according to package directions. Meanwhile, in a bowl, whisk together lemon juice, garlic, salt, pepper, agave nectar, mustard, and oil (starting with 3½ tbsp) (or use hand blender to purée ingredients). Set aside. When pasta is almost done, remove 1 cup of pasta water and reserve. Drain pasta (do not rinse), return to pot, and toss with lemon dressing, toasted nuts, and parsley. If pasta seems too dry, add some pasta water, 1 tbsp at a time. Season to taste, adding extra oil and salt and pepper if desired.

Traditional pesto takes on new life with this recipe. Cashews provide a creamy, buttery contrast to the tangy lemon juice. Be sure to make this dish when fresh basil is abundant. Top with sliced cherry tomatoes, and serve with a salad with Back-to-Basics Balsamic Vinaigrette (page 77) and Simplest Garlic Bread (page 66).

Lemony Cashew-Basil **Pesto** on Pasta

MAKES 3–4 SERVINGS.

1	**large clove garlic**
3–3½ tbsp	**freshly squeezed lemon juice**
¾ tsp	**dry mustard**
¾ tsp	**sea salt**
	freshly ground black pepper to taste
2 tbsp	**olive oil**
1 tbsp	**water**
1 cup + 1–2 tbsp	**raw cashews** (see note)
2½–2¾ cups	(packed) **fresh basil leaves and tender stems**
½–¾ lb	**(225–340 g) dry pasta of choice** (see note)
	olive oil (for finishing)

In a food processor, combine garlic, lemon juice, mustard, salt, pepper, oil, and water, and purée until fairly smooth, scraping down sides of bowl as needed. Add cashews and basil and purée (may leave some texture). Cook pasta according to package directions. When almost done, remove 1 cup of pasta water and reserve. Drain pasta (do not rinse) and toss with pesto, using as much as desired (see note). If pasta seems too dry, add some pasta water, 1 tbsp at a time. Season with additional salt and pepper if desired, and finish with a drizzle of olive oil.

WHEAT-FREE OPTION: Use brown rice, spelt, or quinoa pasta.

Raw almonds may be substituted for cashews, just add extra water or oil to moisten when puréeing.

You can make this pesto in advance and refrigerate in a sealed container until you're ready to cook the pasta. This pesto also makes a dynamite sandwich spread or pizza sauce (or dollop on pesto as a pizza topping).

I like a lot of sauce on my pastas, but you may prefer less; use up to 1 lb (450 g) pasta and add extra cooking water or oil to help distribute the pesto through the pasta.

This recipe was inspired by Julie Farson, a fellow blogger who requested a chimichanga (fried burrito) recipe in this book. This wickedly good chimichanga is not at all traditional; I created it one evening after making a lentil sauce for pasta. If you want a more traditional version, see Gimme Chimis (page 128). Serve drizzled with flax oil and balsamic vinegar and alongside a salad with Creamy Basil Dressing (page 78). Add Cornmeal-Crusted Plantains (page 158) or Rosemary Cornmeal Polenta Fries (page 164) to further impress guests.

Lentil Veggie Chimichangas

MAKES 4–5 SERVINGS.

WHEAT-FREE OPTION: Use hemp or rice tortillas. Regardless, use ones that do not contain hydrogenated oils.

Four tortillas make large chimichangas; for smaller chimis, use another tortilla.

It's best to heat the sauce to simmer before using in recipe to reduce liquid, otherwise, the chimis will be leaky. Allow to cool slightly to fill chimis.

These chimis are crispiest just when fried, but baking heats them thoroughly. If prefer a crispier chimi (but not as hot), skip the baking step.

Whole fennel seeds add a delicate taste and aroma to this sauce. When purchasing fennel seeds, buy a small amount and store tightly sealed in your pantry.

½ tbsp	**olive oil** (for sautéing veggies)
1	**medium zucchini or yellow squash,** sliced lengthwise and chopped (1½–2 cups)
1	**medium-large yellow bell pepper,** sliced (about 1½ cups)
1	**small onion,** thinly sliced (½–¾ cups)
½ tsp	**fennel seeds**
⅛ tsp	(rounded) **sea salt**
	freshly ground black pepper to taste
4–5	**(10-in/25-cm) whole wheat tortillas** (see notes)
2 cups	**"Hide the Lentils" Tomato Sauce** (page 129) (see note)
2 tbsp	**olive oil** (for frying chimi)

In a frying pan on medium-high heat, add ½ tbsp oil, zucchini or squash, bell peppers, onions, fennel seeds, salt, and pepper, and sauté for 6–7 minutes, until veggies are slightly seared and onions soften. Remove from heat to cool slightly. Preheat oven to 425°F (220°C). Line a baking sheet with parchment paper. On a flat surface, spoon ⅓–½ cup lentil sauce down center of each tortilla, leaving 1–2-in (2½–5-cm) space on top and bottom. Spoon ¼–⅕ of veggie mixture on top of sauce. Fold bottom edge over filling and roll up, tucking in sides as you go. In a frying pan on medium-high, heat 2 tbsp oil. Place burritos seam-side down in pan. Cook for 2–3 minutes on each side to lightly brown, then transfer to lined baking sheet (or if frying pan is oven-proof, simply place in oven) and bake for 12–15 minutes.

A double olive whammy, this tomato-based sauce features good quality, cold-pressed extra virgin olive oil and pungent olives. Now we have a vegan pasta for both Popeye (see page 139) and Olive Oyl; I'll get to Bluto next! (Thanks to Leslie for naming this recipe.) Serve with White Bean & Walnut Bruschetta (page 70), or a salad with Living Caesar Dressing (page 83) and Polenta Croutons (page 85).

Olive Oyl Pasta

MAKES 4 SERVINGS.

2–2½ tbsp	**good quality, cold-pressed extra virgin olive oil**
8–10	**large cloves garlic, chopped**
3 tbsp	**shallots,** minced (or ¼ cup white portion of green onions, minced)
1½ tsp	**dried basil**
½ tsp	**dried oregano**
¾ tsp	**sea salt**
	freshly ground black pepper to taste
1–2 tsp	**water** (optional)
1 can	**(28-oz/796-ml) diced tomatoes** (see note)
½ cup	**Kalamata and green olives,** pitted and halved (or olives of choice)
¾–1 lb	**(380–450 g) dry pasta of choice** (see note)
2–2½ tbsp	**good quality, cold-pressed extra virgin olive oil** (for finishing)

Organic diced tomatoes are preferable; a seasoned variety (such as with basil or garlic and onions) will add extra flavor.

WHEAT-FREE OPTION: Use brown rice, spelt, or quinoa pasta.

This sauce can be prepared a couple of hours in advance: after it has simmered, turn off heat, and cover. To serve, simply reheat and toss in pasta.

In a large pot on medium-low heat, add oil, garlic, shallots, basil, oregano, salt, and pepper, and stir to combine. Cover and cook for 5–7 minutes (if needed, reduce heat and/or add water to prevent garlic from burning). Remove cover, increase heat to medium-high, and add tomatoes. Bring to boil, then reduce heat to medium-low and cover again to simmer for 15–20 minutes. Meanwhile, prepare pasta in another large pot according to package directions. When pasta is almost done, remove 1 cup of pasta water and reserve. Drain pasta (do not rinse), return to pot, and toss in tomato sauce and olives. If pasta seems dry, add some pasta water, 1 tbsp at a time. Add remaining 2–2½ tbsp oil (or to taste) and season with additional salt and pepper if desired.

This recipe started off as a generic roasted vegetable phyllo roll, but it lacked pizazz. I remembered the flavors of Moroccan cuisine that I love—cumin, cinnamon, and ginger—so I changed a few elements and ingredients, and the result was vegan magic! Serve as an elegant meal, drizzled with Balsamic Maple Sauce (page 76) and paired with a mixed green salad, or as an impressive appetizer.

Moroccan-Infused Vegetable Phyllo **Rolls**

MAKES 4 SERVINGS (OR MORE AS APPETIZERS).

2 cups	**combination of yellow, red, and orange bell peppers,** chopped
2½–3 cups	**zucchini or yellow squash,** cubed
1–1¼ cups	**onion,** chopped
1½–2 cups	**fennel bulb,** chopped (about 1 medium bulb)
½ cup	**dried apricots** (preferably unsulfured), chopped (or if in season, 1 cup fresh figs, stems removed, and halved)
5–6	**large cloves garlic,** minced
1½–2 tbsp	**olive oil**
1½ tsp	**cumin**
¾ tsp	**ground ginger**
½ tsp	**paprika**
¼ + ⅛ tsp	**cinnamon**
½ tsp	**sea salt**
	freshly ground black pepper to taste
1 cup	**cooked chickpeas or white beans**
½ cup	(packed) **fresh basil (or parsley) leaves,** minced
8–12 sheets	**phyllo pastry sheets** (see notes)
2½–3 tbsp	**olive oil** (to brush phyllo)
¼ cup	**chopped or slivered almonds,** lightly toasted (for garnish)

Preheat oven to 425°F (220°C). Line a wide-rimmed baking sheet with parchment paper. Place bell peppers, zucchini, onion, fennel, apricots, and garlic on sheet, and toss with oil, cumin, ginger, paprika, cinnamon, salt, and pepper. Roast in oven for 35–45 minutes, tossing once or twice, until veggies are caramelized in some spots and softened. Remove from oven, toss in chickpeas or white beans and basil, and let cool slightly. Reduce oven temperature to 375°F (190°C). Line a baking dish or sheet with parchment paper. Place a lightly dampened dish towel over phyllo sheets to keep moist while preparing rolls. Lightly brush top of one sheet with oil. Place another sheet (not brushed with oil) on top. Spread ¾–1 cup roasted veggie mixture (see note) down the center of top sheet, leaving 1–2-in (2½–5-cm) space from edges. Fold left side over filling and roll up, tucking in sides as you go. Brush with additional oil and place in lined baking dish or sheet. Repeat process until all phyllo and mixture are used; you will have 4–6 rolls (see note). Bake for 24–28 minutes, until golden brown. Serve warm, garnished with almonds.

WHEAT-FREE OPTION: Use spelt phyllo pastry.

Use 8 sheets to make generously stuffed rolls or 12 sheets for smaller ones. If the roll is quite full, it may tear while baking. This of course won't ruin them, but will affect the presentation (if that's important to you).

As appetizers: Make smaller rolls or bite-sized phyllo triangles. For the latter, brush one sheet with oil. Then, with a sharp knife, cut 4 strips lengthwise down length of sheet. Place a small spoonful of filling at the base of one strip. Then, fold that corner over to form a triangle, and continue to fold back and forth until you reach the top. Repeat process until you have used up all the filling. Bake at 375°F (190°C) for 15–20 minutes, until golden. Serve with Balsamic Maple Sauce (page 76) as a dip.

My kids love this tofu dish. It's delicious and wholesome when served with a whole grain and salad or steamed veggies, such as Coconut Lime Rice (page 157), and Simple Swiss Chard (page 166) or a salad with "Honey" Mustard Vinaigrette (page 81). Try leftovers in rice paper wraps rolled with fresh veggies.

Orange Sesame Tofu

MAKES 4–5 SERVINGS (ABOUT 24 SQUARES). | **WHEAT-FREE**

2 tsp	**arrowroot powder**
½ cup	**freshly squeezed orange juice** (zest orange first, see below)
1 tsp	**orange zest**
3 tbsp	**tamari**
2 tbsp	**pure maple syrup**
2 tbsp	**apple cider vinegar**
2	**medium cloves garlic,** minced
1 tbsp	**toasted sesame oil**
⅛ tsp	**sea salt**
1 pkg	**(12-oz/350-g) extra-firm tofu,** sliced ¼–½-in (5–10-mm) thick squares, and patted to remove excess moisture
¼ cup	**green onions,** thinly sliced (for garnish)
1–2 tbsp	**sesame seeds** (for garnish)

Preheat oven to 400°F (205°C). In an 8x12-in (20x30-cm) baking dish, combine arrowroot with 2 tbsp orange juice and stir until fully dissolved. Add remaining juice and ingredients, except tofu, green onions, and sesame seeds, and stir to combine. Add tofu and turn to coat both sides. Cover and refrigerate to marinate for 1 hour or more, or bake it immediately. To bake, cover with aluminium foil and bake for 15 minutes. Turn over tofu, gently stir to cover tofu with sauce, and bake again, uncovered, for another 6–9 minutes, or until sauce thickens and is bubbling at edges (sauce will continue to thicken as it cools). Remove from oven, sprinkle with green onions and sesame seeds, and serve.

This is a vegan interpretation of the popular Indian dish Palak Paneer, which is made with spinach, cheese, and a blend of spices. My brother-in-law Brent shared his version of Palak Paneer with me, which used tofu instead of cheese. I simplified his recipe for home cooks, while maintaining the sensational flavors. Brent also suggested this name; Soyabina Panira means "cheese of soybean." Serve with samosas and mango chutney and/or Curry Chickpea Hummus (page 48) to spread on roti or naan bread. Refresh your palate with chopped raw vegetables (e.g., tomatoes, bell peppers, cucumbers), tossed with lemon juice and a touch of oil.

Palak Soyabina **Panira**

MAKES 4–6 SERVINGS. | **WHEAT-FREE**

TOFU:

1 pkg	**(12-oz/350-g) firm or extra-firm tofu,** cubed and gently patted to remove excess moisture (see note)
1½ tbsp	**lemon juice**
1½ tbsp	**tamari**
2 tsp	**coconut or canola oil**

SPICE & VEGGIE MIXTURE:

1½ tbsp	**coconut or canola oil**
2 tsp	**cumin**
1½ tsp	**coriander**
½ tsp	**cinnamon**
¼ tsp	**allspice**

2–3 pinches	**ground cloves**
¼ tsp	(rounded) **sea salt**
	freshly ground black pepper to taste
1¼–1½ cups	**onion,** diced
1–2 tsp	**water** (optional)
1½ tsp	**ginger,** grated
2	**large cloves garlic,** minced
1½–2½ tbsp	**jalapeño peppers,** seeded and minced (or to taste)
1 cup	**tomatoes,** chopped
½ tsp	**agave nectar**
1 lb	**(450 g) fresh spinach**
	fresh cilantro leaves, chopped (for garnish)

In a shallow baking dish, pour lemon juice and tamari over tofu and toss to combine. Marinate for 20 minutes or longer. After marinating, in a deep frying pan or large pot on medium-high, heat 2 tsp oil. Add tofu and cook for 8–10 minutes, tossing occasionally, to lightly brown all sides. Remove tofu and reserve pot. In the same pot on medium-high, heat 1½ tbsp oil. Add cumin, coriander, cinnamon, allspice, cloves, salt, and pepper and sauté for 1–2 minutes, then reduce heat to medium. Add onions, cover, and cook for 2–3 minutes (if needed, reduce heat and/or add 1–2 tsp water if onions are sticking). Add ginger, garlic, and jalapeños and stir to combine. Cover and cook for another 2–3 minutes, then add tomatoes and agave nectar. Cover and cook for another 5–6 minutes, until onions are soft and tomatoes start to break down. Add spinach, cover, and cook for another 2–3 minutes, tossing occasionally, until spinach is just wilted. Using a hand blender or food processor, purée mixture to smooth, or keep more texture if desired. Add tofu, toss to combine, and serve, sprinkling with cilantro if desired.

I like to reserve ¼ of sautéed tofu made in this recipe for two reasons. First, I like this dish with less tofu. Second, the reserved tofu is a great nibbler for kids, or to refrigerate for sandwich mixtures.

I created this dish one night when I had no idea what to make for dinner; I rummaged through the pantry and found prepared polenta, beans, and tomato sauce. This casserole was fast, simple, and tasted great. Serve with generous portions of salad tossed in Back-to-Basics Balsamic Vinaigrette (page 77).

Polenta **Casserole**

MAKES 4–5 SERVINGS. | **WHEAT-FREE**

Use a large-holed grater to grate polenta.

½–1 tsp	**oil** (to coat baking dish)
2½ cups	**cooked beans** (any kind)
1 cup	**tomato sauce**
½ cup	**frozen or fresh corn kernels**
3 tbsp	**onion,** minced
2 tsp	**fresh thyme,** chopped
1½ tsp	**red wine vinegar** (or balsamic vinegar)
½ tsp	**agave nectar**
½ tsp	**paprika**
½–1 tsp	**dried oregano**
½ tsp	**dry mustard**
1 tsp	**tamari**
½ tsp	**sea salt**
	freshly ground black pepper to taste
1 tube	**(18-oz/510-g) prepared polenta,** grated (see note)
1 tbsp	**olive oil**
⅛ tsp	**sea salt**
1 cup	**vegan cheese,** grated (optional, I use "Follow Your Heart" mozzarella)
¼ cup	**fresh basil or parsley leaves, or chives,** chopped (for garnish)

Preheat oven to 375°F (190°C). Lightly oil an 8x12-in (20x30-cm) baking dish. In a bowl, combine beans, tomato sauce, corn kernels, onion, thyme, vinegar, agave nectar, paprika, oregano, mustard, tamari, ½ tsp salt, and pepper. Mix to combine well. Transfer to baking dish and distribute evenly. In a separate bowl, combine polenta, 1 tbsp olive oil, ⅛ tsp salt, and cheese, then sprinkle on top of bean mixture. Bake for 30–35 minutes, until top is golden and cheese is melted, or a little longer for a crunchier topping. Place casserole under broiler for 1–2 minutes to melt cheese if needed. Garnish with sprinkling of herbs if desired.

This pasta dish is chock full of spinach! It has a full, rich flavor and can be embellished with as many modifications as you like. Serve with Pizza Focaccia (page 63) or Simplest Garlic Bread (page 66) slathered with White Bean Spread (page 115).

Popeye Pasta

MAKES 3–4 SERVINGS.

1½–2 tbsp	**olive oil**
½ cup	**onion,** diced (about 1 small onion)
4	**large cloves garlic,** minced (see note)
½ tsp	(rounded) **sea salt**
	freshly ground black pepper to taste
1–2 tsp	**water** (optional)
⅓ cup	**red or white wine**
1 can	**(28-oz/796-ml) crushed tomatoes** (see note)
½ tsp	**dried oregano**
½ tsp	**dried marjoram**
1 tsp	**dried basil**
½–1 tsp	**agave nectar** (optional, or other sweetener)
¾–1 lb	**(340–450 g) dry penne or rotini** (or pasta of choice) (see note)
6–8 cups	**spinach leaves,** chopped (see note)

In a large pot on medium-low heat, add oil, onion, garlic, salt, and pepper and stir to combine. Cover and cook for 5–7 minutes (if needed, reduce heat and/or add water to prevent garlic from burning). Uncover, increase heat to medium-high, and stir in wine. Allow to boil for 1 minute, then add tomatoes, oregano, marjoram, basil, and agave nectar. Reduce heat to medium-low, cover, and simmer for 15 minutes. Meanwhile, cook pasta in a large pot according to package directions. After simmering sauce for 15 minutes, uncover, and reduce heat to further simmer for another 5–7 minutes to thicken. Remove sauce from heat, add spinach, and stir to combine, until spinach is just wilted and still vibrant green. Drain pasta (do not rinse) and spoon sauce over pasta (or toss through). Serve drizzled with extra olive oil, freshly ground black pepper, and any "add-ins" you like (see note).

Kid-friendly tips: You may want to reduce the amount of garlic; although the alcohol in the wine burns off, you can omit wine if you prefer; and you can "hide" the spinach by mincing or pulsing in a food processor before adding to sauce.

If you only have whole or diced canned tomatoes, use a hand blender to purée them. Pour off some liquid from the can into pot first, then insert hand blender directly in can and purée.

WHEAT-FREE OPTION: Use brown rice, spelt, or quinoa pasta.

"Add ons" to this pasta can include: pitted olives, toasted pumpkin seeds or pine nuts, capers, julienned fresh basil, capers, and/or sun-dried tomatoes.

If you want to make this sauce in advance, don't add the spinach. Allow to cool before storing in a sealed container in refrigerator. Reheat sauce and add spinach just before serving.

Instead of cooking quinoa and a legume separately on the stovetop, combine the two and let the oven do the work! This healthy dish is comforting with its delicate, earthy seasoning. Drizzle with Balsamic Maple Sauce (page 76), and pair with a mixed green salad.

Quinoa Chickpea Confetti **Casserole**

MAKES 4–6 SERVINGS. | **WHEAT-FREE**

You can substitute brown rice for quinoa; just add another 2–3 tbsp water and bake for another 20 minutes.

Substitute 1 cup sliced zucchini for fennel if you wish.

After this dish is cooked, keep covered before serving to retain moisture. Also, after removing casserole from oven, the quinoa will continue to cook, so if needed, mix 2–3 tbsp boiled water into casserole before a second helping!

1¼ cups	**uncooked quinoa,** rinsed (see note)
1 cup	**vegetable stock**
2 cups	**water**
1½ cups	**cooked chickpeas (garbanzo beans)**
1½ cups	**fennel bulb,** julienned (about 1 medium bulb) (see note)
1 cup	**red bell pepper,** chopped (about 1 medium pepper)
3–4	**large cloves garlic,** minced
1 tbsp	**extra virgin olive oil**
1 tsp	**fennel seeds**
1 tsp	**dried basil**
1 tsp	**dried rosemary**
½ tsp	**dried thyme**
½ tsp	**sea salt**
⅛ tsp	**allspice**
1	**dried or fresh bay leaf**
	freshly ground black pepper to taste
2–3 tbsp	**freshly squeezed lemon juice** (for finishing)
1½–2 tbsp	**extra virgin olive oil** (for finishing)
¼–½ cup	**fresh basil or parsley leaves,** chopped (for garnish)

Preheat oven to 400°F (205°C). In a lightly oiled, deep casserole dish, combine all ingredients (except lemon juice, oil for finishing, and basil or parsley) and stir to combine well. Cover and bake for 55–60 minutes, stirring occasionally, until quinoa is cooked and has absorbed all liquid. Remove from oven, stir in lemon juice, and season to taste with additional salt and pepper if desired. To serve, drizzle a touch of olive oil on each portion if desired and sprinkle with basil or parsley.

This luscious sauce is made from puréeing roasted squash and garlic with other flavorful ingredients. It is incredible served over gnocchi, and topped with toasted nuts. Serve as part of a romantic meal, along with artisan breads, and mixed greens tossed with Back-to-Basics Balsamic Vinaigrette (page 77).

Roasted Red Kuri **Squash** with Gnocchi

MAKES 4–5 SERVINGS.

1–3 lb	(½–1½ kg) red kuri squash (see notes)		2 tbsp	olive oil
1	bulb garlic		2½–3½ tbsp	freshly squeezed lemon juice
1 tsp	sea salt		1 pkg	(16-oz/450-g) prepared gnocchi of choice (see note)
	freshly ground black pepper to taste		1–2 tbsp	Earth Balance Buttery Spread or extra virgin olive oil (for finishing)
¾ tsp	freshly ground nutmeg		⅓ cup	toasted walnuts, lightly crushed (or chopped pistachios)
½ tsp	freshly rosemary, chopped		2–3 tbsp	fresh basil or parsley leaves, or chives, chopped (for garnish)
1¼–1½ cups	plain soy or rice milk			lemon wedges (for serving)

Preheat oven to 400°F (205°C). On a baking sheet lined with parchment paper, place whole squash. Place garlic bulb in small dish and cover with aluminium foil then place on sheet alongside squash. Bake for 1 hour, or until squash is tender when pierced and garlic is soft (garlic may require less roasting time than squash). Let squash cool enough to handle. Cut squash open, scrape out seeds and strings, and discard. Scoop out 3 cups of flesh and combine in food processor with remaining ingredients except walnuts, margarine or oil, fresh herbs, and lemon wedges (and starting with 2½–3 tbsp lemon juice and 1¼ cups milk). Blend until smooth, scraping down sides of bowl as needed. Transfer sauce to a saucepan on low-medium heat, to warm, stirring occasionally. Meanwhile, cook gnocchi according to package directions. Once sauce is warm, test for seasoning and add remaining lemon juice and milk, and additional salt and pepper if desired. You can also finish the sauce by stirring in 1–2 tbsp margarine or olive oil. When gnocchi is cooked, drain, and generously ladle sauce on top of portions. Sprinkle on walnuts and fresh herbs if desired. Serve with lemon wedges for squeezing.

In total, you will need enough squash to yield 3 cups cooked squash. You can substitute with butternut or another deep orange squash. For butternut squash, you will need about 2¾ lb (1¼ kg) and 1 cup milk or more for desired consistency. Sweet potatoes (yams) can also substitute in part for some of the squash.

WHEAT-FREE OPTION: Use a wheat-free pasta or serve with a robust whole-grain like barley.

This pasta sauce is a cinch to make and it has pizzazz! Give yourself an hour to roast veggies, then toss this pasta together in minutes. Serve with side breads and a green salad.

Roasted Tomato-Fennel **Pasta** with Pine Nuts & Capers

MAKES 2–4 SERVINGS (DEPENDING ON QUANTITY OF PASTA).

WHEAT-FREE OPTION: Use brown rice, spelt, quinoa, or kamut pasta.

I have used fig-balsamic vinegar in this recipe, and the taste was terrific! If you find a specialty seasoned balsamic, give it a try.

2–2½ tbsp	olive oil
3½–4 cups	fresh Roma tomatoes (about 1½ lb/680 g), cut in ⅛ths
1 large	fennel bulb, thinly sliced
4	large cloves garlic, minced
1½ tbsp	balsamic vinegar (or flavored variety)
¾–1 tsp	sea salt
	freshly ground black pepper to taste
1 tsp	dried oregano
½–¾ lb	(225–340 g) dry pasta (see note)
2–3 tbsp	pine nuts, toasted
2 tbsp	capers
½ cup	fresh basil, torn or thinly sliced
1–3 tbsp	olive oil (for finishing)

Preheat oven to 400°F (205°C). On a baking sheet lined with parchment paper, toss together 2–2½ tbsp oil, tomatoes, fennel, garlic, vinegar, salt (start with ¾ tsp), pepper, and oregano. Roast for 40–45 minutes, tossing once or twice, until tomatoes are soft and fennel is golden in spots. During the last 10–15 minutes of roasting, cook pasta according to the package directions. When the pasta is almost done, remove ½ cup of pasta water and reserve. Remove veggies from oven. Drain pasta (do not rinse!) and toss in roasted veggies. If pasta seems dry, add some reserved pasta water, 1 tbsp at a time. Just before serving, toss in pine nuts, capers, and fresh basil, and oil for finishing (or drizzle oil on individual portions). Test for seasoning and add extra salt and pepper if desired.

Sometimes I need a legume recipe that is quick to prepare and doesn't require much chopping. After making this dish the first time, our family loved it so much that it quickly became a mainstay served over brown rice. The French lentils are naturally earthy in flavor, and the savory seasonings suit the lentils just beautifully. Serve with brown basmati rice with Roasted Winter Squash Rings (page 163), or over Autumn Purée (page 155). Also, pair with Lemon Broiled Green Beans (page 160) or steamed veggies drizzled with Balsamic Maple Sauce (page 76).

Savory French (Puy) Lentils

MAKES 3–4 SERVINGS. | **WHEAT-FREE**

¾ cup	**dry French (Puy) green lentils,** rinsed
2¼ cups	**water**
1	**mushroom bouillon cube** (see note)
3	**large cloves garlic,** grated or minced (see note)
1 tsp	**dried rosemary**
¾ tsp	**dried thyme**
½ tsp	**dried savory**
¼ tsp	**dry mustard**
1	**dry or fresh bay leaf**
½ tsp	**blackstrap molasses**
	freshly ground black pepper to taste
	lemon wedges (for garnish)

Use a kitchen rasp (see page 14) to grate garlic cloves directly into pot.

I like using Harvest Sun mushroom bouillon cubes to enhance the earthy flavors in this dish. But, you can use a vegetable bouillon cube if needed.

In a saucepan on high heat, combine all ingredients, except lemon wedges, and stir to combine. Bring to a boil, stir, then reduce heat to medium-low, cover, and cook for 35–40 minutes, or until lentils are tender and have absorbed most of the water. (If more water is needed to soften lentils, add another 3–4 tbsp boiled water). Remove from heat and season with additional pepper if desired. Serve with lemon wedges for squeezing over portions.

You will love the fresh, vibrant elements in this dish—lime, ginger, garlic, toasted sesame oil—tossed with tender soba noodles, and shiitake mushrooms, snow peas, and green onions. Zesty, fragrant, healthy, and entirely delicious! For a protein-rich addition, serve with Tamari-Roasted Chickpeas (page 68) or Pan-Fried Tempt-eh! (page 62).

Sesame Lime Soba **Noodles** with Shiitake Mushrooms & Snow Peas

MAKES 3–4 SERVINGS.

SAUCE:

1 tbsp	hoisin sauce
3½ tbsp	tamari
1½ tbsp	fresh ginger, chopped
2	large cloves garlic (see note)
3 tbsp	freshly squeezed lime juice
2 tbsp	apple cider vinegar
2½ tbsp	toasted sesame oil (see note)
3 tbsp	agave nectar

1 pkg	(8-oz/225-g) soba noodles (I use Sobaya organic kamut/soba noodles)
2 tsp	olive oil
5-6-oz	(170-g) shitake mushrooms (about 2½–3 cups), stems removed, and cut in halves or thirds
4-5-oz	(140-g) snow peas, ends trimmed, and sliced lengthwise in thirds
1 tsp	tamari
1 cup	green onions, chopped
2 tbsp	black sesame seeds, or toasted or raw sesame seeds (optional)
¼–½ cup	fresh cilantro leaves, chopped (optional, but very good!)
	lime wedges (for garnish)
	toasted sesame oil (for finishing)

This sauce benefits from the intense flavor of toasted sesame oil, so don't substitute regular sesame oil.

With a hand blender or in a blender, combine all sauce ingredients (or, finely mince or grate garlic and ginger, then whisk all ingredients by hand in a bowl). Cook noodles according to package directions. Meanwhile, in a deep frying pan or large pot on high, heat oil. Add mushrooms and sauté for 1–2 minutes to slightly sear, then add snow peas and tamari and cook for 2–3 minutes, tossing to slightly sear vegetables, then remove from heat and toss in green onions. Drain pasta (do not rinse!) and add to mushrooms and snow peas, along with prepared sauce. Toss to warm sauce and distribute through the noodles. Add sesame seeds and cilantro, toss again, and serve. Serve each portion with a lime wedge and a drizzle of toasted sesame oil if desired.

Lemony Cashew-Basil Pesto on Pasta (page 131)

Moroccan-Infused Vegetable Phyllo Rolls (page 134) with
Balsamic Maple Sauce (page 76)

Orange Sesame Tofu (page 136) with Simple Swiss Chard (page 166)
on Coconut Lime Basmati Rice (page 157)

"Spicoli" Burgers (page 145) with
Potato Squashers (page 162)

These patties are crisp on the outside, soft and moist on the inside. If you don't like hemp seeds, you'll change your mind after a bite of these totally "awesome" patties. (Thanks to Angela for the name!) Serve on their own with a slurry of balsamic vinegar and flax oil, or inside pita breads with veggies and condiments. Popcorn Fries (page 161) or Potato Squashers (page 162) make this meal sing, as well as a salad with Back-to-Basics Balsamic Vinaigrette (page 77).

"Spicoli" Burgers

MAKES 8–10 PATTIES. | **WHEAT-FREE**

2 tsp	olive oil
1¼–1½ cups	onion, diced
⅛ tsp	sea salt
	freshly ground black pepper to taste
¾ cup	red bell pepper, diced
2 cups	cooked short-grain brown rice (see note)
1 cup	shelled hemp seed nuts (I use Manitoba Harvest brand)
2	medium cloves garlic, quartered
2 tbsp	ketchup
1 tbsp	tamari
1 tsp	Dijon mustard
1 tsp	dried oregano
½ tsp	dried thyme
¼ tsp	dried ground sage (or ½ tsp dried sage leaves)
¼ tsp	sea salt
1 cup	cooked short-grain brown rice
¼ cup	white rice flour (to coat patties, may use another flour)
1½–2 tbsp	olive oil (for frying)

You need 3 cups total cooked brown rice for this recipe. I like these patties tender, but you can make them firmer adding oats or breadcrumbs after chilling if you prefer.

Don't know what to do with leftover cooked patties? Refrigerate for a sandwich filling; mash and stir in chopped fresh veggies and vegan mayonnaise to taste.

In a frying pan on medium heat, add oil, onions, salt, and black pepper and sauté for 3–4 minutes until onions start to soften. Add bell peppers, and sauté for another 5–6 minutes, until onions are fully softened. In a food processor, combine 2 cups rice, hemp seeds, garlic, ketchup, tamari, mustard, oregano, thyme, sage, and salt and purée until fairly smooth, scraping down sides of bowl if needed. Transfer to a bowl and stir in remaining rice. Refrigerate for at least 30 minutes to firm up. Remove from fridge and form patties with your hands. Place flour evenly on a plate and lightly dust both sides of each patty, shaking off excess. In a frying pan on medium-high, heat oil. Add patties, 3 or 4 at a time, and lightly flatten with a spatula. Cook for 6–9 minutes on each side, until golden and a crust has formed.

This is one of the easiest pestos you can make, and its flavor is by no means sacrificed by its simplicity. I like lots of pesto to coat the noodles—but feel free to use more noodles and thin out the sauce to your liking. Serve with salad or lightly steamed or broiled veggies (e.g., asparagus, broccolini, green beans) and Pizza Focaccia (page 63).

Sun-Dried Tomato **Pesto** with Toasted Almonds & Pine Nuts

MAKES 4–5 SERVINGS.

WHEAT-FREE OPTION: Use a spelt, quinoa, or kamut pasta.

If you have extra pesto left over, spread it on sandwiches or pizza crusts, dollop on baked white or sweet potatoes, or mash into baked tempeh or tofu for a pita sandwich filling.

1⅛–1¼ cups	**oil-packed sun-dried tomatoes,** drained
2	**medium cloves garlic,** quartered
1 tbsp	**capers**
¾ cup	**water**
1 tbsp	**olive oil**
½ tsp	**agave nectar**
⅛ tsp	(rounded) **sea salt**
	freshly ground black pepper to taste
⅓ cup	**toasted slivered almonds**
⅛ cup	**toasted pine nuts**
½ cup	**fresh basil leaves**
¾–1 lb	(340–450-g) **dry pasta** (see note)
	olive oil (for finishing)
	fresh basil leaves, shredded (for garnish)
	toasted pine nuts (for garnish)

In a blender or food processor, combine sun-dried tomatoes, garlic, and capers and purée, scraping down sides of bowl as needed. Add water, oil, agave nectar, salt, and pepper and purée again until fairly smooth. Add almonds, pine nuts, and basil and blend, keeping some texture. Cook pasta according to package directions. Once pasta is almost done, remove 1 cup of pasta water and reserve. Drain pasta (do not rinse!) and immediately toss in pesto. If pasta seems dry, add some pasta water, 1 tbsp at a time. Season with salt and pepper is desired. Serve with a drizzle of oil, and garnish with basil and pine nuts if desired.

Tangy, thick sauce with just a hint of smoky chipotle peppers coats tender pieces of sweet potato and tempeh. Slivers of green bell peppers and onion soften the sauce, and cashews finish the dish with a crunch. Serve over Coconut Lime Basmati Rice (page 157) and a salad with Cumin-Cinnamon Vinaigrette (page 80).

Sweet & Sour Chipotle Tempeh with Sweet Potatoes

MAKES 4–5 SERVINGS. | **WHEAT-FREE**

2 tbsp	arrowroot powder
1 cup	water
¼ cup	unrefined sugar
½ cup	ketchup
¼ cup	unseasoned rice vinegar
¼ cup	pure maple syrup
2 tbsp	tamari
2 tbsp	olive oil
1 tsp	blackstrap molasses
2	medium-large cloves garlic, quartered
1½–2 tsp	chipotles in adobo sauce, or chipotle hot sauce (or to taste, see note)
¼ tsp	(rounded) sea salt
2½ cups	sweet potatoes (yams), peeled, quartered, and sliced ¼-in (5-mm) thick (about ½ lb/225 g)
1½ cups	green bell pepper, sliced (about 1 medium pepper)
1¼–1½ cups	onions, thinly sliced (1 medium-large onion)
1-8-oz	(227-ml) can pineapple, crushed or in chunks (lightly drained) or 1 cup fresh pineapple, chopped)
1 pkg	(8-oz/227-g) tempeh, cubed (see note)
½ cup	cashews, lightly crushed or chopped (for garnish)

You can make this sauce without chipotle for a more classic sweet and sour sauce, or drizzle individual servings with chipotle-flavored oil—like Wildy Delicious Fine Foods Chipotle Grapeseed Oil.

To help remove any bitter undertones that might be in tempeh, simmer it in 2 cups vegetable broth for 20 minutes before cubing. Also, you may substitute tempeh with cubed tofu or seitan.

Omit tempeh to make this recipe a terrific side dish.

Preheat oven to 425°F (220°C). With a hand blender or in a blender, combine arrowroot, water, sugar, ketchup, vinegar, maple syrup, tamari, oil, molasses, garlic, chipotle, and salt and purée (or mince garlic, then whisk ingredients by hand in a bowl). Transfer to an 8x12-in (20x30-cm) baking dish, add sweet potatoes, green peppers, onions, pineapple, and tempeh and mix to combine. Cover with aluminium foil and bake for 60–70 minutes, stirring occasionally, until sweet potatoes are soft and sauce has thickened. Serve, sprinkled with cashews.

Pizza has crossed over into almost every cuisine; this is my take on the popular Thai chicken pizza. If serving with a salad, include cooling vegetables such as celery, cucumber, tomatoes, jicama, and toss with a simple dressing like Back-to-Basics Balsamic Vinaigrette (page 77).

Thai Chick-Un **Pizza**

MAKES 2–3 SERVINGS (10-IN/25-CM PIZZA) OR 4–6 SERVINGS (12-IN/30-CM PIZZA).

PEANUT SAUCE (SEE NOTE):

⅔ cup	natural peanut butter
⅓ cup	ketchup
2 tbsp	rice vinegar
2 tbsp	tamari
2	large cloves garlic, quartered
1½ tbsp	fresh ginger, chopped
¼ tsp	crushed red pepper flakes (or to taste)
¼ cup	light coconut milk (or plain non-dairy milk)
1–2 tbsp	water (or additional milk)
1½–2 tsp	agave nectar

1	**(10–12-in/25–30-cm) pizza shell** (see note)
1 cup	**cooked chickpeas (garbanzo beans)** (see note)
1–1½ cups	**red bell pepper,** thinly sliced (1 medium-large pepper)
¾ cup	**fresh pineapple,** chopped (may use canned pineapple chunks, drained)
½ cup	**green onions,** sliced (or sweet red onions, very thinly sliced)
½ cup	**mung bean sprouts**
	peanuts, chopped (for garnish)
	fresh cilantro leaves (for garnish)

Since this sauce is rich, the pizza shell should not be too thin. Also, you may not want to use all of the sauce, refrigerating any leftovers.

WHEAT-FREE OPTION: Use a non-wheat pizza shell.

I like to flatten the chickpeas before adding them, but you can leave them whole. Mock chicken strips or vegetarian chicken ground round can be substituted for chickpeas.

Kid-friendly tip: Reduce ginger to ½ tbsp, and omit crushed red chili pepper flakes and perhaps onions.

To prepare peanut sauce: In a food processor, add peanut butter, ketchup, rice vinegar, tamari, garlic, ginger, and red pepper flakes and purée until smooth, scraping down sides of bowl as needed. Add coconut milk and purée again until smooth (add 1–2 tbsp water to thin if desired—sauce should be thick enough to spread on pizza and not runny). Taste test, and if you would like a touch of sweetness, add agave nectar.

Preheat oven to 425°F (220°C). If using pizza stone, place in oven to preheat, or line a pizza pan with parchment paper. Spread peanut sauce evenly on pizza shell. In a bowl, lightly flatten chickpeas with a large spoon (or in palm of your hand), and distribute evenly over sauce. Distribute bell pepper and pineapple evenly. Place pizza on pizza stone or pan and bake for 17–20 minutes, sprinkling on green onions for last minute of cooking, until the crust is golden and toppings have heated through. Serve sprinkled with the bean sprouts, and a handful of chopped peanuts and cilantro if desired.

These burritos are modeled after one I used to order at a local restaurant that was stuffed with boldly seasoned sautéed veggies. They are excellent with vegan cheese melted on top, and serve with Cornmeal-Crusted Plantains (page 158) or tortilla chips and Guacamole con Alga Marina (page 61).

Veggie-Sizzle Burritos

MAKES 3–4 SERVINGS.

1½ tbsp	**coconut or olive oil**
1 cup	**onion,** thinly sliced (1 small-medium onion)
1 tbsp	**mild chili powder**
1 tbsp	**paprika**
¼ tsp	**sea salt**
	freshly ground black pepper to taste
1¾–2 cups	**zucchini,** sliced lengthwise then chopped in ½-moons
1 cup	**green bell pepper,** sliced (about 1 small pepper)
3½–4	cups **Portobello mushrooms,** sliced (about 2–3 large caps; may use white button)
1–2 tsp	**tamari** (see note)
1–1½ cups	**cooked beans** (see note)
4	**(10-in/25-cm each) whole wheat tortillas** (or tortillas of choice) (see note)
½–¾ cup	**non-dairy mozzarella cheese,** grated (optional)

Beans are an optional ingredient. If using beans, use the full 2 tsp tamari, since beans will benefit from the extra seasoning in the vegetables. You may also need another tortilla.

WHEAT-FREE OPTION: Use a wheat-free tortilla like hemp or rice. Be sure to check tortilla ingredients to ensure they do not contain hydrogenated oils.

Preheat oven to 400°F (205°C). In a frying pan on medium-high, heat oil. Add onions, chili powder, paprika, sea salt, and pepper and cook for 2–3 minutes. Add zucchini, bell peppers, mushrooms, and tamari, increase heat slightly and cook for another 4–5 minutes to sear veggies but not completely soften them. Stir in beans, remove from heat, and let cool slightly. Line a baking sheet with parchment paper. Spoon ¼ of mixture down center of each tortilla, leaving 1-in (2½-cm) space on top and bottom. Fold bottom edge over filling and roll up, tucking in sides as you go. Place burritos, seam-side down on sheet. Bake for 15–20 minutes, sprinkling on cheese during last 5 minutes. Serve with suggested accompaniments above, or a slurry of balsamic vinegar and flax oil.

These phyllo rolls have a delectable filling made with puréed cannellini (white kidney) beans, toasted walnuts, fresh spinach, and roasted red peppers. If you're new to phyllo, don't be shy! It's easier to use than you might think, and very forgiving. Serve drizzled with a slurry of balsamic vinegar and flax oil (or Balsamic-Garlic Flax Oil, from *Vive le Vegan!*) or with a dollop of Traditional Cranberry Sauce (page 89).

Walnut, White Bean & Spinach Phyllo **Rolls**

MAKES 3–4 SERVINGS.

WHEAT-FREE OPTION: Use spelt phyllo.

Be aware that if rolls are over-stuffed, they may break open while baking. This of course won't ruin the rolls for eating, but will affect the presentation.

Transform this dish into an impressive appetizer, making small rolls or triangles. For the latter, brush 1 sheet with oil. Then, with a sharp knife, cut 4 strips down the length of sheet. Place a small spoonful of filling at base of one strip. Then fold corner over to form a triangle and continue to fold back and forth until you reach the top. Repeat process until you have used up all the filling. Bake at 375°F (180°C) for 15–20 minutes, until golden. Serve with Traditional Cranberry Sauce (page 89) for a contrasting, tart dip.

2½ tbsp	**freshly squeezed lemon juice**
2 tbsp	**tamari**
2	**medium cloves garlic,** chopped
¼ tsp	**sea salt**
	freshly ground black pepper to taste
3 cups	(packed) **fresh spinach,** roughly chopped
½ cup	(packed) **fresh basil leaves**
1 tsp	**fresh thyme** (optional; do not use dried)
½ cup	**whole walnuts, toasted**
1 can	**(14-oz/398-ml) cannellini (white kidney) beans,** drained and rinsed (about 1¾ cups)
¼–⅓ cup	**toasted walnuts,** lightly crushed or chopped
½ cup	**roasted red peppers** (from jar), drained, patted dry, and chopped
15–18 sheets	**phyllo pastry** (see note)
3 tbsp	**olive oil** (to brush the phyllo)

In a food processor, combine lemon juice, tamari, garlic, salt, and pepper and purée. Add spinach, basil, thyme, whole walnuts, and half of beans and pulse, keeping some texture. Remove the blade from processor and stir in crushed or chopped walnuts, remaining beans, and roasted red peppers. Preheat oven to 375°F (190°C). Line a baking dish or sheet with parchment paper. Place a lightly dampened dish towel over phyllo sheets to keep them moist. Lightly brush the top of 1 sheet with oil. Stack another sheet on top, and brush with oil. Top with a third sheet (but do not brush with oil). Spread ⅓–½ cup filling down the center of sheet, leaving 1–2-in (2½–5-cm) space from edges. Fold edge over the filling and roll up, tucking in sides as you go. Brush tops and sides with oil and place in baking dish or sheet. Repeat process until filling is used, making 5–6 rolls (see note); leave a small space between each roll so they don't stick. Bake for 24–28 minutes, until golden brown.

This curry is fragrant and flavorful, but not overly spicy (which is how we like it). Serve over a whole grain, alongside Cucumber Mint Raita (page 79), roti or naan bread, mango or tamarind chutney (see note), and a fresh salad.

Zucchini Chickpea Tomato **Curry**

MAKES 4–6 SERVINGS. | **WHEAT-FREE**

1 tbsp	**coconut oil** (may use olive oil)
1–1¼ cup	**onion,** diced
2 cups	**yellow-flesh sweet potatoes,** cut in small chunks (about ½ lb/225 g) (may use red or Yukon potatoes)
2	**large cloves garlic,** minced
1 tsp	**sea salt**
1½–2 tsp	**fresh ginger,** grated
1 tbsp	**curry powder**
½ tsp	**whole fenugreek seeds** (optional)
1 tsp	**coriander seeds**
1 tsp	**cumin seeds**
½ tsp	**turmeric powder**
⅛ tsp	**ground cloves**
1½–2 cups	**zucchini,** sliced lengthwise then chopped
1 can	**(28-oz/796-ml) crushed tomatoes** (see note)
1 can	**(14-oz/398-ml) chickpeas (garbanzo beans),** drained and rinsed (about 1¾ cups cooked chickpeas)
½ tsp	**agave nectar**
½ cup	**green beans,** frozen or fresh (chopped if fresh)
	fresh cilantro leaves, chopped (for garnish)
	lime wedges for serving (optional)

I serve this curry with the Taj Mahal brand (by Everland Natural Foods) of tamarind or mango chutney. It's delicious and made with all-natural ingredients.

If you only have whole or diced canned tomatoes, use a hand blender to purée them. Pour off some liquid from the can into pot first, then insert hand blender directly in can and purée.

In a large pot on medium-low heat, add oil, onion, potatoes, garlic, salt, ginger, curry powder, fenugreek, coriander, cumin, tumeric, and cloves, and stir to combine. Cover and cook for 7–8 minutes, stirring occasionally. If the mixture is sticking, add a few drops of water. Add zucchini and cook another 2–3 minutes. Add tomatoes, chickpeas, and agave nectar, increase heat to a boil, then reduce heat to simmer for 20–25 minutes, until sweet potatoes are soft when pierced. Add green beans and cook for another 5–7 minutes until tender. Garnish with cilantro and lime wedges for squeezing on portions.

Sidekicks

Side Dishes & Accompaniments

HERE ARE A NUMBER of simple side dish ideas to accompany your meals all year round. Some of these "Sidekicks" work equally well as appetizers or nibblers, such as the Seared Portobello Mushrooms (page 165) and Rosemary Cornmeal Polenta Fries (page 164). Also, in the recipes for the main courses (in the Main Events chapter), you can find suggested side dish pairings to create dynamite meals; for example, the Teriyaki Quinoa (page 167) is delicious alongside Pan-Fried Tempt-eh! (page 62) and a crisp salad tossed with Cumin-Cinnamon Vinaigrette (page 80). Give these recipes a try, and you'll want to keep them at your "side" for years to come.

Once roasted, sweet potatoes become candy-like, and the flavor of roasted winter squash becomes concentrated when their natural sugars caramelize. Serve with Blackened Tofu (page 121), Cumin Lime Tofu (page 126), or another bean, tofu, seitan, or tempeh dish of choice. This purée is also delicious drizzled with Thick 'n' Rich Gravy (page 88).

Autumn **Purée**

MAKES 3–4 SERVINGS. | **WHEAT-FREE**

2½–3 lb	**(1–1½ kg) yellow-flesh sweet potatoes and winter squash** (e.g., delicate or butternut) (see note)
⅓ cup	**regular or light coconut milk** (may use plain non-dairy milk) (see note)
½ tsp	**sea salt**
¼ tsp	(rounded) **freshly grated nutmeg**
⅛ tsp	**cinnamon**

Preheat oven to 425°F (220°C). Line a baking sheet with parchment paper. Pierce sweet potatoes and squash with a knife, place on baking sheet, and bake for 45–60 minutes (or longer, depending on size of sweet potatoes and squash), until very soft when pierced. Remove from oven and let cool enough to handle, then remove and discard skins. In a large bowl, combine sweet potatoes and squash with remaining ingredients and use a hand blender (or food processor) to purée until very smooth (or transfer to a food processor to blend). Season with additional salt if desired; if you want a thinner texture, add another 1–2 tbsp milk and purée to incorporate. Serve warm, or reheat in baking dish until hot.

I like to use a combination of ⅔ sweet potatoes and ⅓ squash; just ensure that at least half of the combination is sweet potatoes, since they add a smooth, rich texture and naturally sweet flavor.

Regular coconut milk adds fat to the purée, providing a rich flavor. If using plain non-dairy milk, add 1–2 tbsp olive oil.

This recipe peps up quinoa with light spices, sweet dried fruit, and toasted almonds for additional flavor and a subtle crunch. Pair with Cashew-Ginger Tofu (page 124) or Orange Sesame Tofu (page 136).

Cinnamon Lime **Quinoa** with Apricots & Almonds

MAKES 4 SERVINGS. | **WHEAT-FREE**

If making with cranberries, use ¼ cup plus ¼ cup another dried fruit, since cranberries are tart. When buying dried fruit, be sure to avoid those preserved with sulfites.

1 cup	**dry quinoa**
1 ¾ cups	**water**
3–4 tbsp	**freshly squeezed lime juice** (zest limes before juicing, see below)
1 tbsp	**tamari**
½ tsp	**cinnamon**
¼ tsp	**freshly ground nutmeg**
¼ tsp	**sea salt**
½ cup	**chopped dried apricots or other dried fruit** (see note)
1 tsp	**lime zest**
⅓ cup	**toasted almond slivers or toasted almonds,** chopped
1–2 tbsp	**extra virgin olive oil** (optional)

Rinse quinoa in cold water for 1–2 minutes. In a saucepan, combine quinoa, water, lime juice (start with 3 tbsp), tamari, cinnamon, nutmeg, and salt. Bring to a boil on high heat, stir, then reduce heat to low, cover, and cook for 12–14 minutes. Turn off heat and stir in apricots or other dried fruit and lime zest. Cover again and let sit for 5 minutes. Stir in almonds and oil. Taste test, add remaining lime juice and a sprinkle of sea salt if desired, and serve.

This is one of my favorite side dishes, particularly with spicy entrées. Light coconut milk gives a subtly rich taste, and the hint of lime adds a tangy acidity. Serve with Sweet & Sour Chipotle Tempeh with Sweet Potatoes (page 147), Orange Sesame Tofu (page 136), or Zucchini Chickpea Tomato Curry (page 151).

Coconut-Lime Basmati **Rice**

MAKES 4 SERVINGS. | **WHEAT-FREE**

1 cup	**dry brown basmati rice**
1 can	**(13½-oz/400-ml) light coconut milk**
½ cup	**water**
2–2½ tbsp	**freshly squeezed lime juice** (zest limes before juicing, see below)
¼ tsp	**sea salt**
1½ tsp	**lime zest**
	lime wedges (for serving)

If needed, have 1–2 tbsp boiled water on hand to moisten rice as it sits before serving.

In a saucepan, combine rice, coconut milk, water, lime juice (start with 2 tbsp), and salt. Bring to a boil on high heat, stir, then reduce heat to low, cover, and cook for 35–45 minutes, until liquid is absorbed and rice is cooked through. Turn off heat, stir in lime zest, and let sit for 4–5 minutes. Taste test, add additional lime juice if desired, and serve with lime wedges to squeeze on individual portions.

You know those funny-looking blackened bananas you see in the grocery store? Well, they're actually plantains, and you can prepare them in a flash with this recipe. They make an outstanding counterpart to a burrito, taco, or other spicy dish.

Cornmeal-Crusted **Plantains**

MAKES 2–3 SERVINGS. | **WHEAT-FREE**

¼ cup	**fine cornmeal** (not corn grits)
⅛ tsp	**sea salt**
¾–1 lb	**(375–450 g) ripe plantains** (fairly blackened), peeled and sliced ¼-in (5-mm) thick
2–3 tbsp	**coconut oil or olive oil** (or more if desired)
	lime wedges (for serving)

On a plate, combine cornmeal and salt. Toss in plantain slices to coat both sides. In a large frying pan on medium-high, heat oil. Carefully place coated plantains in pan and cook for 4-6 minutes each side, until golden brown. Serve hot with lime wedges.

Use the simple Mulled Cran-Apple Cider recipe (page 227) to make this fragrant and festive quinoa dish. You can also substitute other whole grains, adjusting cooking times as needed (see page 228).

Cran-Apple Quinoa

MAKES 4 SERVINGS. | **WHEAT-FREE**

1 cup	**dry quinoa**
1½ cups	**Mulled Cran-Apple Cider** (page 227)
½ cup + 2–4 tbsp	**water**
½	**vegetable bouillon cube** (see note)
⅛ tsp	**sea salt**
3 tbsp	**dried cranberries** (see note)
¼ cup	**pistachios or other nuts/seeds of choice** (see note)

Rinse quinoa in cold water for 1–2 minutes. In a saucepan, combine quinoa, cider, water (start with ½ cup + 2 tbsp), bouillon cube, and salt. Bring to a boil on high heat, stir, reduce heat to low, cover, and cook for 14–15 minutes. (If quinoa needs to cook longer, add 1–2 tbsp water and cook for another couple of minutes.) Once quinoa is cooked, turn off heat, stir in cranberries, and let sit covered for 5 minutes. Stir in pistachios, season with additional salt if desired, and serve.

For more details on vegetable bouillon cubes, see page 93. If you don't have any, you can use a scant ½ tsp sea salt.

Look for dried cranberries that are unsulphured. Other dried fruits can be used, including chopped dried apricots or apples.

Pistachios are a colorful addition to this dish, and also taste delicious. However, you can substitute with other nuts or seeds, including slivered almonds, chopped pecans, or pumpkin seeds.

This is one of our favorite ways to eat green beans. It's quick, and the fresh tangy lemon and touch of salt shows that with vegetables, simplicity in seasoning is sometimes best.

Lemon-Broiled Green **Beans**

MAKES 2–3 SERVINGS. | **WHEAT-FREE**

Instead of green beans, you can use yellow wax beans or dragon tongue beans, which may be purchased in whole foods stores or at farmers' markets. Dragon tongue beans have a flat shape and light yellow base with purplish streaks. You may also substitute with asparagus; be sure to adjust cooking time accordingly to cook until just tender and retaining fresh green color.

¼ lb	**(100 g) green beans,** ends trimmed (see note)
1 tsp	**olive oil**
1 tsp	**freshly squeezed lemon juice**
¹⁄₁₆ tsp	**sea salt**
	freshly ground black pepper to taste

Set toaster oven or regular oven to broil. Line a baking pan with parchment paper. Add beans and toss with oil, lemon juice, salt, and pepper. Broil for 7–11 minutes, tossing once or twice, until beans blister and are tender. Serve immediately.

The first time I made these fries, my husband said the house smelled like popcorn. Coconut oil, which has a popcorn-like aroma, is more stable than olive oil at high cooking temperatures. Serve these fries with veggie burgers such as "Spicoli" Burgers (page 145), wraps, or sandwiches … or enjoy them as a movie snack!

Popcorn Fries

MAKES 4 SERVINGS. | **WHEAT-FREE**

2½ tbsp	coconut oil
2½–2¾ lb	(1–1⅓ kg) **Russet or white potatoes,** washed
½ tsp	sea salt
¼–½ tsp	**ground turmeric** (optional) (see note)
2–3 tbsp	**nutritional yeast** (optional)

The turmeric is for color, enhancing the appearance of these fries.

Preheat oven to 400°F (205°C). Line a baking sheet with parchment paper. Cut potatoes (peeling optional) into strips ½-in (1-cm) thick. Add coconut oil to baking sheet and place in oven for 2–3 minutes until oil is just melted, then remove from oven and add potatoes, salt, and turmeric and carefully toss to combine. Bake for 60–70 minutes, until potatoes are golden in spots and fully cooked. If desired, toss in nutritional yeast 5 minutes before end of baking.

Potatoes reign supreme in our home; my kids squeal with delight when they see me pull these easy-to-make spuds out of the oven! Serve as is or with condiments of choice, including vinegar, ketchup, vegan sour cream, and/or hot sauce.

Potato **Squashers**

MAKES 3–4 SERVINGS. | **WHEAT-FREE**

1½ lb	**(680 g) red or Yukon Gold potatoes** (5–7 small-medium potatoes), washed
2 tbsp	**olive oil**
⅛ tsp	(rounded) **sea salt**

Preheat oven to 400°F (205°C). Line a baking sheet with parchment paper. Pierce whole potatoes with a knife, place on baking sheet, and bake for 45–60 minutes, until tender when pierced. Remove from oven and increase heat to 450°F (230°C). Use a wooden spoon or spatula to flatten each potato. (The flesh will "squish" out, making each potato an uneven round.) Drizzle with 1 tbsp oil and sprinkle with half the salt. Return to oven and bake for another 10–12 minutes. Remove and flip potatoes over, drizzle with remaining oil and sprinkle on remaining salt, and bake for another 10–15 minutes, until outer edges and skins are crispy and golden. Remove from oven, season with additional salt if desired, and serve.

When fall arrives and the bounty of beautiful winter squash appears in your market, pick up a small butternut or delicata squash for this recipe. It is such a nice side dish, though I often have a hard time not eating it all myself along with a bowl of rice or beans!

Roasted Winter Squash **Rings**

MAKES 2–4 SERVINGS. | **WHEAT-FREE**

1¼–1½ lb	**(510–680 g) butternut or delicata squash** (see note)
2–2½ tsp	**olive oil or coconut oil**
¼ tsp	**sea salt**
¾–1 tsp	**fresh rosemary,** minced (or ½ tsp dried)
2–2½ tsp	**freshly squeezed lemon juice**

An easier and safer way to cut squash is to lay it on its flattest side (if there is one) on the cutting board. If needed, slice a strip off the squash to create a flat edge (or cut in half-moons instead of rings).

Preheat oven to 425°F (220°C). Use a vegetable peeler to remove the thick rind from squash. Cut squash in half or in thirds to get rounds that you can hollow out, scraping out seeds and strings using a spoon. Slice squash further into ¼-in–½-in (5–10-mm) thick rings. Line a baking sheet with parchment paper. If using coconut oil, add oil to baking sheet and place in oven for 1–2 minutes until just melted, then remove from oven. Add squash and toss in pre-heated coconut oil or olive oil, salt, rosemary, and 1½ tsp lemon juice. Bake for 35–45 minutes, flipping once or twice, until golden on both sides. (Thinner rings cook faster, so remove these when browned and reheat just before other rings are ready.) Taste test, and add remaining lemon juice if desired, returning pan to oven for 1 minute. Serve hot, drizzled with a touch more olive oil if desired.

If you haven't tried polenta fries, you'll want to try these! If you have, you'll enjoy the added crunch and seasoning in this recipe—not to mention the ease of using prepared polenta. Serve plain or with vinegar, ketchup, or Smoky Avocado Sauce (page 87).

Rosemary Cornmeal Polenta **Fries**

MAKES 3–4 SERVINGS. | **WHEAT-FREE**

Use a vegetable peeler to remove the thin coating from the packaged polenta.

For kids, you can omit the rosemary or substitute with other seasonings, or add 1–2 tbsp nutritional yeast with the cornmeal to coat the fries.

1 tube	**(18-oz/510-g) prepared polenta,** "peeled" (see note)
1 tbsp	**olive oil**
1½ tbsp	**fine cornmeal**
⅛ tsp	**sea salt**
1 tsp	**fresh rosemary,** chopped

Preheat oven to 450°F (230°C). If you have a pizza stone, place it in oven to preheat, or line a baking sheet with parchment paper and set aside. After peeling polenta, trim it into a rectangular shape, then cut in half lengthwise and slice into ⅓–½-in (5–10-mm) thick strips. In a bowl, gently toss polenta strips in oil, then in cornmeal, and transfer to pizza stone or baking sheet, and sprinkle with salt and rosemary. Bake for 23–30 minutes, turning once or twice, until lightly browned. The fries become crispier and chewier once cooled.

These fried mushrooms have a crispy, very lightly battered coating. They are juicy and succulent inside, with a hint of lime in each irresistible bite.

Seared Portobello **Mushrooms**

MAKES 3–4 SERVINGS.

2–3	**large Portobello mushrooms,** caps cleaned and gills scraped (about ½ lb/225 g)
2 tbsp	**freshly squeezed lime juice**
1½ tbsp	**vegan Worcestershire sauce**
2–4 pinches	**freshly ground black pepper**
4–5 tbsp	**potato starch** (if unavailable, use arrowroot powder or cornstarch)
2–3 pinches	**sea salt**
3–4 tbsp	**olive oil or coconut oil**
	sea salt (for finishing)

Slice mushrooms into 1–1½-in (2½–4-cm) thick strips. In a large shallow dish, combine lime juice and Worcestershire sauce. Add mushrooms, season with pepper, and marinate for at least 20 minutes, flipping mushrooms halfway through. Once mushrooms are marinated, on a large dish, combine potato starch and 2–3 pinches salt. In a non-stick frying pan on high, heat 3 tbsp oil. Coat marinated mushrooms in starch mixture, lightly tapping them to remove any clumps. Carefully add mushrooms to pan, searing one side for 4–5 minutes, until brown and crispy. Flip over and cook for another 3–4 minutes, until crispy, adding more oil if needed. If mushrooms stick together, use a heat-proof spatula to separate and flip again if needed. Serve hot, sprinkled with additional salt if desired. (If needed, transfer to a lined baking pan to reheat at 450°F [230°C] for serving.)

Preparing leafy greens is not difficult, and should not be intimidating. This is one of my favorite ways to quickly prepare Swiss chard—lightly sautéed to preserve its vibrant taste and nutritional value.

Simple **Swiss Chard**

MAKES 2–3 SERVINGS. | **WHEAT-FREE**

If you substitute chard with other leafy greens, be sure to adjust cooking time (e.g., kale requires longer sautéing), being sure not to overcook them.

Store cleaned, julienned Swiss chard in the refrigerator for up to 3 days. Toss into pasta dishes or stir-fries during the last minute of cooking; stir into soups just before serving; or finely chop and add to Romaine lettuce for a nutrient-boosted salad.

I often use add sautéed kale or chard to my sandwiches; the warmth of greens with other sandwich fillings is wonderful.

1 bunch	**red, green, or rainbow Swiss chard,** rinsed and dried (see note)
1 tsp	**olive oil or toasted sesame oil**
2-3 pinches	**sea salt**
	freshly ground black pepper to taste
½–1 tsp	**toasted sesame oil**
½ tsp	**tamari**
½ tsp	**freshly squeezed lemon juice** (optional)

Remove thick stem and spine from each chard leaf by folding leaf over and cutting stem and spine out down length of leaf. Stack the leaves, roll them up tightly in a cylinder shape, and julienne. In a large frying pan on medium-low, heat 1 tsp olive or sesame oil. Add chard, season with salt and pepper, and toss to lightly coat. Sauté for 4–5 minutes, tossing occasionally, until chard reduces slightly, but is still vibrant green. Do not overcook. Toss in ½–1 tsp sesame oil, tamari, and lemon juice if desired. Serve immediately.

This dish is effortless, and infuses everyday quinoa with a sweet and salty, garlicky essence that gives this delicate grain more flavor without overpowering it. This is terrific served with tofu or Pan-Fried Tempt-eh! (page 62).

Teriyaki Quinoa

MAKES 3–4 SERVINGS. | **WHEAT-FREE**

1 cup	**dry quinoa**
2 cups	**water**
4	**large cloves garlic,** minced
1 pinch	**sea salt**
¾–1 tsp	**fresh ginger,** grated (may use ½ tsp dried)
3½ tbsp	**tamari**
2½ tbsp	**agave nectar**
2–3 tsp	**freshly squeezed lemon juice** (or rice or apple cider vinegar, or combination of both)
2 tsp	**toasted sesame oil**
1 tbsp	**toasted or raw sesame seeds** (for finishing)
⅛–¼ cup	**green onions,** sliced (for finishing)

Rinse quinoa in cold water for 2 minutes. In a saucepan, add quinoa, water, garlic and salt. Bring to a boil on high heat, stir, then reduce heat to low, cover, and cook for 12–14 minutes. Turn off heat and stir in ginger, tamari, agave nectar, lemon juice (start with 2 tsp), and sesame oil. Cover again and let sit for 5 minutes. Remove cover and stir. Taste test, add remaining lemon juice and sprinkle with sesame seeds and green onions if desired, and serve.

Kept chilled, this salad is perfect for picnics, potlucks, and brunches, though it tastes especially good when freshly made and served warm.

Warm Potato Spinach **Salad** with Pine Nut **Dressing**

MAKES 4–5 SERVINGS. | **WHEAT-FREE**

1½ lb	**(680 g) new potatoes or fingerling potatoes** (see note)

VINAIGRETTE:

2½ tbsp	**red wine vinegar**
1 tsp	**Dijon mustard**
1½ tsp	**agave nectar**
½ tsp	**sea salt**
	freshly ground black pepper to taste
4 tbsp	**extra virgin olive oil**
⅛ cup	**toasted pine nuts**

SALAD MIXTURE:

2½ cups	(loosely packed) **fresh baby spinach leaves,** whole or chopped
¼ cup	(packed) **fresh basil leaves,** julienned
¾–1 cup	**artichokes,** chopped (may use marinated in a jar or canned, rinsed and patted dry)
½–¾ cup	**red bell peppers,** diced
¼–⅓ cup	**pitted Kalamata or green olives,** halved or chopped
2 tbsp	**toasted pine nuts**
½–1 tbsp	**olive oil** (optional)

In a large pot of salted water, add potatoes and bring to a boil on high heat. Reduce heat to simmer for 12–15 minutes, or until potatoes are tender when pierced with a knife. Meanwhile, in a blender or mini-food processor, or with a hand blender, combine all vinaigrette ingredients and purée until fairly smooth. Once potatoes are tender, drain, let cool just enough to handle, and cut in half or in quarters (see note). In a large bowl, toss hot potatoes with vinaigrette, then add salad ingredients, except oil, and toss again. (If you don't want spinach to wilt, toss in once entire salad has cooled considerably). Taste test, and season with additional salt and pepper and ½–1 tbsp oil if desired. Serve warm, or refrigerate in a covered container and serve chilled (if salad seems dry after refrigeration, add an additional 1 tsp vinegar and ½–1 tbsp olive oil).

You could use the larger, whole red potatoes for this recipe, but the cooking time will be longer. Russet potatoes are not suitable because they do not hold their shape once cooked.

The potatoes will absorb the flavors of vinegar and olive oil best when they are warm or hot.

Sugar 'n' Spice & All Things Nice

Desserts & Baking

DESSERTS! MY FAVORITE CHAPTER. What better way to reward our healthy and compassionate lifestyle than with a sweet? Here I'll tempt you with Coconut Cake (page 190) with Coconut Dream Frosting (page 191), or perhaps decadent Chocolate Pumpkin Pie (page 188) topped with Macadamia Maple Butter Cream (page 201) is more to your liking. Do cookie monsters rule your domain? Feed them Chocolate Chunk Spice Cookies (page 184), 5-Spice Almond Cookies (page 180), Jam-Print Cookies (page 197), and Lemon Poppy Seed Crackle Cookies (page 198). Like things a little sour? Cut yourself a slice of Lime Sucker Coconut Pie (page 200). And, beware of the Maple Pecan Sticky Blondies (page 203) … you'll be leaving evidence of your sweet indulgence with sticky fingerprints everywhere you go! Whatever your weakness, there is a dessert here for you.

I love creating luscious, delicious vegan desserts for several reasons. First, non-vegans assume we must really miss desserts in our plant-based diet. But we can make some of the most delectable sweets without butter, milk, and eggs. Not only do they taste incredible, they do not require the intricacies of creaming butter and sugar, or adding eggs of the right size and at the precise moment. While vegan baking still requires precision in measurements, it is far less finicky. And you can always taste test the batters because there are no raw eggs in the ingredients.

I think vegan desserts are the only ones that can be truly deemed "sweet," because ours are always free of animal products: sweet rewards for our palates and our planet. So indulge, if you can decide which one to make first!

Baking Notes

FLOURS

You will notice that most of my recipes do not call for white flour. I do use this flour on occasion, such as in cakes or cupcakes, but if I do, I make sure it is unbleached, and organic if possible.

WHEAT-FREE: For everyday baking, I prefer to use wholesome, wheat-free flours. Over the years, I have received many requests for baking recipes using whole-grain and wheat-free flours. Although I do not have a wheat sensitivity, when I included wheat-free baking recipes in *Vive le Vegan!* I received overwhelmingly positive feedback.

The wheat-free flours I use most are spelt, oat, and barley. I sometimes use kamut flour, but it has a coarser texture that only works well in small amounts or in particular recipes. Spelt is one of my favorite flours. I purchase it pre-sifted because it has a lighter and finer texture, but you can always sift spelt flour yourself. But, substituting spelt flour for wheat flour may require an adjustment in measure. For example, if substituting spelt flour for all-purpose, you will probably need a little more spelt; in general, if 1 cup unbleached all-purpose, is the original ingredient, I usually substitute with 1 cup + 2–4 tbsp spelt flour.

MIXING BATTERS

When mixing wet ingredients with dry ingredients for cake, muffin, and quick bread batters, it is important to mix until well blended to fully incorporate ingredients and activate the gluten in the flours—but do not overmix. Wheat flours contain more gluten than non-wheat flours; overmixing wheat-based can cause the gluten to get overworked. Other flours, like spelt, barley, oat, and kamut, can be mixed a little more because they have a lower gluten content.

EGG REPLACERS

One of the questions I'm asked most often by non-vegans is: "How do you bake without eggs?" While some baked goods need a "replacement" binding agent, others do not. Wheat flours contain a lot of gluten, which provides enough binding in certain recipes, but wheat-free recipes will often need a binding agent in lieu of eggs. Also, leavening ingredients are sometimes required to lighten and lift vegan batters. There are a number of egg replacers now considered "standard" in vegan baking. Below is a quick summary:

Flax meal: This is one of my favorite egg replacers for providing softness and structure. Flax meal, when combined with a liquid such as water or non-dairy milk, becomes gelatinous, or "eggy." The general rule is to combine 1 tbsp flax meal with 3 tbsp liquid, and mix through for 1 "egg." It is helpful to allow the mixture to sit for a few minutes and become "gooey" before using it. Whole flax seeds can be ground to make flax meal yourself, or you can buy it (I use Bob's Red Mill brand) in the refrigerated section of the grocery store. Whether store-bought or homemade, ensure that it is stored at home in the freezer. It does not need to be thawed before using.

Soy yogurt: Soy yogurts have improved in taste and texture in recent years. They are smooth and delicious, and do wonders in certain vegan baked goods, adding moisture and density. Depending on the recipe, use plain or flavored varieties. In general, ¼ cup soy yogurt replaces 1 egg.

Silken tofu: As with soy yogurt, ¼ cup blended silken tofu replaces 1 egg, adding moisture and density required for some dessert recipes.

Applesauce or mashed banana: These are staples I almost always have on hand because even organic varieties are available at most grocery stores. Also, they are non-allergenic for many people (unlike soy yogurt and silken tofu), add a great deal of moisture and stability to baked goods, and help reduce the fat content. Finally, they add delightful flavor, and in the case of bananas, a great deal of natural sweetness. Typically, ¼ cup applesauce or mashed bananas replaces 1 egg (although I usually add more for muffin or quick bread recipes). Other fruit purées can be used in certain recipes as egg replacers, such as puréed canned pumpkin or pumpkin pie mix, and crushed pineapple.

Baking soda (and powder) with an acid: Many vegan dessert and baking recipes use either baking soda, or a combination of baking soda and baking powder together with an acid such as citrus juice, vinegar, applesauce, and even molasses or regular cocoa powder (not Dutch-processed; see page 177). These acidic elements react with the alkaline baking soda, creating air bubbles that leaven, or lighten and lift, the batter. The addition of baking powder, once it becomes wet in a batter and then heated, produces air bubbles, allowing the batter to rise better.

Additional baking powder: Sometimes a recipe requires nothing more than a little extra baking powder for leavening, particularly if it already includes mashed bananas or another fruit purée. Be sure to use a non-aluminium baking powder.

Xanthan gum: Although xanthan gum is more obscure than the other egg replacers listed here, it's a marvelous ingredient for wheat-free and gluten-free baking. Xanthan gum is a natural vegan starch made from a fermentation process, and can be purchased in health food stores. In addition to helping to bind ingredients, when it also works well in frostings and puddings to provide structure without adding other starches, or more importantly, without adding shortenings and/or extra sugar. It doesn't need heat to thicken, and a little goes a very long way. Most recipes use between ½–2 tsp.

Ener-g Egg Replacer: This is an ingredient used in a lot of vegan baking (although I don't use it in these recipes). It is can be found in most grocery stores.

CHOCOLATE 101

Chocolate is a commonly misunderstood ingredient in the vegan diet. Many of us grew up eating milk chocolate, but most varieties of dark chocolate are dairy-free (although some brands sneak in "milk solids," so be sure to read the labels). Dark chocolate is actually good for us in small quantities, and the darker the chocolate the better. Dark chocolate contains heart-healthy compounds called flavanoids. Look for chocolate with high percentages of cocoa (70% or greater) for the greatest health benefits—and flavor. Experiment with different varieties; the darkest chocolate may seem bitter at first, but your palate will later appreciate it. There are several types of chocolate, including:

Unsweetened: This is chocolate that is not sweetened at all. It is simply the chocolate liquor molded into blocks and solidified.

Semisweet or bittersweet: The chocolate liquor has been combined with sweetener, cocoa butter, and often vanilla. This is often known as dark chocolate and contains at least 35% chocolate liquor (or "cocoa"). Most good-quality chocolate has around 50–60%. Bittersweet usually has more chocolate liquor (around 70%) than semi-sweet and therefore a more intensely chocolate taste.

Sweet chocolate: This is similar to semisweet, but has more sweeteners and has at least 15% chocolate liquor.

Milk chocolate: Milk ingredients are added to this chocolate and sometimes its flavorings. The content of chocolate liquor is at least 10%.

White chocolate: Not really chocolate at all, since this confection does not contain any chocolate liquor. It is made of cocoa butter, milk ingredients, sweeteners, and flavorings.

When shopping for dark chocolate, there are many brands that offer dairy-free varieties, including Endangered Species, Dagoba, Green and Black's, Cocoa Camino, Terra Nostra, and Tropical Source. You can also find other brands of dark chocolate bars, as well as dark chocolate chips and larger baking bars through gourmet chocolate suppliers. Always check the label to ensure they are dairy-free.

Twenty (or so) Random Baking Tips

(Also see page 15 for tips related to cooking and food preparation.)

Parchment ease!: Parchment paper is brilliant for lining baking sheets for cookies and scones, but can also be used for cake, brownie, and loaf pans. Simply cut a square or circle to fit the bottom of your pan; it doesn't even need fill the entire area. Apply a small amount of oil (I use canola) over the bottom and inner sides of your pan, then insert the parchment paper. Baked goods can then be removed with ease.

In a sticky situation?: Before measuring sticky ingredients like nut butters and thick syrups (like brown rice syrup), use any oil needed in that recipe to coat the measuring cup or spoon first. That light coat of oil will help the nut butter or thick syrup easily slide out.

Smooth-sicles: Make popsicles with leftover smoothies or shakes by pouring the extras into popsicle molds and freeze. You can also make popsicles out of flavored soy milks that might be otherwise wasted, such as strawberry soy milk.

Sift, please: Always sift baking powder, baking soda, and cocoa powder. Any lumps that exist in these ingredients can be hard to work out simply through mixing. Use a fine strainer (see page 13) for quick and easy sifting.

Bug off!: Place a dried bay leaf in your canisters of flours and grains to repel insects.

Baking powder fresh test: To check whether your baking powder is stale or fresh, combine about 1 tsp baking powder with about 3 tbsp hot water. If it bubbles, it's fresh. If not, time for a new batch!

Baking soda fresh test: To test the freshness of your baking soda, combine about 1 tsp baking soda with about 2 tbsp white vinegar. If it bubbles, it's fresh. (Baking soda combined with vinegar is also a good natural cleaner for sinks and other surfaces.)

Keep it cool!: When baking with frozen berries and fruits, stir them into the batter at the very end of mixing, then bake straight away. This prevents the berries from "bleeding" into your batter, discoloring it.

Ziploc piping trick: If you want to pipe frosting on cakes or cupcakes and don't have a decorating piping bag, use Ziploc bags. Spoon frosting into a clean bag, then twist to pack it in and remove air pockets. Invert the bag so the packed bottom corner faces up. Cut a small opening in this corner, and you're ready to pipe.

Top of the muffin to you!: Always use muffin liners for baking cupcakes and muffins for easy removal from the pan. Also, wipe the surface area of your muffin pans with a smidgen of oil so the muffin caps do not stick.

Arrowroot vs. cornstarch: Arrowroot and cornstarch can be substituted measure for measure. Arrowroot is sometimes preferred to cornstarch because it can be heated longer (and reheated) without breaking down, is considered more neutral in flavor, and freezes and thaws more successfully in sauces than cornstarch. Also, arrowroot works better than cornstarch when thickening a sauce with acid (e.g., citrus juices). Just be sure to first combine the starch with a liquid component before heating. Whisk together until smooth (or the sauce will become lumpy), then continue to whisk as it reaches a boil.

Cookie know-how: Be sure not to overbake cookies. In most instances, recipes in this book will direct you to remove cookies when they may appear to need more baking, but cookies will continue to set and firm as they sit on the cooling rack. So be sure to follow the directions. In general, let cookies cool briefly, for 1 minute or so, on the baking sheet, then transfer to a cooling rack.

Frosting cakes: When preparing cakes, it is optimal to frost it the day or night before serving. This allows the frosting to set with the cake layers, making it easier to cleanly slice.

Transporting cakes: If you don't have a cake container and need to tote a cake, don't despair. If you have a large enough Rubbermaid, Tupperware, or other similar container that will fit the width and depth of your cake, simply place your cake on the underside of the container lid (put a small piece of parchment under cake). You can frost the cake right on the lid, then invert the bottom of the container to cover the cake. Carefully secure the container, and you are ready to move!

Cookie portioning: For uniformly sized cookies, use a small cookie scoop, small measuring cup (e.g., 1/8 cup), or rounded tablespoon for the batter.

Dried fruit caution: When buying dried fruits (including shredded coconut), check the ingredients to ensure they do not contain sulfites, which are a preservative. Organic varieties typically do not contain sulfites, but always check the label.

Pie time saver: Make pies much quicker and easier by using pre-made pie crusts and shells. Wholly Wholesome brand offers traditional pie shells and graham and chocolate cookie pie crusts that do not have any hydrogenated oils. The company also offers frozen vegan pies, which can be stored in the freezer then baked (and paired with non-dairy ice creams) for last-minute desserts. Their products are exceptional, and will save you time and effort!

Cocoa powder confusion: When a recipe calls for cocoa powder, use regular rather than Dutch-processed. While Dutch-processed cocoa powder has a richer, milder flavor, it has been processed to reduce its acidity. Regular cocoa powder is more bitter but is also acidic, and thus reacts differently during baking. The two varieties can sometimes be substituted for one another, particularly when the recipe does not include much or any baking soda (since baking soda reacts with acidic components). When in doubt, though, use regular cocoa powder unless Dutch-processed is specifically listed.

Storing chocolate: Store chocolate in a cool, dry place. When stored in temperatures above 75°F (25°C), cocoa butter can separate from the solids, causing grey streaks to appear on the surface, called chocolate "bloom," although it doesn't affect the taste. Don't store chocolate in the refrigerator; it can absorb food odors.

Melting—not burning—chocolate: Melting chocolate requires some care. Chocolate can burn easily, and while some people use a microwave for melting, I recommend melting chocolate in a double boiler (I use a large metal or glass bowl fitted over a saucepan with water). Keep the heat at medium-low, allowing the water to simmer, not boil. Ensure that not even a drop of water from excess steam gets into the chocolate, otherwise it will seize up.

Process—don't mix—that silken tofu: For recipes like Chocolate Hazelnut Cream Frosting (page 185) and Strawberry Cream Kids' Frosting (page 208), which require you to purée silken-firm tofu, use a food processor—not a stand or hand-mixer—please! Silken tofu must be puréed with the sharp blade of a food processor to produce that very silky smooth texture important for frostings. This takes a couple of minutes, and the sides of the bowl will need to be scraped down a couple of times during the process to fully incorporate it.

What better treat than an ice cream cookie sandwich? The 5-Spice Almond Cookies used in this recipe are scrumptious with vanilla ice cream, and perfect for a summer day (or any day).

5-Star Ice Cream Cookie Sandwiches

MAKES 5–6 ICE CREAM SANDWICHES. | **WHEAT-FREE**

1 batch	**5-Spice Almond Cookies** (see next page), cooled
2½–3 cups	**vanilla non-dairy ice cream** (I use So Delicious Creamy Vanilla) (see note)

Allow ice cream to soften just enough to easily scoop out of the container. Scoop ⅓–½ cup ice cream (depending on cookie size), and mound it on the underside (flat side) of one cookie. Gently distribute ice cream, then top with another cookie of similar size (with underside touching ice cream). Repeat process with remaining cookies and ice cream, placing finished sandwiches in a sealable container keep in the freezer until ready to serve. Allow sandwiches to thaw for a couple of minutes before serving.

Try any favorite cookie and non-dairy ice cream combination, such as the Chocolate Chunk Spice Cookies (page 184) with chocolate ice cream, or "Tickled Pink" Vanilla Sprinkle Cookies (page 211) with strawberry ice cream.

The number of ice cream sandwiches you make depends on how many cookies the batch yields.

These delicately spiced cookies are a welcome change from chocolate treats.

5-Spice Almond **Cookies**

Makes 10–12 cookies. | **WHEAT-FREE**

Five-spice powder usually contains cassia, star anise, fennel, cloves, and ginger.

For something more exotic, try substituting pine nuts for almonds and anise flavoring for almost extract.

1 cup + 2 tbsp	**barley flour** (or 1 cup all-purpose flour)
1 tsp	**baking powder**
¼ tsp	**baking soda**
¼ cup	**unrefined sugar**
2 tbsp	**almond slices**
¼ tsp	**sea salt**
1½ tsp	**five-spice powder** (see note)
⅓ cup	**pure maple syrup**
¾ tsp	**pure almond extract**
¼ cup	**canola oil**
1–1½ tbsp	**unrefined sugar** (for topping)

Preheat oven to 350°F (180°C). In a bowl, combine dry ingredients, sifting in baking powder and baking soda, and stir until well combined. In a separate bowl, combine syrup, almond extract, and oil and stir until well mixed. Add wet mixture to dry, and stir until just well combined (do not overmix). Line a baking sheet with parchment paper. Scoop rounded tablespoons of batter on baking sheet, evenly spaced apart. Sprinkle 1–1½ tbsp sugar on top of cookies. Bake for 11 minutes (no longer, or they will dry out). Remove from oven, and let cool on baking sheet for 1 minute (no longer), then transfer to a cooling rack.

It's so much fun creating unique new vegan recipes that sometimes we forget about the classics. You can add natural food colorings to this cake or substitute other extracts for the vanilla (e.g., cherry, lemon, almond). Allow cake layers to cool completely before covering with Creamy Vanilla Frosting (page 192), Chocolate Hazelnut Cream Frosting (page 185), or other frosting of choice.

All-Purpose Vanilla **Cake**

MAKES 2 ROUND CAKE LAYERS.

1 cup	**unrefined sugar** (fine-granule is best)
½ tsp	**sea salt**
2 cups	**unbleached all-purpose flour**
2½ tsp	**baking powder**
½ tsp	**baking soda**
1½ cups	**plain soy milk**
3 tbsp	**unsweetened applesauce**
1 tsp	**freshly squeezed lemon juice**
2½ tsp	**pure vanilla extract**
¼ cup	**canola oil**

To remove baked cakes from pans with ease, cut a round piece (it doesn't have to be perfectly round or the exact size) of parchment to place in bottom of each oiled pan.

Preheat oven to 350°F (180°C). In a large bowl, combine dry ingredients, sifting in flour, baking powder, and baking soda, and stir until well combined. In a separate bowl, combine milk, applesauce, lemon juice, and vanilla. Add oil, and stir to combine. Add wet mixture to dry, and stir until just well combined (do not overmix). Lightly oil 2 round cake pans (see note). Pour batter evenly into pans. Bake for 23–25 minutes, until a toothpick inserted in center comes out clean.

Blueberry grunt is a traditional recipe from Atlantic Canada. My vegan adaptation is made with a blend of blueberries, strawberries, apples, and without white flour or white sugar. Serve with non-dairy ice cream, soy yogurt, Celestial Cream (page 29), or Macadamia Maple Butter Cream (page 201).

Berry Apple **Grunt**

MAKES 4–6 SERVINGS. | **WHEAT-FREE**

BATTER:

¾ cup	**barley or oat flour**
½ cup	**spelt flour**
¼ cup	**unrefined sugar**
2 tsp	**baking powder**
¼ tsp	**sea salt**
½ tsp	**cinnamon**
¼ tsp	**freshly grated nutmeg**
⅓ cup	**plain or vanilla non-dairy milk**
1 tsp	**pure vanilla extract**
1 tsp	**lemon zest**
2 tbsp	**canola oil**

FRUIT MIXTURE:

2 cups	**frozen or fresh blueberries** (see note)
1 cup	**frozen or fresh strawberries** (or raspberries, or more blueberries)
1–1½ cups	**apple,** cored, peeled, and chopped
¼ cup	**pure maple syrup**
⅓–½ cup	**water** (depending on amount of apples used)
½–1 tsp	**lemon zest** (zest lemon before juicing, see below)
1 tbsp	**freshly squeezed lemon juice**
¹⁄₁₆ tbsp	**sea salt**

For a more traditional blueberry grunt, use only blueberries (4–4½ cups) instead of a blend of fruits.

To prepare batter: In a large bowl, combine flours, sugar, baking powder, salt, cinnamon, and nutmeg. In a small bowl, combine milk, vanilla, lemon zest, and oil. Add wet mixture to dry and stir, until just well combined. The batter should be fairly thick. To prepare fruit mixture: In a large saucepan (that can be fitted with a lid) on medium-high heat, combine all ingredients. Stir occasionally as mixture comes to a boil, then reduce heat to medium-low and simmer, covered, for 3–4 minutes. Remove lid, scoop large spoonfuls of batter, and gently drop into fruit mixture. (The scoops can be uneven, since these "dumplings" will expand to touch as they cook.) Continue until all batter is used, filling any exposed areas in fruit mixture. Cover with lid and cook for another 13 minutes (do not remove cover!). Remove cover, and if a toothpick inserted in center of a dumpling comes out clean, it is ready, otherwise cover and cook for another 1–2 minutes. Remove from heat and let cool slightly before serving.

This is an unbelievably simple "ice cream" that does not require an ice cream maker. The cashew butter lends a creamy, rich taste to the frozen bananas. The overall flavor is so delightful, it's surprising that it's homemade and dairy-free.

Cashew Banana Ice Cream

MAKES ABOUT 2½ CUPS. | **WHEAT-FREE**

3 cups	**frozen sliced bananas** (4–5 medium bananas) (see notes)
½ cup	**cashew butter** (or in combination with macadamia butter)
⅛ tsp	**sea salt**
¼–⅓ cup	**pure maple syrup** (or agave nectar)

In a food processor, process bananas until they are roughly chopped. Add cashew butter, salt, and syrup (starting with ¼ cup) and purée until very smooth, scraping down sides of bowl as needed. Taste test, adding remaining syrup if desired. Serve immediately, and store leftovers in the freezer.

When I have overripe bananas, I slice them, measure 3 cups to a container, then store in the freezer so they are readily available to make this ice cream.

The more overripe your bananas, the sweeter this ice cream will be. Also, softer ice cream is sweeter to our tastebuds than hard, frozen ice cream.

You can modify this ice cream as you like. I prefer the simplicity of bananas and cashews, but you could add vanilla extract (or paste), almond extract, cinnamon, and/or nutmeg. Also, try pulsing in some raw cashews or macadamia nuts, or some chocolate chips.

These moist chocolate chunk cookies are enhanced by the warmth of cinnamon, nutmeg, allspice, and cloves. Spice up your cold-weather chocolate cravings with one of these decadent delights!

Chocolate Chunk Spice Cookies

MAKES 10–14 COOKIES. | **WHEAT-FREE**

Transform these cookies into outrageously good ice cream sandwiches (see page 179), using non-dairy vanilla, mocha, or chocolate ice cream.

⅓ cup	**unrefined sugar**
⅓–½ cup	**dark chocolate chunks**
¼ tsp	**sea salt**
1¼ tsp	**cinnamon**
½–¾ tsp	**freshly grated nutmeg**
1/16 tsp	**ground allspice**
1–2 pinches	**ground cloves**
1 cup	**barley flour** (may use 1 cup, less 2 tbsp, all-purpose flour)
3 tbsp	**cocoa powder**
1 tsp	**baking powder**
½ tsp	(scant) **baking soda**
⅓ cup	**maple syrup**
¼ cup + 1 tsp	**canola oil**

Preheat oven to 350°F (180°C). In a bowl, combine all ingredients, except for syrup and oil (reserving a small amount of chocolate chunks to top cookies if desired), sifting in the flour, cocoa powder, baking powder, and baking soda, and stir until well combined. In a separate bowl, mix maple syrup and oil. Add wet mixture to dry, and stir until just well combined (do not overmix). Line a baking sheet with parchment paper. Scoop rounded tablespoons of batter onto baking sheet, and press in reserved chocolate chunks on top of each cookie if desired. Bake for 11 minutes (no longer, or they can dry out). Remove from oven and let cool for 1 minute (no longer) on sheet, then transfer to a cooling rack.

If you love chocolate and hazelnut like I do, you'll be eating this frosting with a spoon! Be sure to try it with Chocolate Sin-namon Cake (page 189) and serve with a scoop of non-dairy vanilla ice cream and Warm Raspberry Sauce (page 39) drizzled around plate. Divine!

Chocolate Hazelnut Cream **Frosting**

MAKES PLENTY OF FROSTING FOR ONE 2-LAYER CAKE. | **WHEAT-FREE**

1²⁄₃–1¾ cups	**non-dairy chocolate chips** (see note)
1 pkg	**(12-oz/340-g) + ¾ cup silken extra-firm tofu** (see note)
¼ cup	**hazelnut butter** (see note)
½ cup	**brown rice syrup**
1½ tsp	**pure vanilla extract**
¼ tsp	**almond extract** (optional)
⅛ tsp	**sea salt**

Fit a metal or glass bowl over a saucepan on medium-low heat and filled with several inches of water (or use a double-boiler). Add chocolate to bowl and stir occasionally as water simmers (do not allow to boil), letting chocolate melt. Meanwhile, pat tofu with a paper towel to remove excess moisture. In a food processor, purée tofu until smooth, scraping down sides of bowl as needed. Add hazelnut butter, syrup, vanilla and almond extracts, and salt, and purée again until smooth. Once chocolate is melted, add to tofu mixture and purée again until very smooth, scraping down sides of bowl as needed. Refrigerate until cool before using.

Use 1²⁄₃ cups chocolate chips for a creamier, more pudding-like texture, and use the full 1¾ cups for denser, thicker frosting.

You will need 2 packages (12 oz/340 g each) silken firm tofu for this recipe, but only a ¾-cup portion from the second package. Refrigerate remainder in water in a sealed container for up to 5 days, replacing water each day.

If hazelnut butter is not available, use cashew or peanut butter.

I first served these at my daughter's birthday party and they disappeared in a flash. Minty cool and choco-latey—magical!

Chocolate Mint **Melties**

MAKES 11–14 COOKIES. | **WHEAT-FREE**

Use a dark chocolate bar that is mint flavored, rather than a mint cream-filled dark chocolate bar. For this recipe, try the Endangered Species brand "Dark Chocolate with Deep Forest Mint."

If you want to use unbleached all-purpose flour instead of spelt, use just 1 cup. If batter seems too dry or thick, stir in another 1–2 tsp each of oil and maple syrup.

For the holidays, make these cookies festive by sprinkling 1–2 tbsp crushed or chopped candy canes on cookies before baking, and lightly press in.

1 bar	**(3-oz/85-g) mint dark chocolate** (see note)
1⅛ cups	**spelt flour** (see note)
3 tbsp	**cocoa powder**
1 tsp	**baking powder**
½ tsp	**baking soda**
¼ cup	**unrefined sugar**
¼ tsp	**sea salt**
¼ cup	**pure maple syrup**
2 tbsp	**agave nectar**
1 tsp	**pure vanilla extract**
½ tsp	**mint extract**
¼ cup	**canola oil**

Preheat oven to 350°F (180°C). Break off 9 squares from chocolate bar (about ⅔ of bar, reserve remaining squares to top cookies) and place in mini-food processor, processing until finely chopped (or chop by hand). Transfer to a bowl and combine with dry ingredients, sifting in flour, cocoa powder, baking powder, and baking soda, and stir until well combined. In a separate bowl, combine syrup, agave nectar, vanilla and mint extracts, and oil and stir until well mixed. Add wet mixture to dry, and stir until just well combined (do not overmix). Line a baking sheet with parchment paper. Spoon batter onto baking sheet, spacing evenly. Break up or roughly chop reserved chocolate and place on top of each cookie, pressing in a little. Bake for 11 minutes (no longer, or they will dry out). Remove from oven, and let cool for 1 minute (no longer) on the sheet, then transfer to a cooling rack.

This is one of the easiest, quickest desserts you can make, and it looks so pretty no one will know how effortless it was!

Chocolate **Pudding** Cups

MAKES 8 CHOCOLATE CUPS (SEE NOTE). | **WHEAT-FREE**

1 pkg	**Mori-Nu Pudding Mates** (vanilla or chocolate) (see note)
1 pkg	**(12-oz/340-g) silken extra-firm tofu**
1–2 tbsp	**vanilla soy milk**
½–1 tsp	**vanilla paste** (see note)
¼ tsp	**pure almond extract** (optional)
1 pkg	**(3¾-oz/105-g) non-dairy dark chocolate dessert cups** (see note)
	garnishes (e.g., 1–2 tbsp fresh berries, chopped nuts, grated dark chocolate, minced dried cranberries, and/or toasted coconut)

Prepare pudding mix according to package directions, using silken tofu and puréeing until smooth, and adding milk, vanilla paste, and almond extract. In a food processor, purée tofu with pudding until smooth, adding milk, vanilla paste, and extract as needed. Transfer mixture to a pastry bag (or see Ziploc piping tip on page 176) to pipe pudding into dessert cups, or simply spoon pudding directly into cups. About ¼ cup of pudding will fill each cup. Repeat until all cups are used (some pudding may be left over). Garnish as desired. Refrigerate until ready to serve (see note).

I use Mori-Nu Pudding Mates for this recipe because it makes a very thick pudding which works well in these cups. If you have a recipe for a very thick pudding, you can use that.

Vanilla paste is a fragrant, flavorful baking ingredient in which the seeds of the vanilla bean are combined with water, sugar, and vanilla extract. It is more intense than vanilla extract, but you can use 1 tsp vanilla extract as a substitute.

There are many different brands and sizes of non-dairy chocolate dessert cups. The ones used here hold about ¼ cup filling; making 8 chocolate pudding cups. If you prefer, use smaller dessert cups that each hold about 1 tbsp pudding.

After filling chocolate cups, the moisture from pudding will slowly soften the chocolate, so be sure to serve the same day you make them.

This pie is rich and decadent, so a little slice will do. Serve portions topped with Celestial Cream (page 29), Macadamia Maple Butter Cream (page 201), or vanilla non-dairy ice cream.

Chocolate Pumpkin **Pie**

MAKES 6–8 SERVINGS.

You can also use a graham cracker crust if you prefer, or a traditional pastry pie crust.

WHEAT-FREE OPTION: Use a spelt pastry crust.

FILLING:

1¼ cups	**non-dairy chocolate chips**
1 can	**(14-oz/415-ml) organic pumpkin pie mix** (I use Farmer's Market Organic brand)
2 tbsp	**unrefined sugar**
2 tsp	**arrowroot powder**
⅛ tsp	(rounded) **sea salt**
1	**prepared chocolate cookie-crust pie crust** (see notes)
2 tbsp	**non-dairy chocolate chips,** optional (for garnish)

Preheat oven to 425°F (220°C). Fit a metal or glass bowl over a saucepan on medium-low heat and filled with several inches of water (or use a double-boiler). Add 1¼ cups chocolate chips to bowl and stir occasionally as water simmers (not boils), letting chocolate melt. While chocolate is melting, in a food processor, add pumpkin pie mix (scraping out everything from can), sugar, arrowroot powder, and salt. Purée until very smooth, scraping down sides of bowl as needed. Once chocolate is melted, add to food processor and purée with pumpkin mixture, scraping down sides of bowl as needed. Pour mixture into pie crust (scraping out all filling) and tip pie back and forth gently to evenly distribute filling. Sprinkle on 2 tbsp chocolate chips. Bake for 15 minutes, then reduce heat to 350°F (180°C) and bake for another 35 minutes, until pie is set (the center may be soft, but it will set further as it cools). Carefully remove from oven and place on cooling rack. Let cool completely before slicing, refrigerating if desired.

Now that I think about it, without dairy, eggs, and refined sugar, this cake is not that "sinful" after all! Frost with Chocolate Hazelnut Cream Frosting (page 185) or Creamy Vanilla Frosting (page 192).

Chocolate Sin-namon Cake

MAKES 2 ROUND CAKE LAYERS.

1¼ cups	**spelt flour** (see note)
1 cup	**unbleached all-purpose flour**
½ cup	**regular cocoa powder** (not Dutch-processed)
1 tsp	**baking powder**
1½ tsp	**baking soda**
1⅛ cups	**unrefined sugar**
½ tsp	(scant) **sea salt**
2–2½ tsp	**cinnamon**
¼ tsp	**freshly grated nutmeg** (optional)
1¾ cup	**water**
⅛ cup	**balsamic vinegar**
1½ tsp	**pure vanilla extract**
¼ cup	**canola oil**

If you want to use only all-purpose flour in this recipe, use 2 cups + 1–2 tbsp. Do not make this cake with only spelt flour, at least not for special occasions, the texture will be a little heavy.

To remove baked cakes from pans with ease, cut a round piece (it doesn't have to be perfectly round or the exact size) of parchment to place in bottom of each oiled pan.

Preheat oven to 350°F (180°C). In a large bowl, combine dry ingredients, sifting in flour, cocoa powder, baking powder, and baking soda, and mix until well combined. In a separate bowl, combine water, vinegar, vanilla, and oil. Add wet mixture to dry, and stir until just well combined (do not overmix). Lightly oil 2 round cake pans (see note). Pour batter evenly into pans. Bake for 23–25 minutes, until a toothpick inserted in the center comes out clean. Transfer cakes to cooling racks to cool completely before frosting.

This moist, light cake is perfect for birthdays or other special occasions (hmmm, like any weekend?!). Once the finished cakes have completely cooled, top with Coconut Dream Frosting (opposite page)—the coconut taste is subtle, but the overall flavor and texture is blissful!

Coconut Cake

MAKES 2 ROUND CAKE LAYERS.

To remove baked cakes from pans with ease, cut a round piece (it doesn't have to be perfectly round or the exact size) of parchment to place in bottom of each oiled pan.

Even though this is a coconut cake, the addition of just a small amount of almond extract adds a distinctive, but not overpowering, flavor.

1¾ cups	unbleached all-purpose flour
2½ tsp	baking powder
½ tsp	baking soda
¾ cup	unsweetened shredded coconut
1 cup	unrefined sugar
½ tsp	sea salt
1½ cups	plain soy milk
¼ cup	unsweetened applesauce
1 tsp	pure vanilla extract
¼–½ tsp	almond extract (or ¼ tsp each of almond and coconut extracts)
1½ tsp	freshly squeezed lemon juice
⅓ cup	canola oil

Preheat oven to 350°F (180°C). In a large bowl, combine dry ingredients, including coconut, sifting in flour, baking powder, and baking soda, and mix until well combined. In a separate bowl, combine soy milk, applesauce, vanilla and almond extracts, lemon juice, and oil. Add wet mixture to dry, and stir until just well combined (do not overmix). Lightly oil 2 round cake pans (see note). Pour batter evenly into cake pans. Bake for 23–26 minutes, until a toothpick inserted in center comes out clean. Transfer cakes to cooling racks to cool completely before frosting.

This frosting is like a thick, lightly flavored sweet coconut pudding. When my good friend Vicki tried it, she said I should change the name to Coconut Dream Frosting! Use on Coconut Cake (opposite page) for a dreamy result.

Coconut Dream **Frosting**

MAKES ABOUT 3¾ CUPS. | **WHEAT-FREE**

1 pkg	**(12-oz /340-g) silken extra-firm tofu**
1 pkg	**(8-oz/235-g) Tofutti cream cheese** (see note)
1½ cup	**organic powdered sugar** (see note)
⅛ cup	**macadamia nut butter**
1–1½ tsp	**freshly squeezed lemon juice**
¼ tsp	**sea salt**
¾ tsp	**coconut extract**
½ tsp	**pure vanilla extract**
½ tsp	**almond extract**
1½ tsp	**xanthan gum** (see note)

Pat tofu with a paper towel to remove excess moisture. In a food processor, purée tofu with cream cheese until smooth, scraping down sides of bowl as needed. Add remaining ingredients and process for 1–2 minutes until very smooth, scraping down sides of bowl. Refrigerate until completely cool before using.

Tofutti makes two varieties of cream cheese, one with hydrogenated oils and the other without (use the latter).

I use Wholesome Sweeteners brand Organic Powdered Sugar, which is made from unrefined cane sugar. If you cannot find organic powdered sugar, make your own: in a blender, combine 1¼–1½ cups unrefined sugar with 1 tbsp arrowroot powder or cornstarch. Blend on high speed until powdery, scraping down sides of bowl as needed. (Omit arrowroot or cornstarch if using a very high-powered blender such as Vita-Mix.)

When blending frosting, it may appear too loose, but the xanthan gum will thicken it when refrigerated.

Make this frosting the day or night before, since refrigeration will help it firm. Or chill for several hours before frosting cakes or cupcakes, which you can then refrigerate overnight to set.

This is a thick and creamy frosting that is brilliant on cupcakes, cakes, or just a spoon!

Creamy Vanilla Frosting

MAKES ABOUT 2⅓ CUPS. | **WHEAT-FREE**

Make this frosting the day or night before, since refrigeration will help it firm up. Or chill for several hours before frosting cakes or cupcakes, which you can then refrigerate overnight to set.

1 pkg	**(12-oz/340-g) silken extra-firm tofu**
1–1½ tsp	**pure vanilla extract**
½–¾ tsp	**pure almond extract** (to taste)
¼ cup	(packed) **Earth Balance Buttery Spread** (or other non-hydrogenated vegan margarine)
¼ tsp	**xanthan gum**
¼ cup	**agave nectar**
⅔ cup	**unrefined sugar** (fine granule is best)
⅛ tsp	(rounded) **sea salt**
2¼ tsp	**agar powder**
2–3 tbsp	**non-dairy milk**
1–3 tsp	**non-dairy milk** (if needed)

Pat tofu dry with a paper towel to remove excess moisture. In a food processor, purée tofu with vanilla and almond extracts until smooth, scraping down sides of bowl as needed. Add margarine and xanthan gum and purée again to combine. In a saucepan on low-medium heat, combine agave nectar, sugar, and salt, stirring continually to dissolve sugar. In a small bowl, combine agar powder and milk. Once the sugar-agave mixture has dissolved, add agar-milk mixture and stir to combine. Increase heat to medium-high and stir continually as mixture thickens and comes to a boil, then reduce heat to low and simmer for 1–2 minutes to fully dissolve agar. Remove from heat and add to tofu purée in food processor. Purée again until smooth, scraping down sides of bowl as needed. Refrigerate until completely cool. When ready to use, purée again until completely smooth. (After chilling, the frosting may appear too thick, but after several minutes of puréeing, it will smooth out. If needed, add non-dairy milk, a teaspoon at a time, and purée again.)

Thai Chick-Un Pizza (page 148)

5-Star Ice Cream Cookie Sandwiches (page 179)

Sunny Pineapple Yogurt Cake with Orange Glaze (page 209)
and Warm Raspberry Sauce (page 39)

Chocolate Pumpkin Pie (page 188) with Macadamia Maple Butter Cream (page 201)

Why should chocolate have all the fun? These are delicious, rich cookies that anyone will enjoy—especially those with chocolate sensitivities.

Double Carob Cashew Cookies

MAKES 10–12 COOKIES. | **WHEAT-FREE**

1 cup	**spelt flour**
¼ cup	**carob powder** (raw or roasted; see Glossary, page 233)
1 tsp	**baking powder**
¼ tsp	**baking soda**
¼ tsp	**cinnamon**
¼ cup	**unrefined sugar**
¼ tsp	**sea salt**
⅓ cup	**carob chips**
3 tbsp	**maple syrup**
3 tbsp	**agave nectar** (or more maple syrup)
2 tbsp	**cashew butter**
1½ tsp	**pure vanilla extract**
¼ cup + 1–2 tsp	**canola oil**
¼ cup	**raw or toasted cashews,** crushed

Preheat oven to 350°F (180°C). In a bowl, sift in flour, carob powder, baking powder, and baking soda. Add cinnamon, sugar, and salt and stir until well combined, then stir in carob chips. In a separate bowl, combine syrup, agave nectar, cashew butter, and vanilla, stirring until well combined and then stir in oil. Add wet mixture to dry and stir until just well combined (do not overmix). Line a baking sheet with parchment paper. Spoon batter onto baking sheet and evenly space apart. Press a few pinches of crushed cashews on each cookie, ever so slightly flattening each cookie. Bake for 11 minutes (no longer, or they will dry out). Remove from oven and let cool on baking sheet for 1 minute (no longer), then transfer cookies to a cooling rack.

I've made this pie many times over the years at Christmas. I love it because it's easy and can be made in advance. Also, with the generous amount of nutmeg and fragrant vanilla beans, it has an egg-nog-like flavor that's perfect for the holidays. The Butter Rum Sauce is a cinch to make, and, after all, what is "egg"-nog without a little "rum"?

Egg-Nog Ice Cream **Pie**

MAKES 6–8 SERVINGS.

Baking the pie crust is optional. It will give it a nuttier, toasted flavor, but this step can be skipped.

1	**prepared graham cracker pie crust** (I use Wholly Wholesome brand)

FILLING:

1 qt	**(1 l) non-dairy vanilla ice cream** (I use So Delicious)
1	**vanilla bean** (seeds only)
1 tsp	**freshly grated nutmeg**
1 batch	**Butter Rum Sauce** (opposite page)

Preheat oven to 350°F (180°C). Bake pie crust (see note) for 7–12 minutes until slightly golden and aromatic. Remove and let cool. Meanwhile, place ice cream in refrigerator or countertop until just softened. Slice open vanilla bean and scrape out all seeds. In a food processor, add ice cream, vanilla seeds, and nutmeg. Process until seeds and nutmeg are incorporated into ice cream, working quickly so ice cream does not melt much. (Alternatively, ice cream, nutmeg, and vanilla seeds can be mixed by hand in a large bowl.) Transfer into cooled pie crust, distributing evenly with a spatula. Cover pie (with Wholly Wholesome lid or plastic wrap) and immediately place in freezer for at least 1 hour to harden. To serve, let pie sit at room temperature for 5 minutes, then slice and drizzle with Butter Rum Sauce.

A rich, buttery, "boozy" sauce that is heavenly served hot over Egg-Nog Ice Cream Pie (opposite page), ice cream sundaes, or any dessert you choose.

Butter Rum Sauce

MAKES 5–7 SERVINGS (1¼–1⅓ CUPS). | **WHEAT-FREE**

¾ cup	**plain or vanilla non-dairy milk** (see note)
1–1½ tbsp	**arrowroot powder** (see note)
⅓ cup	**unrefined sugar**
3–3½ tbsp	**Earth Balance Buttery Spread** (or other non-hydrogenated vegan margarine)
1½ tsp	**pure vanilla extract**
¼ tsp	**blackstrap molasses**
¼ tsp	**sea salt**
2 tbsp	**rum** (gold or dark)

Soy milk is better suited for this recipe than rice milk, but you may use any non-dairy milk of choice, even coconut milk for a much richer sauce.

If you want a thinner sauce, use 1 tbsp arrowroot. For a thicker sauce, use the full 1½ tbsp.

In a small bowl, combine 3 tbsp non-dairy milk with arrowroot, mixing until well combined. In a saucepan on medium heat, combine arrowroot mixture with remaining ingredients, whisking to combine well. Bring mixture to a boil, stirring occasionally, then let it bubble slowly while stirring for another 30 seconds before turning off heat. Serve hot or warm.

Vive le Vegan! includes a Homestyle Chocolate Chip Cookie recipe that has become very popular. I received so many emails and website comments, I decided to do a gluten-free version so they could be enjoyed by just about everyone!

"Gluten-Be-Gone" Homestyle Chocolate Chip **Cookies**

MAKES 11–13 COOKIES.

Amaranth flour has a grainier texture than brown rice flour but I prefer amaranth's flavor; use either flour for this recipe, or a combination of both. White rice flour can also be substituted.

¾ cup + 1 tbsp	**amaranth flour or brown rice flour** (see note)
1 tsp	**xanthan gum**
1 tsp	**baking powder**
¼ tsp	**baking soda**
2 tbsp	**tapioca starch flour**
¼ cup	**unrefined sugar**
¼ tsp	**sea salt**
⅓ cup	**pure maple syrup**
¼ tsp	**blackstrap molasses**
1–1½ tsp	**pure vanilla extract**
3–3½ tbsp	**canola oil**
⅓–½ cup	**non-dairy chocolate chips**

Preheat oven to 350°F (180°C). In a bowl, combine dry ingredients, sifting in flour, xanthan gum, baking powder, and baking soda, and stir until well combined. In a separate bowl, combine syrup, molasses, and vanilla, then stir in oil until well combined. Add wet mixture to dry, along with chocolate chips, and stir until just well combined (do not overmix). Line a baking sheet with parchment paper. Scoop rounded tablespoons of batter onto baking sheet, evenly spaced apart, and ever so slightly flatten. Bake for 11 minutes (no longer, or they will dry out). Remove from oven and let cool on baking sheet for 1 minute (no longer), then transfer to a cooling rack.

These are festive, delicious, and fun to make. What more could you want in a cookie; wholesome ingredients? They've got those too! No excuses, now go bake!

Jam-Print Cookies

MAKES 11–13 COOKIES. | **WHEAT-FREE**

¾ cup	**barley flour**
⅔ cup	**oat flour**
½ cup	**crushed walnuts** (or shelled hemp seed nuts) (see notes)
3 tbsp	**unrefined sugar**
1 tsp	**baking powder**
¼ tsp	**cinnamon**
¼ tsp	**sea salt**
¼ cup	**pure maple syrup**
2 tbsp	**brown rice syrup**
1 tsp	**pure vanilla extract**
¼ tsp	**almond extract**
¼ cup	**canola oil**
3–4 tbsp	**raspberry jam** (or jam of choice)

Preheat oven to 350°F (180°C). In a bowl, combine flours, walnuts, sugar, baking powder, cinnamon, and salt and stir until well combined. In a separate bowl, combine maple syrup with brown rice syrup, stirring until well incorporated. Add vanilla and almond extracts and oil and stir to combine. Add wet mixture to dry, and stir until just well combined (see note). Line a baking sheet with parchment paper. Spoon batter onto baking sheet and evenly space apart. Using the handle of a wooden spoon, make an indentation in the center of each cookie and fill with ¾–1 tsp jam. Bake for 14 minutes, until slightly golden around the edges. Remove from oven, and let cool for 1–2 minutes on the sheet until the cookies have firmed a little. Remove and transfer to a cooling rack.

To crush walnuts, lightly pulse in a food processor, or place in a small Ziploc bag and move rolling pin or mug back and forth over bag until finely crushed (some small pieces are okay).

Use shelled hemp seed nuts (I use Manitoba Harvest brand) in place of the walnuts for a nut-free version.

Depending on brands of flours and sugars used, the density of the batter can vary. This batter should be fairly thick, and not crumbly. If it is a little too wet, stir in 1–2 additional tbsp oat flour. If it is too crumbly, mix in another 1–2 tsp each brown rice syrup and oil.

These cookies have a refreshing lemon tang and a crispy, sugary crust. They are particularly good served with vanilla non-dairy ice cream or lime or coconut sorbet (or try making into ice cream sandwiches, see page 179).

Lemon Poppy Seed Crackle Cookies

MAKES 16–19 COOKIES. | **WHEAT-FREE**

These cookies will naturally spread out while baking, so don't press down batter to flatten them. The portions of batter should be round and plump on the baking sheet. Because they spread, some cookies may touch during baking, so you may prefer to divide batter between two baking sheets.

1 ⅛ cups	**spelt flour**
1–1½ tbsp	**poppy seeds**
⅓ cup	**unrefined sugar**
2 tsp	**lemon zest** (zest lemons before juicing, see below)
¼ tsp	**sea salt**
1 tsp	**baking powder**
½ tsp	**baking soda**
⅛ cup	**brown rice syrup**
1½ tbsp	**pure maple syrup**
2 tbsp	**freshly squeezed lemon juice**
1½ tsp	**pure vanilla extract**
3–3½ tbsp	**canola oil**
1½–2 tbsp	**unrefined sugar** (for topping)

Preheat oven to 350°F (180°C). In a bowl, combine flour, poppy seeds, sugar, lemon zest, and salt, and sift in baking powder and baking soda. Stir until well combined. In a separate bowl, combine brown rice syrup, maple syrup, lemon juice, and vanilla. Stir until brown rice syrup is well incorporated, then stir in oil until well combined. Add wet mixture to dry, gently folding until just well combined (do not overmix). Line a baking sheet with parchment paper. Scoop rounded tablespoons of batter onto baking sheet and even space apart (do not flatten, see note). Sprinkle tops of cookies with sugar. Bake for 11 minutes (no longer, or they will dry out). Remove from oven and let cool on baking sheet for 1 minute (no longer), then transfer to a cooling rack.

I created these one day when my oven wasn't working but I needed cookies! They have a pecan-coconut-cocoa base and a thick and nutty chocolate ganache topping. On my blog, I described them as bad ... but oh so good. Visitors liked the name, and suggested that these bars be dedicated to Leslie, a fellow blogger, who made all of her vegan food without need for an oven.

Leslie's Bad But Good Bars!

MAKES 12–16 SQUARES. | **WHEAT-FREE**

BASE LAYER:

1 cup	**pecans,** finely chopped (see note)
1 cup	**quick oats**
½ cup	**unsweetened shredded coconut**
2 tbsp	**Dutch-processed cocoa powder**
⅛ tsp	**sea salt**
⅓ cup	**brown rice syrup**
3 tbsp	**Earth Balance Buttery spread,** melted (or other non-hydrogenated vegan margarine) (see note)

CHOCOLATE TOPPING:

1 cup	**non-dairy chocolate chips**
⅔ cup	**silken extra-firm tofu**
1 tsp	**pure vanilla extract**
2 tbsp	**nut butter of choice**

In a large bowl, combine all base layer ingredients until well combined; the mixture should be crumbly yet somewhat hold together when pressed. Line an 8x8-in (20x20-cm) pan with parchment paper (see note). Transfer mixture to pan, pressing down evenly, then set aside. Fit a metal or glass bowl over a saucepan on medium-low heat and filled with several inches of water (or use a double-boiler). Add chocolate chips to bowl, stirring occasionally until water simmers (not boils), letting chocolate melt. Meanwhile, in a food processor, add tofu and purée until very smooth, scraping down sides of bowl as needed. Add vanilla and nut butter and purée again until smooth. Once chocolate is melted, add to food processor (scraping out all chocolate from bowl), and blend until tofu is fully incorporated and smooth, scraping down sides of bowl as needed. Pour this mixture over pecan base, smoothing with a rubber spatula to evenly distribute. Refrigerate for about 2 hours until completely cooled and chocolate topping is set, then cut into squares and serve.

Chop pecans by pulsing in a food processor. Or chop with a knife, or place in a Ziploc bag and use a rolling pin or mug to crush.

You may use walnuts (which contain healthy omega-3 oils) instead of pecans, but note that pecans are sweeter and more buttery than walnuts. You can also toast them in advance if you prefer, to enhance their flavor.

Melt margarine (I place it in a small bowl in the toaster oven) until it is almost liquefied.

Lining your pan with parchment paper makes removing the bars so simple! Cut two long sheets to fit bottom and sides of pan so the paper hangs slightly over the edges. Once cooled, simply lift edges of parchment to remove in whole, then slice in squares.

This, tangy-sour-sweet pie will convince you that not all great desserts have chocolate in them! Give this easy pie a try … cut a wedge and pucker up! Top with Macadamia Maple Butter Cream (opposite page) or with Warm Raspberry Sauce (page 39) along with some vanilla soy ice cream or soy whipped topping.

Lime Sucker Coconut **Pie**

MAKES 7–8 SERVINGS.

WHEAT-FREE OPTION: Use a spelt pastry crust; pre-bake and cool it before filling.

If you prefer, you can also make this pie using lemons instead of limes … reminiscent of lemon meringue pie!

1	**prepared graham cracker pie crust** (I use Wholly Wholesome brand) (see note)
½ cup	**freshly squeezed lime juice** (zest limes before juicing, see below)
¼ cup	**arrowroot powder**
1¾–2 tsp	**agar powder**
1 can	**(13-oz/400-ml) regular coconut milk** (not light)
½ cup + 3 tbsp	**unrefined sugar**
¼ tsp	(rounded) **sea salt**
½ cup	**unsweetened shredded coconut**
1½ tsp	**pure vanilla extract**
¼ tsp	**coconut extract**
2½ tsp	**lime zest**

First pre-bake pie crust to give it a nuttier, toasted flavor: Preheat oven to 350°F (180°C). Bake crust for 7–12 minutes until lightly golden and aromatic. Remove from oven and let cool on a cooling rack. To prepare filling: In a saucepan (not yet on stove), combine lime juice, arrowroot, and agar powder, whisking until well combined with a uniform consistency. Add coconut milk, sugar, salt, and coconut, and whisk to combine. Place saucepan on medium heat, stirring continually. Once it has reached a steady, slow boil, remove from heat and stir in vanilla and coconut extracts and lime zest. Let mixture sit until almost cooled, stirring occasionally. (You may transfer mixture to a bowl to cool in refrigerator.) Pour mixture into pie crust and refrigerate again for 1 hour or more until set.

This cream is good stuff! It's creamy, infused with pure vanilla bean seeds and a hint of maple and macadamia. Serve on pies or cakes, or as a dip for fruit, cookies, or … your fingers!

Macadamia Maple Butter Cream

MAKES 4–6 SERVINGS (ABOUT 1½ CUPS). | **WHEAT-FREE**

1 pkg	**(12-oz/340-g) silken extra-firm tofu**
¼–⅓ cup	**maple butter or cream** (see notes)
2½ tbsp	**macadamia nut butter**
¼ tsp	**sea salt**
1	**vanilla bean** (seeds only)

In a food processor, combine tofu, maple butter (starting with ¼ cup), macadamia nut butter, and salt and blend until very smooth, scraping down sides of bowl as needed. Slice open vanilla bean lengthwise and use a butter knife to scrape out all the seeds. Add seeds to tofu mixture in food processor and blend again until well incorporated. Taste test, and add remaining maple butter if desired.

"Maple butter" or "maple cream" is concentrated maple syrup, produced by heating and cooling the syrup. It is important to check the label to ensure the maple butter or cream is vegan; some manufacturers add butter and some make it with 100% maple syrup.

If maple butter is not available, you may substitute with 1/3–½ cup maple syrup (or ¼ cup maple syrup and 2–3 tbsp organic powdered sugar); just note that the cream will be thinner.

Vegan white chocolate chips can be purchased from online sources or specialty grocery stores. If they're not available, you can make this recipe with dark chocolate chips and it will not disappoint!

Macadamia White Chocolate Chip Cookies

MAKES 11–14 COOKIES. | **WHEAT-FREE**

Depending on the density of the flour you use, and the time of year, you may need more or less liquid in this recipe. If the batter is too dry, stir in another 1–2 tsp each brown rice syrup and oil.

1 cup + 2 tbsp	**spelt flour** (or 1 cup all-purpose flour)
1 tsp	**baking powder**
¼ tsp	**baking soda**
2 tbsp	**unrefined sugar**
¼ tsp	**sea salt**
⅓ cup	**macadamia nut butter**
⅓ cup	**pure maple syrup**
2 tbsp	**brown rice syrup** (or more maple syrup or agave nectar)
1 tsp	**pure vanilla extract**
3 tbsp	**canola oil** (see note)
¼ cup	**macadamia nuts,** lightly chopped or crushed
3–4 tbsp	**vegan white chocolate chips** (or dark chocolate chips)

Preheat oven to 350°F (180°C). In a bowl, sift in flour, baking powder, and baking soda, stir in sugar and salt, and mix until well combined. In a separate bowl, combine macadamia nut butter, maple syrup, brown rice syrup, vanilla, and stir until very well combined. Stir in oil, nuts, and chocolate chips. Add wet mixture to dry, and stir until just well combined (do not overmix). Line a baking sheet with parchment paper. Spoon batter onto baking sheet and evenly space apart. Bake for 11–12 minutes (no longer, or they will dry out). Remove from oven and let cool on baking sheet for 1 minute (no longer), then transfer to a cooling rack.

These blondies live up to their name, with a sticky gooey-ness that is irresistible. They will have you reaching for "just one more."

Maple Pecan Sticky **Blondies**

MAKES 12–16 SQUARES. | **WHEAT-FREE**

BASE:

1 ⅛ cups	spelt flour
1 tsp	baking powder
¾ cup + 2 tbsp	unrefined sugar
½ tsp	sea salt
1 tbsp	arrowroot powder
3 tbsp	plain soy milk or other plain non-dairy milk
⅓ cup	vanilla soy yogurt
2 tbsp	pure maple syrup
1½ tsp	blackstrap molasses
2 tsp	pure vanilla extract
3½ tbsp	canola oil
¼ cup	dark chocolate or white chocolate chips (for garnish)

TOPPING:

¾ cup	pecans, lightly crushed or chopped
2 tbsp	pure maple syrup
1 pinch	sea salt
½ tsp	canola oil

Preheat oven to 400°F (205°C). Line a baking sheet with parchment paper. In a small bowl, combine pecans, syrup, salt and oil. Transfer mixture to baking sheet, using a spatula to spread out evenly, and bake for 4–5 minutes. Remove from oven and let cool while preparing base. Reduce oven temperature to 350°F (180°C). In a bowl, sift in flour and baking powder. Add sugar and salt, and stir until well combined. In a separate bowl, combine arrowroot with 1 tbsp milk, whisk until smooth, then add remaining milk, yogurt, 2 tbsp syrup, molasses, vanilla, and oil, and stir until well combined. Add wet mixture to dry, and stir for about 30 seconds. Line an 8x8-in (20x20-cm) brownie pan with parchment paper. Transfer batter to pan and use a spatula to distribute as evenly as possible. Sprinkle on maple pecan topping and chocolate chips, lightly pressing into batter. Bake for 30–34 minutes, until the center is just set (it will set more after cooling). Remove from oven, transferring pan to a cooling rack to cool completely before removing and cutting into squares. (If you can wait, refrigerate blondies before cutting into them—they will then be easier to cut).

Lining your pan with parchment paper makes removing the bars so simple! Cut two long sheets to fit bottom and sides of pan so the paper hangs slightly over the edges. Once cooled, simply lift edges of parchment to remove in whole, then slice in squares.

This is my vegan adaptation of the classic Rice Krispie squares that have become an all-time favorite treat.

Nice Krispie Squares

MAKES 12–16 SQUARES. | **WHEAT-FREE**

Use an entire 10-oz (285-g) bag of Vegan Sweets marshmallows or use the Sweet and Sara brand (keep in mind they are sold in smaller portions, so you will need enough for 10 oz/285 g marshmallows). I prefer using the Sweet and Sara brand in this recipe because it tastes more similar to the squares I ate as a child.

For chewier, more "marshmallowy" squares, use 3 cups cereal; for denser squares, use the full 4 cups.

¼ cup	**Earth Balance Buttery Spread** (or other non-hydrogenated vegan margarine)
10 oz	**(285 g) vegan marshmallows** (see note)
1 tsp	**pure vanilla extract**
3–4 cups	**rice crisp cereal** (I use Nature's Path "Crispy Rice") (see note)

Line an 8x8-in (20x20-cm) pan with parchment paper (or lightly grease with Earth Balance spread). In a large saucepan on low heat, melt margarine (ensure it does not burn). Add marshmallows, stirring for 10–15 minutes until melted (do not increase heat to quicken process). Stir in vanilla, then quickly stir in rice cereal and transfer mixture to pan, pressing it down evenly (use an edge of parchment paper to press without sticking). Refrigerate to cool completely, then cut into squares.

This recipe mimics the flavors and textures of Rice Krispie squares using more natural ingredients that are easier to find. These taste phenomenal, with the buttery richness of the macadamia nut butter and the sweetness of brown rice syrup. They aren't sticky or gooey like traditional Rice Krispie squares, but the flavor is remarkably similar. Also try the variation with cranberries, pistachios, and white chocolate chips—suggested on my website by Mrs Carlson.

"Nicer" Krispie Squares

MAKES 12–16 SQUARES. | **WHEAT-FREE**

½ cup	**macadamia nut butter**
½ cup	**brown rice syrup**
3 tbsp	**unrefined sugar**
¼ tsp	**sea salt**
¼ tsp	**agar powder** (see note)
1½ tsp	**pure vanilla extract**
4 cups	**rice crisp cereal** (I use Nature's Path "Crispy Rice")

OPTIONAL PISTACHIO CRANBERRY CHIP VERSION:

¼–⅓ cup	**pistachios,** lightly crushed or chopped (see note)
2–3 tbsp	**dried cranberries**
¼ cup	**white chocolate chips** (or carob or dark chocolate chips)

If agar powder is not available, you can omit it. The squares will just lose some firmness.

You can use other nuts in place of pistachios, or substitute ½ the pistachios with pumpkin seeds.

Line an 8x8-in (20x20-cm) pan with parchment paper (or lightly grease pan with canola oil or Earth Balance spread). In a large saucepan on low-medium heat, combine macadamia butter, syrup, sugar, salt, agar powder, and vanilla. Stir continually as mixture heats until agar powder is fully dissolved (reduce heat if mixture starts bubbling). Remove from heat and stir in cereal and optional pistachios, cranberries, and chips, quickly incorporating ingredients so chocolate chips don't melt too much. Transfer mixture to pan and press in evenly (use an edge of parchment paper to press without sticking). Refrigerate to cool completely, then cut into squares.

This lightly spiced recipe makes a small enough batch for treats for your little ones (or yourself)!

Oatmeal Raisin Cookies

MAKES 9–12 COOKIES. | **WHEAT-FREE**

¾ cup + 1 tbsp	spelt flour
1 tsp	baking powder
¼ tsp	baking soda
½ cup	quick oats
¼ cup	unrefined sugar
¼ cup	raisins
½ tsp	cinnamon
1 pinch	allspice (or ¼ tsp nutmeg)
¼ tsp	sea salt
¼ cup	pure maple syrup
¼–½ tsp	blackstrap molasses
1½ tsp	pure vanilla extract
¼ cup	canola oil

Preheat oven to 350°F (180°C). In a bowl, sift in flour, baking powder, and baking soda. Add oats, sugar, raisins, cinnamon, allspice, and salt, and stir until well combined. In a separate bowl, combine syrup, molasses, and vanilla, then stir in oil to incorporate. Add wet mixture to dry and stir until just well combined (do not overmix). Line a baking sheet with parchment paper. Spoon batter onto baking sheet, evenly space apart, and slightly flatten. Bake for 11 minutes (no longer, or they will dry out), until lightly golden. Remove from oven, and let cool on baking sheet for 1 minute (no longer), then transfer to a cooling rack.

Using a prepared crust, you can make this delightful pumpkin pie in minutes, then let the oven do the rest of the work! A cross between a pumpkin pie and cheesecake, it's a must-make for the holidays. Top with Celestial Cream (page 29), Macadamia Maple Butter Cream (page 201), vanilla non-dairy ice cream, or soy whipped topping.

Pumpkin Cheese-Pie

MAKES 6–8 SERVINGS.

FILLING:

1 can	**(14-oz/400-ml) organic pumpkin pie mix** (I use Farmer's Market Organic brand)
1 container	**(8-oz/240-g) soy cream cheese** (I use Tofutti brand; non-hydrogenated)
3 tbsp	**unrefined sugar**
2 tsp	**arrowroot powder**
1 tsp	**freshly squeezed lemon juice**
1/8 tsp	**sea salt**
1	**prepared graham cracker pie crust** (I use Wholly Wholesome brand) (see notes)
1–2 tbsp	**unrefined sugar** (coarse granule, if possible) (for topping)

You can also use a traditional pastry pie crust if you prefer, either prepared or made from scratch.

WHEAT-FREE OPTION: Use a spelt pastry crust.

Preheat oven to 425°F (220°C). In a food processor, combine pumpkin pie mix (scraping out everything from the can), cream cheese, 3 tbsp sugar, arrowroot powder, lemon juice, and salt. Purée until very smooth, scraping down sides of bowl as needed. Pour mixture into pie crust (scrape out bowl) and gently tip back and forth to distribute evenly. Sprinkle with 1–2 tbsp sugar. Bake for 15 minutes, then reduce heat to 350°F (180°C) and continue to bake for 35–37 minutes, until the pie is set (the center may be soft, but it will set further as it cools). Let cool before serving.

This started out as a butter-cream frosting for kids that would be sweet with a light pink hue. But as I developed the recipe, I reduced the amount of sugar and eliminated the butter and it became "berry" luscious, and creamier than my original version!

Strawberry Cream Kids' Frosting

MAKES ENOUGH FOR ONE 2-LAYER CAKE OR 20–24 CUPCAKES (2½ CUPS). | **WHEAT-FREE**

For thicker frosting, use 2¼ tsp agar powder.

Use regular coconut milk since you need to skim off ¼ cup of the thick cream that sits at the top of the milk when you open the can; so don't shake the can before opening! Refrigerate remaining milk in a sealed container.

I use Wholesome Sweeteners Organic Powdered Sugar, which is made from unrefined cane sugar (unlike icing sugar, which is made from refined white sugar). If you cannot find it, make your own: In a blender, combine 1¼–1½ cups unrefined sugar with 1 tbsp arrowroot powder or cornstarch. Blend on high until powdery, scraping sides of blender as needed. (Omit arrowroot or cornstarch if using a high-powered blender such as Vita-Mix.)

If possible, frost cake or cupcakes the night before, and refrigerate overnight to help it set. But if using for Vanilla Cupcake Cones (page 213), do not frost in advance, as the moisture in the icing will soften the ice cream cone shell.

1 cup	**strawberry jam or berry jelly** (I use Crofters organic strawberry brand)
1 tsp	**lemon juice**
2–2¼ tsp	**agar powder** (see note)
1 pkg	**(12-oz/340-g) silken extra-firm tofu**
¼ cup	**cream from can of regular coconut milk** (see note)
½ tsp	(scant) **sea salt**
¾ tsp	**pure almond extract**
½ tsp	**pure vanilla extract**
2–3 pinches	**beet powder** (optional, for color)
3–4 tbsp	**organic powdered sugar** (optional) (see note)

In a small pot on medium-low heat, whisk together jam, lemon juice, and agar powder, allowing mixture to come to a slow boil. Reduce heat and cook for about 3 minutes, until agar powder is fully dissolved. Remove from heat and set aside. In a food processor (do not use a mixer), combine tofu, coconut cream, salt, almond and vanilla extracts, and beet powder, and purée until smooth, scraping down sides of bowl as needed. Add jam mixture and purée again until smooth. Refrigerate until completely cooled. When ready to use, purée again until completely smooth, and taste test, adding 3–4 tbsp powdered sugar if desired.

This one-layer cake is similar to a coffee cake, perfect for afternoon tea or a light dessert. It is flavorful and supremely moist, even though it contains only 3 tbsp of oil! Serve as is, or with a scoop of non-dairy vanilla ice cream and an elegant drizzle of Warm Raspberry Sauce (page 39).

Sunny Pineapple Yogurt Cake with Orange Glaze

MAKES 6–8 SERVINGS. | WHEAT-FREE

1½ cups	spelt flour
½ cup + 2 tbsp	unrefined sugar
¼ tsp + ⅛ tsp	sea salt
¼ tsp	cinnamon
1½ tsp	baking powder
½ tsp	baking soda
1 tbsp	plain or vanilla non-dairy milk
1 tbsp	arrowroot powder
2 tbsp	pure maple syrup
¾ cup	vanilla soy yogurt
2 tsp	pure vanilla extract
1 can	(8-oz/235-ml) crushed pineapple (including juice)
3 tbsp	canola oil

GLAZE:

⅓ cup	organic powdered sugar (see note)
1 tbsp	freshly squeezed orange juice (zest before juicing, see below)
½–1 tsp	orange zest

I use Wholesome Sweeteners Organic Powdered Sugar, which is made from unrefined cane sugar (unlike icing sugar, which is made from refined white sugar). If it is not available, make your own: In a blender, combine 1¼–1½ cups unrefined sugar with 1 tbsp arrowroot powder or cornstarch. Blend on high until powdery, scraping sides of blender as needed. (Omit arrowroot or cornstarch if using a high-powered blender such as Vita-Mix.)

You can bake this cake in a larger pan, just be sure to adjust baking time, checking for doneness between 27–30 minutes, until a toothpick inserted in center comes out clean.

Preheat oven to 350°F (180°C). In a large bowl, combine flour, sugar, salt, and cinnamon, and sift in baking powder and baking soda. Stir to combine well. In a separate bowl, combine milk and arrowroot, whisking until smooth, then whisk in syrup. Add yogurt, vanilla, and pineapple, and stir until well combined, then stir in oil to incorporate. Add wet mixture to dry, and stir until just well combined (do not over-mix). Line an 8x8-in (20x20-cm) baking pan with parchment paper (or lightly grease with canola oil). Pour batter evenly into pan. Bake for 35–40 minutes, until a toothpick inserted in center comes out clean (see note). Remove from oven and transfer pan to a cooling rack. In a small bowl, whisk glaze ingredients until very smooth. When cake is completely cool, transfer to a serving plate and drizzle on glaze. Serve immediately.

After our eldest daughter played her first soccer league game, the players were handed enormous pre-wrapped cookies that were full of hydrogenated fats, white flour, and sugar, and weighed ¼ lb each! It occurred to me that we don't need to super-size our kids' food … we need to super-charge it! So I created these incredibly healthy, delicious cookies.

Super-Charge Me! Cookies

MAKES 11–12 COOKIES. | **WHEAT-FREE**

1 cup	**quick oats**
⅔ cup	**spelt flour**
¼ tsp	(rounded) **sea salt**
¼–½ tsp	**cinnamon**
⅛ cup	**unsweetened shredded coconut**
¼–⅓ cup	**raisins or chopped dried fruit**
3–4 tbsp	**carob or chocolate chips** (optional; or use more dried fruit, nuts, or seeds)
1 tsp	**baking powder**
⅓ cup	**flax meal**
½ cup	**pure maple syrup**
3 tbsp	**almond butter** (may use cashew, peanut, hemp seed butter)
1½ tsp	**pure vanilla extract**
2 tbsp	**canola oil**

Preheat oven to 350°F (180°C). In a bowl, combine oats, flour, salt, cinnamon, coconut, raisins, and carob or chocolate chips, sift in baking powder, and stir until well combined. In a separate bowl, combine flax meal, syrup, almond butter, and vanilla and stir until well combined. Stir in oil. Add wet mixture to dry, and stir until just well combined (do not overmix). Line a baking sheet with parchment paper. Spoon batter onto baking sheet evenly space apart, and lightly flatten. Bake for 13 minutes (no longer, or they will dry out). Remove from oven and let cool on baking sheet for 1 minute (no longer), then transfer to a cooling rack.

Kids will adore these naturally pink-tinted cookies with a vanilla flavor and topped with sprinkles. Be sure to make a double or triple batch for birthday parties!

"Tickled Pink" Vanilla Sprinkle Cookies

MAKES 11–14 COOKIES. | **WHEAT-FREE**

¼ cup	**unrefined sugar**
¼ tsp	**sea salt**
1 cup + 2 tbsp	**spelt flour** (or 1 cup all-purpose flour)
1 tsp	**baking powder**
¼ tsp	**baking soda**
¼ + ⅛ tsp	**beet powder**
⅓ cup	**pure maple syrup**
2 tsp	**pure vanilla extract**
¼ cup	**canola oil**
2–3 tbsp	**naturally colored sprinkles** (I use Let's Do … Sprinkelz brand)

Preheat oven to 350°F (180°C). In a bowl, combine sugar and salt, sift in flour, baking powder, baking soda, and beet powder, and stir until well combined. In a separate bowl, combine syrup, vanilla, and oil and stir until well mixed. Add wet mixture to dry, and stir until just well combined (do not overmix). Line a baking sheet with parchment paper. Spoon batter onto baking sheet and evenly space apart. Top with sprinkles, lightly pressing them into batter. Bake for 11 minutes (no longer, or they will dry out). Remove from oven and let cool on pan for 1 minute (no longer), then transfer to a cooling rack.

You will amaze your friends (and yourself) with this confection! These truffles are not as good as their dairy counterparts—they're better. Honestly, these are heavenly with a rich smooth texture, not overly sweet, and blissfully chocolatey!

Unbelievably Rich Chocolate **Truffles**

MAKES 20–24 TRUFFLES. | **WHEAT-FREE**

The easiest way to finely chop or shave chocolate is with a serrated knife. Place chocolate on a cutting board, and guide knife along edge of chocolate to shave off fine pieces.

To grind the nuts, place a small quantity in a mini-food processor and blend through until fairly fine.

¾ cup	**regular coconut milk** (not light)
10–10½ oz	**(295–310 g) good quality dark chocolate,** finely chopped (about 2 cups) (see note)
½ tsp	**almond extract** (or ½–1 tsp other extract of choice)
1 tbsp	**liquor** (e.g., brandy, Grand Marnier, Kahlua) (optional)
2–3 tbsp	**Dutch-processed or regular cocoa powder or ground nuts** (see note)

In a small pot on medium, heat coconut milk, stirring until very hot but not boiling. Place chocolate in a glass bowl. Pour hot milk over chocolate and use a heat-proof spatula to stir until chocolate is fully melted and mixture is well combined. (If it needs to melt more, place bowl over a pot of simmering water and stir continually until melted.) Stir in extract and liquor. Refrigerate for 1 hour or more, until completely cooled and firm. Scoop using a melon baller or small spoon, then lightly roll into balls using your hands. (You will need to rinse your hands a few times throughout.) Place truffles on a plate or baking sheet lined with parchment paper (you can refrigerate in small batches if desired while finishing rolling). Place cocoa or nuts on a plate and lightly roll truffles on to coat. Serve as is, or refrigerate until serving.

This is the ultimate treat for birthday parties: ice cream cones filled with cake batter instead of ice cream, then topped with frosting. Top with Strawberry Cream Kids' Frosting (page 208) or your favorite icing, and just before serving, top with a scoop of non-dairy ice cream. Thanks to Julie Hasson for the recipe idea.

Vanilla Cupcake Cones

MAKES 12 CUPCAKE CONES.

12	**flat-bottomed ice cream cones** (see note)
½ cup	**unrefined sugar** (fine granule is best)
¼ tsp	**sea salt**
1 cup	**unbleached all-purpose flour**
1 tsp	**baking powder**
¼ tsp	**baking soda**
²/₃ cup + 1–2 tbsp	**plain soy or other non-dairy milk** (see note)
½ tsp	**freshly squeezed lemon juice**
1 tsp	**pure vanilla extract**
2 tbsp	**canola oil**

Make regular cupcakes with this batter: use muffin liners, and fill about halfway full with batter. Bake for 21–23 minutes to yield 9–12 cupcakes.

If using Strawberry Cream Kids' Frosting or other tofu-based frosting, wait to frost cones within 1 hour before serving since moisture from the tofu will soften the cone.

Preheat oven to 350°F (180°C). Using a muffin pan, place a cone in each compartment. In a bowl, combine sugar and salt, sift in flour, baking powder, and baking soda, and stir until well combined. In a separate bowl, combine milk (starting with ²/₃ cup + 1 tbsp), lemon juice, and vanilla. Stir in oil until incorporated. Add wet mixture to dry, and stir until just well combined (do not overmix). (If batter seems too thick, add remaining tablespoon of milk.) Spoon ¹/₈ cup of batter into each cone. Bake for 21–23 minutes. Remove from oven and let cool in pan for 1–2 minutes before transferring cones to a cooling rack to cool completely before topping with frosting.

This is one of those rare cookie recipes that was perfect the very first time I baked them. Toasted walnuts add a lot of flavor, but you can use raw walnuts or pecans if you prefer.

Walnut-Carob-Cranberry **Clusters**

MAKES 13–14 COOKIES. | **WHEAT-FREE**

1 cup	**toasted walnuts,** crushed just a little
¼ cup	**unsweetened shredded coconut**
¼ cup	**dried unsweetened cranberries**
⅓ cup	**carob chips**
¼ tsp	**sea salt**
¾ cup	**spelt flour**
½ tsp	**baking powder**
¼ cup	**pure maple syrup**
1 tsp	**pure vanilla extract**
3 tbsp	**canola oil**

Preheat oven to 350°F (180°C). In a large bowl, combine walnuts, coconut, cranberries, carob chips, and salt, sift in flour and baking powder, and stir to combine. In another bowl, combine syrup, vanilla, and oil until well mixed. Add wet mixture to dry and stir until well combined. Line a baking sheet with parchment paper. Scoop about 1½–2 tbsp batter and roughly form each into a ball with your hands. (You will need to rinse your hands a few times throughout.) Place clusters on baking sheet. Bake for 12–13 minutes (no longer, or they will dry out). Remove from oven and let cool on pan for 1 minute (no longer), then transfer to a cooling rack.

When I posted the photo of these peanut-butter chocolate cookies on my website, Chris from the Eat Air blog said they reminded him of a Reese's commercial from the 1980s with the memorable lines, "You got peanut butter on my chocolate!" "No, you got chocolate in my peanut butter!" I couldn't resist Chris's recipe title suggestion!

"You Got Peanut Butter in My Chocolate" Cookies

MAKES 10–14 COOKIES. | **WHEAT-FREE**

¼ cup	**unrefined sugar**
¼ cup	**dark chocolate chips**
¼ tsp	**sea salt**
1 cup + 1 tbsp	**barley or spelt flour** (or 1 cup all-purpose flour)
3 tbsp	**cocoa powder**
1 tsp	**baking powder**
½ tsp	**baking soda**
¼ cup	**pure maple syrup**
2–2½ tbsp	**agave nectar** (or more maple syrup)
1 tsp	**pure vanilla extract**
¼ cup	**canola oil**
¼–⅓ cup	**natural peanut butter** (smooth or chunky)

Preheat oven to 350°F (180°C). In a bowl, combine sugar, chocolate chips, and salt, sift in flour, cocoa powder, baking powder, and baking soda, and stir until well combined. In a separate bowl, combine maple syrup, agave nectar, vanilla, and oil until well mixed. Add wet mixture to dry, and stir until just well combined (do not overmix). With a knife, cut in peanut butter into batter, but just a little, so peanut butter remains in chunks and swirls in batter. Line a baking sheet with parchment paper. Scoop rounded tablespoons of batter onto baking sheet evenly spaced apart. Bake for 11 minutes (no longer, or they will dry out). Remove from oven and let cool on pan for 1 minute (no longer), then transfer to a cooling rack.

A Toast to Being Vegan!

Beverages

LET'S RAISE A GLASS to healthy, compassionate eating! This chapter presents some fun and tasty drinks that are simple to prepare. You'll want to include certain recipes into your daily repertoire, such as Ginger Immunity Tea (page 223) and Drink Your Greens Smoothie (page 222). Others will suit parties and celebrations, such as Sugar-Free Lemonade (page 225) or Lemon Rooibos Iced Tea (page 225) in the warmer months, and Mulled Cran-Apple Cider (page 227) to take the chill out of in the winter months.

These drink recipes are all free of alcohol. You can enhance some with a splash of spirits if you choose, or just pick up some vegan beers and wines for your intimate dinners or larger parties.

Açai ("ah-sigh-ee") is an antioxidant-abundant berry that is also a source of protein and omega fatty acids. Açai has a unique berry-cocoa flavor, and combines beautifully with the frozen blueberries and cocoa powder, which also happen to be antioxidant-rich foods! You'll be glowing after enjoying this nutritional powerhouse smoothie.

Açai Antioxidant Smoothie

MAKES 2 SERVINGS (ABOUT 2½ CUPS).

1½ cups	plain or vanilla non-dairy milk
½ cup	frozen blueberries
½ cup	frozen sliced bananas (see note)
1 tbsp	Dutch-processed cocoa powder (can omit or use carob powder)
1–2 tbsp	agave nectar (or to taste)
1 packet	Sambazon "Pure Açai" frozen pulp (see note)
1½ –3 tbsp	extra non-dairy milk (to thin as needed)

With a hand blender or in a blender, combine milk, blueberries, bananas, cocoa, agave nectar, and Açai pulp (break up pulp by hand first if using hand blender) and purée until smooth. If smoothie is too thick, add extra milk, 1 tbsp at a time, to thin as desired (smoothie will also thin as frozen elements thaw).

For a purely raw smoothie, use fresh nut milk, or use freshly squeezed apple or other juice instead of milk. Also, use raw cocoa or carob powder and raw agave nectar.

Let bananas get overripe; when ready, they can be sliced, placed in Ziploc bags, and frozen.

I use Sambazon brand of Açai berries for this recipe. The berries are processed into a pulp, then frozen and sold in packets. I use the "Pure Açai" unsweetened variety. If using the "Original Açai," note that they are pre-sweetened.

If you want to make this smoothie even more substantial, add 1–2 tbsp raw almond butter or hemp seed nut butter.

Keep fruit juice and sparkling mineral water on hand, and you can make a refreshing natural "soda" anytime of the year. With the wide variety of pure, organic fruit juices available in natural health food stores, experiment with different flavor combinations to create your personal favorite spritzer!

Berry Spritzer

MAKES 2 SERVINGS (ABOUT 2 CUPS).

Any pure juices can be used, such as cherry, raspberry, pomegranate, or cranberry, or lemonade blends such as strawberry lemonade.

For a twist, use flavored natural sodas, such as black cherry, raspberry vanilla, or natural ginger ale, in place of sparkling mineral water.

1 cup	**pure berry juice** (e.g., Bremner's Pure Blueberry Juice or Santa Cruz Raspberry Lemonade) (see note)
1 cup	**sparkling mineral water** (see note)
2 tbsp	**agave nectar** (or more to taste)
	ice (for serving)
	fresh orange or lemon wedges (for garnish)

In a small pitcher, combine juice, mineral water, and agave nectar and mix well. Serve in individual glasses over ice, garnished with an orange or lemon wedge if desired.

The question all vegans love to hear, again and again! Of course, we know that protein is ample in so many plant-based foods, and that most non-vegans get too much protein, but let's answer that question with one simple, protein-packed, delicious, on-the-go, breakfast smoothie!

"But Where Do You Get Your Protein?" Smoothie

MAKES 2 SERVINGS.

2 cups	**plain or vanilla soy milk**
¾–1 cup	**frozen sliced bananas** (see note)
½ cup	**frozen blueberries** (optional)
1 tbsp	**almond, cashew, or peanut butter**
1 tbsp	**hemp seed nut butter** (or other nut butter)
2–2½ tbsp	**brown rice protein powder** (I use NutriBiotic brand)

With a hand blender or in a blender, combine all the ingredients and purée until smooth.

Let bananas get overripe; when ready, they can be sliced, placed in Ziploc bags, and frozen.

One serving of this smoothie provides 20–25 grams of protein, depending on the type of nut butter and soy milk used.

If serving only one, pour leftovers into popsicle molds and freeze to enjoy any time of the day. Our daughters love them!

This is an easy way to get those über-healthy greens in your diet. I first tried a greens smoothie at a raw cooking demo by raw vegan enthusiast Agathe Mathieu, whose recipe I adapted here. The secret to a delicious "green" smoothie is to use enough sweet and creamy fruits to camouflage the bitter greens, and then blend until extremely smooth.

Drink Your Greens **Smoothie**

MAKES 1–2 SERVINGS (ABOUT 2 CUPS).

Use another fruit juice or watered-down juice if you prefer. The better quality of juice, the better tasting the smoothie. Also, freshly squeezed juice provides an entirely raw smoothie.

Let bananas get overripe; when ready, they can be sliced, placed in Ziploc bags, and frozen.

Other greens can be substituted for kale, such as baby spinach or Swiss chard. Kale, however, is more nutritious, in that calcium and iron are better absorbed by the body. Dinosaur kale leaves are more tender than the common curly green variety, but any variety can be used.

Ripe avocado adds creaminess to this smoothie (along with bananas), and healthy fats. Store avocados on your counter until ripe, then refrigerate.

I like to use Ataulfo mangoes for smoothies because they are less stringy and less sweet than the more common Tommy Atkins variety.

½ cup	**freshly squeezed orange juice** (see note)
½ cup	**water**
1–1¼ cups	**frozen sliced bananas,** (see note)
1 cup	**dinosaur or curly green kale,** stems removed and chopped (see note)
¼–⅓ cup	**ripe avocado,** chopped (see note)
½ cup	**cantaloupe or honeydew melon, or mango,** cut in chunks or slices (see note)
1–2 tbsp	**agave nectar** (optional)

With a hand blender or in a blender, combine all ingredients, except agave nectar, and purée 1–2 minutes until very smooth and only specks of kale are visible. Taste test, and add agave nectar as desired. Add extra water or juice to thin as desired.

I buy a lot of fresh ginger, and every morning, I steep some in my green tea. Ginger has anti-viral compounds that are particularly effective at combating viruses that cause colds, and is also a natural decongestant. It has also been studied for its anti-bacterial, anti-fungal, pain-relieving, anti-ulcer, and anti-tumor properties. If that's not enough, ginger also has anti-inflammatory properties, and can ease digestive troubles and nausea.

Ginger Immunity Tea

MAKES 1 SERVING. | **WHEAT-FREE**

1½ tbsp	**fresh ginger,** peeled and chopped (see note)
	tea bag or loose tea of choice (I use green tea)
1½ cups	**boiling water** (or more if desired)
2–3 pinches	**stevia or other sweetener** (or to taste)

In a large mug, add ginger and tea bag (or loose tea in a tea ball). Add boiling water and let steep for several minutes. Add stevia or other sweetener if desired.

This recipe is very flexible in terms of how much ginger to use, depending on your taste. The more ginger you use, the more "heat" the tea will have. Also, the finer you chop it, the "hotter" the drink. If you don't want ginger loose in your tea, strain it after steeping or put ginger in a tea ball. Drink this tea a few times during the day if you are fighting off a cold.

Fresh lemon juice is a nice addition to this tea, and also very healthy.

Hot cocoa takes on a new life in this recipe with the addition of light coconut milk. Creamy, rich tasting, and satisfying, this hot drink can also be served as a dessert.

Hot Coco-**Cocoa**!

MAKES 4–5 SERVINGS (3¼–3½ CUPS).

Light coconut milk provides a rich coconut flavor without the extra fat of regular coconut milk. If using regular, you may need to reduce the measurement and increase the non-dairy milk to make it less rich.

You can use regular cocoa powder, but Dutch-processed cocoa powder has a richer, milder flavor since it has been processed to reduce its acidity.

Try this hot cocoa topped with thinly sliced fresh strawberries. Also, as a light dessert item, serve topped with soy whipped cream and sprinkled with toasted coconut, grated dark chocolate or fresh berries. Of course, who could forget vegan marshmallows in that rich hot chocolate? Individual servings can be enhanced with a shot of orange, coffee, hazelnut, or other liqueur.

Pour into popsicle molds and freeze for later. Kids will love them!

1 can	**(13½-oz/400-ml) light coconut milk** (see note)
1¼–1½ cups	**vanilla non-dairy milk**
¼ cup	**Dutch-processed cocoa powder** (see note)
⅛ tsp	**sea salt**
3½–4 tbsp	**agave nectar or pure maple syrup** (or to taste)

In a pot on medium heat, combine all ingredients (starting with 1¼ cups of non-dairy milk) and whisk until cocoa is well incorporated. Continue to whisk occasionally until very hot but not boiling. Taste test, and add remaining non-dairy milk to thin if desired. Reheat if needed, and serve in individual glasses.

On muggy summer days, brew some Rooibos tea and follow this simple recipe to chill out with a refreshing, energizing sugar-free iced tea.

Lemon Rooibos Iced Tea

MAKES 3–4 SERVINGS. | **WHEAT-FREE**

4 cups	**steeped Rooibos tea,** cooled (see note)
⅓ cup	**freshly squeezed lemon juice**
¾–1 tsp	**stevia powder** (or to taste; I use Herbal Select brand)
	ice (for serving)

In a pitcher, combine tea, lemon juice, and stevia and stir well to incorporate stevia, adjusting to taste with extra stevia if desired. Chill, and serve over ice.

Rooibos is one of my favorite teas. I drink it and green tea daily. My favorite brand is Ronnefeldt. For this iced tea, I particularly like using the raspberry vanilla flavor.

Rooibos is naturally caffeine-free and rich in antioxidants. It has been used to reduce the risk of cancer, heart disease, and stroke, and slows the aging process. It also aids digestion, and improves sleep and skin conditions.

It's easy to make lemonade. This homemade and sugar-free recipe is healthier and more refreshing than store-bought brands.

Sugar-Free Lemonade

MAKES 3–4 SERVINGS. | **WHEAT-FREE**

3 cups	**cold water**
½ cup	**freshly squeezed lemon juice**
½–¾ tsp	**stevia powder** (or to taste; I use Herbal Select brand)
	ice cubes (for serving)

In a pitcher, combine water, lemon juice, and stevia (start with ½ tsp), stirring well to incorporate stevia. Adding more stevia if desired, then add ice, and serve.

You may substitute lime juice for lemon juice to create a lime-ade.

This is an adaptation of the Indian beverage Mango Lassi. Instead of soy yogurt, lime juice is added for tartness, and also making it a little lighter to drink (and also suitable for those with soy allergies). If you'd like it a little more authentic, feel free to add about ½ cup of plain soy yogurt to the mix!

Mango Sassy!

MAKES 2–3 SERVINGS. | **WHEAT-FREE**

I like to use Ataulfo mangoes for smoothies because they are less stringy than the more common Tommy Atkins variety. To remove mango flesh, first peel, then cut pulp away from the pit. Or, cut along each side of the flat, oval-shaped pit, and with each half, score (cut criss-cross) mango flesh. Use your thumbs to press in on the mango from the outer skin side to turn halves inside-out, exposing mango cubes which you can cut away from the skin. You can peel and cut the remaining mango flesh surrounding the pit.

If serving adults, use the full 6 tsp lime juice. For children, use just 4 tsp.

For a twist, add a handful of frozen or fresh raspberries or strawberries to the mix.

Pour leftovers into popsicle molds and freeze for "Sass-icles"!

1 cup	**mango,** cut in chunks (see note)
1 cup	**plain or vanilla rice milk or other non-dairy milk**
4–6 tsp	**freshly squeezed lime juice** (see note)
⅓ cup	**ice cubes** (for blending)
1–2 tsp	**agave nectar** (or to taste)
	ice cubes (for serving)

With a hand blender or in a blender, combine mango, milk, lime juice (starting with 4 tsp), and ice cubes and blend until smooth. Taste test, and add more lime juice or agave nectar if desired. Pour into individual glasses with a few ice cubes and serve.

This lightly spiced cider will warm and soothe through chilly winter months. The addition of cranberry juice adds a slight tartness to the sweet apple cider, as well as a beautiful red color that is particularly festive for holiday parties.

Mulled Cran-Apple **Cider**

MAKES 4 SERVINGS (3–3 ¼ CUPS).

3 cups	**sweet apple cider** (I use Santa Cruz Organic brand)
1 cup	**pure unsweetened cranberry juice**
2	**cinnamon sticks**
4–7	**whole cloves**
½ tsp	**whole cardamom** (see note)
1 tsp	**orange rind**
¼ tsp	**freshly grated nutmeg,** (optional)
1–2 tbsp	**agave nectar** (or 2–3 pinches stevia) to taste (optional)
	cinnamon sticks (for garnish)

Whole cardamom is a wonderfully fragrant spice, but if you don't have it, substitute about ¼ tsp ground cardamom, or omit altogether.

Try this cider in Cran-Apple Quinoa (page 159).

Add a few splashes of rum or brandy to individual servings of cider if you like.

In a pot on medium-high heat, combine apple cider, cranberry juice, and cinnamon sticks. In a fine mesh tea ball, place cloves, cardamom, and orange rind (alternatively, use a cheesecloth to hold spices, or leave spices loose and strain mixture before serving). Add tea ball and nutmeg to cider mixture. Bring to a low boil, then reduce heat to low and simmer uncovered for about 20 minutes, stirring occasionally. Taste test, and sweeten with agave nectar if desired. Serve in mugs, with a cinnamon stick to swizzle!

GRAIN & BEAN COOKING GUIDES

I included these reference guides to cooking grains and beans in my last cookbook, *Vive le Vegan!* Readers found them very helpful, so I have included them again in this book, with some additional notes.

COOKING WHOLE GRAINS

Grain (1 cup dry)	Water Needed	Cooking Time
Amaranth	2½–3 cups	20–25 min
Barley, pearl	3 cups	40–50 min
Barley, whole (hulled)	3 cups	60–75 min
Buckwheat	2 cups	15–20 min
Kamut berries	3 cups	70–90 min
*Millet	2½–3 cups	18–25 min
Oats	2–2½ cups	15–25 min
**Quinoa	2 cups	12–15 min
Rice, brown basmati	2 cups	35–45 min
Rice, brown short-grain	2 cups	40–50 min
Rice, brown long-grain	2 cups	40–50 min
Rye berries	3–3½ cups	60 min
Spelt berries	3 cups	55–70 min
Wheat berries	3 cups	55–70 min
Wild rice	3 cups	45–60 min

* For millet, more water (3 cups+) and longer cooking time (25 minutes+) will yield a softer, creamier texture; do not stir millet while simmering. For a fluffier texture like rice, use less water and a shorter cooking time.

** Rinse quinoa before using to remove its natural bitter coating. Certain brands are pre-rinsed, but some bitterness may still remain. To be sure, rinse for several minutes.

For all grains, rinse before cooking to remove any dust or other particles (amaranth and quinoa will need to be rinsed in a very fine strainer). To cook, simply combine the grain and cooking water, bring to a boil, then reduce heat to low, and cover to simmer for specified time (as per the chart above). About 5 minutes before cooking time is complete (avoid peeking before this time), check for doneness. Remove from heat and let stand covered for 4–5 minutes.

Cooking times are meant as a guide, and can vary slightly. In general, if you shorten the cooking time, grains will be firmer and chewier. If you increase the cooking time (plus a little more water), grains will be softer.

Some grains have a nuttier flavor (e.g., quinoa, amaranth, millet) and are more separate and less sticky (e.g., millet, amaranth) if toasted before cooking: simply add the dry grains to a dry frying pan on medium heat for 2–3 minutes, stirring occasionally, until there is a nutty aroma. You can also sauté them with a little olive oil before adding water.

COOKING BEANS

Bean	Cooking Time
Adzuki beans	45–60 min
Black beans	60–90 min
Black-eyed peas	45–60 min
Cannellini (white kidney) beans	60–90 min
Chickpeas (Garbanzo beans)	1½–2 hr
*Kidney beans (red)	1½–2 hr
**Lentils, brown/green	30–40 min
**Lentils, red	15–25 min
**Lentils, French (Puy)	35–45 min
**Mung beans	40–50 min
Navy beans	1½–2 hr
**Split peas (green)	40–60 min

* Red kidney beans contain a high concentration of a toxin called lectin, which is found in other bean varieties, but in much lower levels. Red kidney beans must therefore be thoroughly cooked at a high temperature. Undercooked red kidney beans can induce nausea. Cooking from dried form in crock pots is not recommended because the low cooking temperature does not destroy the toxin, and undercooked beans are actually more toxic than raw form. Canned red kidney beans are perfectly fine, and I recommend using them instead of dry.

** Lentils, mung beans, and split peas do not need to be pre-soaked. Just sort to remove any dirt, stones, or particles, rinse and cook.

With the exception of lentils, mung beans, and split peas, beans should be soaked before cooking—it shortens cooking time and helps improve the digestibility of beans. You can either soak beans overnight or do a "quick soak" (explained below). To soak overnight, first rinse dry beans and remove any dirt, stones, particles, or beans that are split or shriveled. Combine 3–4 parts water to 1 part beans and soak for at least 6 hours. Then, drain, rinse again, and proceed with cooking, as per below.

To "quick soak" beans, first rinse dry beans and remove any dirt, stones, particles, or beans that are split or shrivelled. Combine 3–4 parts water to 1 part beans in a large pot. Bring to a boil on high heat, and let boil for 5–7 minutes. Turn off heat, cover, and let sit for 1½–2 hours. Drain beans and rinse again. Also, rinse out cooking pot and wipe clean to remove cooking residues. Then proceed with cooking, as per below.

A note about digestibility: In general, beans that are classified as softer are easier to digest than those classified as hard. Softer beans include lentils, adzukis, and black-eyed peas. Harder beans include cannellini, kidney, and chickpeas. Soybeans are the hardest bean to digest, but soy products like tempeh and tofu are more digestible.

To cook beans, combine 3–4 parts water to 1 part rinsed (or pre-soaked beans) in a large pot. Bring to a boil on high heat, then reduce heat to low and simmer partially covered until tender, using above chart as reference. Ensure beans simmer, not boil, throughout cooking time to prevent skins from splitting. In general, 1 cup of dried beans will yield 2– 2½ cups of cooked beans. Do not add salt or acidic ingredients such as lemons, vinegar, or tomatoes to cooking water as they will lengthen the cooking time; add them when beans are tender. Aromatics such as onion and garlic can be added at the beginning of cooking, however.

Once beans are cooked, they can be frozen for later use. (Be sure to cook beans in large enough batches that you can freeze extra portions.) I usually freeze in 2- or 3-cup portions in Ziploc or other containers, since these are the amounts needed for most recipes. Ensure they have an airtight seal and are labelled to identify the type of bean and quantity.

To use frozen beans, simply thaw. To hasten the process, hold the container under hot running water for a few seconds to loosen. Alternatively, add a whole chunk of frozen beans to soups or stews, letting them thaw as the dish cooks. If you plan to purée them, you can place the frozen beans in a bowl and cover with some boiled water. Let sit until thawed, then drain before use.

Of course, canned beans can be used, but your own cooked beans (particularly organic) usually taste better. If using canned, always drain and rinse before using.

Measurement Conversion Table

Teaspoons	Tablespoons	Cups	Fluid Ounces	Milliters	Other
¼ tsp				1 ml	
½ tsp				2 ml	
¾ tsp				4 ml	
1 tsp	⅓ tbsp			5 ml	
3 tsp	1 tbsp	1/16 cup	½ oz	15 ml	
	2 tbsp	⅛ cup	1 oz	30 ml	
	4 tbsp	¼ cup	2 oz	60 ml	
	5⅓ tbsp	⅓ cup	2½ oz	75 ml	
	8 tbsp	½ cup	4 oz	125 ml	
		⅔ cup	5 oz	150 ml	
		¾ cup	6 oz	175 ml	
	16 tbsp	1 cup	8 oz	237 ml	½ pt
		2 cups	16 oz	473 ml	1 pt
		3 cups	24 oz	710 ml	1½ pt
		4 cups	32 oz	946 ml	1 qt/1 l

Glossary

Açai: Pronounced "ah-sigh-ee," this highly nutritious berry grows in the Amazon rainforest in Brazil. Açai have a unique cocoa-berry flavor, more antioxidants than blueberries and pomegranates, and provide omega fatty acids, protein, iron, and fiber. Açai berries resemble small purple grapes, and have a large inedible nut inside from which the berry pulp must be separated. This pulp can be purchased frozen (I use Sambazon brand) and used in drinks, smoothies, frozen desserts, eaten with cereals like granola, and other recipes where you might use frozen berries or fruit purées. Açai products also include pre-made smoothies and freeze-dried powder for mixing in drinks. Available in health food stores.

Adzuki beans: Small, reddish beans with a slightly sweet flavor that digest more easily than other beans. Adzuki beans cook rather quickly (see Cooking Beans, page 229).

Agar powder: Also called "agar-agar," this powder is derived from seaweed and is used in place of gelatin. It has no flavor, can be easily dissolved in liquid, and gels upon cooling. Agar comes in different forms including flakes and strands; I use the powdered form. Available in health food stores and some grocery stores.

Agave nectar: Pronounced "uh-gah-vay," this is a liquid sweetener made from the juice of the agave cactus plant native to Mexico. It has a mild flavor, more neutral than honey and maple syrup. It is an excellent substitute for honey, but unlike honey, agave nectar pours and dissolves easily. It also has a low glycemic index, meaning it is absorbed slowly into the bloodstream. Available in health food stores and some groceries.

Amaranth flour: Since amaranth is a non-gluten grain, its flour is gluten-free. Available in health food stores or in natural food sections of grocery stores (e.g., Bob's Red Mill brand).

Annie's Naturals Goddess Dressing: A brand of thick, flavorful, all-natural dressing that is tahini-based and does not have any added sweeteners.

Apple cider vinegar: This light brown vinegar is made from fermented apples, and has a mild fruity taste. Look for organic, unpasteurized apple cider vinegar that has some edible sediment (known as "the mother") floating at the bottom of the bottle.

Arrowroot powder: This tasteless thickener comes from the root of a tropical plant, and substitutes equally for cornstarch. Like cornstarch, it dissolves in liquid then must be brought to a boil to activate as a thickening agent. When dissolved, it is cloudy but turns clear once cooked.

Balsamic vinegar: A popular Italian vinegar that has a wonderfully sweet robust flavor and relatively mild acidity. Look for organic varieties without sulfites.

Barley flour: From the barley grain, this flour is light in color and mild in flavor and works well in baking and in combination with other flours. Available in health food stores and some grocery stores.

Barley malt syrup: A thick, dark-colored liquid sweetener used as an alternative to honey (though not as sweet), molasses, or brown rice syrup. Available in health food stores and grocery stores.

Blackstrap molasses: A syrup produced during the final stage of boiling sugar cane juice to make sugar. It is dark brown, thick, and has a strong, slightly bitter flavor. Regular molasses can be substituted and is less bitter, although it is not as nutritious. I often use blackstrap molasses in soups and savory dishes as well as baking.

Brown basmati rice: Unhulled, thus retaining more fiber, brown basmati rice takes longer to cook than white basmati (refer to Cooking Whole Grains, page 228). Brown basmati is light and dry when cooked, not sticky like other varieties. The grain lengthens as it cooks and has a delicate nutty, buttery flavor and aroma similar to popcorn. Available in health food stores and grocery stores.

Brown lentils: These are also called green lentils, and are the most common variety of lentils you see in stores. They are khaki in color, and about the size of green peas, but shaped like flat discs. They have a pleasant earthy flavor, and cook quickly (about 25 minutes). Like all varieties of lentils, they do not need to be soaked or precooked. Before using lentils, rinse to remove any small stones or particles.

Brown rice flour: Made from grinding the whole kernel of brown rice, brown rice flour is gluten-free. Available in health food stores or natural foods sections in grocery stores.

Brown rice syrup: A thick, light brown sweetener made from rice; it sometimes also contains barley malt. It is less sweet than honey or sugar, and its sugars are absorbed more slowly in the bloodstream than other sweeteners.

Cannellini beans: The Italian name for white kidney beans, these are large, white, oval-shaped beans with a smooth, creamy texture and a nutty flavor.

Capers: The unripened buds of a Mediterranean plant that are pickled in a brine to give them a salty, pungent taste. They are dark olive green, have a small roundish shape, and come in different sizes; the smaller ones can be more expensive and are considered better quality. Rinse and drain capers before using. Widely available in grocery stores.

Cardamom (ground): A member of the ginger family, cardamom is ground from the seed that is encased in a cardamom pod. Wonderfully aromatic with a sweet flavor, this spice can be used in both sweet and savory dishes, and is a common ingredient in Indian cuisine. While the ground form is less flavorful than grinding straight from the seed, it is more readily available.

Carob: Available in powder and chip form, carob comes from the pod of a legume-family tree native to the Mediterranean region. It is often used as a substitute for chocolate, although it really doesn't have the same flavor. Carob is sweet whereas pure chocolate is bitter. But unlike chocolate, carob does not contain caffeine. Carob powder and chips are available in health food stores and some grocery stores.

Chili sauce: A blend of seasonings that may include tomatoes, onions, chili peppers, garlic, vinegar, sugar, and salt. I use a very mild tomato-based sauce that adds just a little heat and some sweet and sour taste. Available in grocery stores.

Chipotle hot sauce: Chipotle chili peppers are smoked and dried jalapeño chili peppers. They have a smoky, spicy flavor but are not as hot as other chili peppers. Look for chipotle hot sauces among other hot sauces in your grocery store. I use Tabasco brand.

Chipotle in adobo sauce: Another form of chipotle chili peppers (see above) is canned in adobo sauce. These chili peppers are soft, much like roasted red bell peppers, and are marinated in the adobo sauce that consists of tomatoes, seasonings, and spices. The sauce has a spicy and smoky flavor, but combined with chipotles, the spice is more intense.

Cocoa powder: Sometimes simply called "cocoa," this is the dry powder that remains after pressing the cocoa butter out of chocolate liquor. When a recipe calls for cocoa powder, use regular cocoa powder rather than Dutch-processed. Cocoa powder is available in grocery stores, often in the hot beverages or baking aisles. *See also* Dutch-processed cocoa powder.

Coconut oil: Extracted from the "flesh" of coconut, this oil works well for frying and sautéing since it can be heated to higher temperatures before breaking down. Coconut oil is solid at room temperature. Sold in jars or plastic containers, purchase the refrigerated brand of organic extra virgin coconut oil. Available in health food stores or natural foods section in grocery stores.

Coriander seeds: This spice comes from the plant of the cilantro (or coriander), a leafy herb. It is commonly used in Indian cuisine, and has a very fragrant, lemony, and slightly floral-like flavor. They can be found in grocery stores, in the spice or Indian food sections.

Curry paste: These pastes range from mild to hot (I use only the mild variety), and are a blend of different ingredients, such as coriander, turmeric, chili, onion, ginger, garlic, cumin, tomato paste, and vegetable oil. A good curry paste brings out the complexity of flavors in a dish, and is easier to use than creating your own mixture of dried spices and seasonings. Patak's is a popular brand, and I also like Minara's. You can find small jars of curry pastes in grocery stores, usually in the Indian foods section.

Dutch-processed cocoa powder: Cocoa powder that has been processed to reduce its acidity. Dutch-processed cocoa powder has a richer, milder flavor than regular, but cannot always be substituted for standard cocoa powder in recipes. To be certain, use Dutch-processed cocoa powder only when specifically listed in recipes. Available in natural foods stores and some grocery stores.

Earth Balance Buttery Spread: A brand of non-hydrogenated vegan margarine made from cold-pressed, non-genetically modified oils including soy, canola, and olive oils. It is one of the best vegan dairy substitutes for both cooking and baking. Available in health food stores and most grocery stores (either in the dairy case or in natural foods refrigerated section).

Fennel: If you like the flavor of licorice or anise, as I do, you will love fennel. Eaten raw, its flavor is very pronounced, but mellows greatly as you sauté, grill, or cook it. Fennel looks somewhat like celery, with light green stalks, and a white bulbous base. To use, trim the stalks to where they meet the bulb (fronds can be used as an herb similar to dill). Cut bulb in half and remove the core, then slice or chop as needed. When shopping, look for firm, compact clean bulbs without any blemishes, and stalks that are fresh, green, and firm.

Fennel seeds: This spice adds a sweet, licorice or anise flavor to dishes, and is often found in Italian cuisine. Available in grocery stores, either in the spice section or the ethnic foods section.

File powder: This powder is made from dried, ground sassafras leaves. It is often used in Creole and Cajun cuisine originating in Louisiana, in dishes such as Gumbo and Jambalaya.

Flax meal: Flax meal is made from whole flax seeds ground fine into a powdery or mealy form. Grinding enhances the nutritional absorption of flax seeds (high in omega-3 fatty acids). Flax meal also makes a wonderful egg substitute (see page 174), since it becomes quite gelatinous when combined with water or other liquid. You can grind your own flax seeds, or buy ready-made flax meal (e.g., Bob's Red Mill) at health food stores or grocery stores. Flax meal has a high oil content, so it can go rancid quickly. Be sure it is either refrigerated or frozen (not at room temperature) when purchased, and store in an airtight container in your freezer to retain its nutritional value and fresh flavor. Fresh flax meal has a pleasant, sweet, nutty flavor and aroma, whereas old or rancid flax meal has a strong oily smell.

Flax oil: Derived from flax seed, flax oil is rich in omega-3 fatty acids. It must be kept refrigerated, and cooking destroys its nutritional value, so use it cold in salad dressings, to drizzle on food, or blend into drinks. It doesn't have a long shelf life, so check the expiry date on labels when shopping and be sure to buy it refrigerated. A good quality flax oil should not have much, if any, bitter aftertaste.

Gnocchi: Potato-based dumplings that also contain flour (whole-wheat varieties are available in certain stores) and sometimes seasonings and herbs. Gnocchi originated in Italy, and these bite-sized dumplings work well with pasta sauces as well as dishes that might include pasta, such as soups. Gnocchi can be made from scratch, but can also be found refrigerated or frozen in vacuum-sealed packages in grocery stores. Check the labels to ensure they are vegan, since some brands may contain cheese or other dairy.

Hemp seed nuts: The hard outer shell of the hemp seed is removed to reveal the highly nutritious inner nut. Similar to sesame seeds in size with a light yellow-green color, they have a light, soft texture with a little crunch. They can be sprinkled onto salads, sandwiches, or cereals, or used in baking and other recipes. I use Manitoa Harvest brand, available in health food stores and some grocery stores.

Hemp seed nut butter: This is a butter made from puréeing the shelled hemp seed nut. It can be used much like other nut butters in recipes. It has a greenish color and tastes somewhat like sunflower seeds. I use Manitoa Harvest brand, available in health food stores and some grocery stores.

Hemp seed oil: Cold-pressing the hemp seed nut produces hemp seed oil. It has a green color and a mild, nutty taste. It works wonderfully in salad dressings and drizzled on meals, but like flax oil, it should not be used for cooking and requires refrigeration. I use Manitoa Harvest brand, available in health food stores and some grocery stores.

Hoisin sauce: A thick, dark, flavorful sauce often used in Chinese cooking. It is sweet and mildly spicy, made from such ingredients as soybeans, garlic, chiles, sugar, vinegar, and other seasonings. Available in small jars in grocery stores, usually in Asian foods section.

Jicama: A tan-colored tuber that is shaped similar to a turnip, but a little squat. It has a pleasant, crunchy texture that is similar to water chestnuts with a flavor like very mild green peas. When selecting jicama, look for one that is firm with unwrinkled skin and no blemishes.

Kalamata olives: A popular purple-black Greek olive, Kalamatas are salty and flavorful (far more than common black olives). Buy the pitted variety for convenience. Available in grocery stores, often in bulk in the deli section or bottled in brine or vinegar.

Lemongrass: Often used in Thai cooking, lemongrass slightly resembles a large scallion, having a slender stalk with a bulbous base. It is light green and yellow in color, with the outer leaves rather stiff and woody in texture. Lemongrass has a very unique lemon flavor that is distinct from the lemon itself. Lemongrass is often added whole to soups and stews, to impart its marvelous flavor. After trimming the stalk, the lower bulbous portion is then often "bruised" to help release its flavor, and added whole to simmer in recipes. Available in the produce section in most grocery stores.

Liquid smoke: A liquid seasoning made from burning hardwood chips (e.g., hickory) and condensing the smoke into a liquid product. Liquid smoke is very intense, so it should be used very conservatively; a few drops go a long way. Available in grocery stores.

Macadamia nut butter: A paste or nut butter made from puréeing macadamia nuts. Available in health food stores or natural foods section in grocery stores.

Maple butter: A thick paste made from cooking, cooling, and whipping maple syrup. Since it is very thick and concentrated, it is quite sweet, but this thick consistency lends itself well to certain sauces and toppings for desserts. Maple butter is packaged in small jars, and is usually found near bottles of pure maple syrup in grocery or health food stores. Check the label to ensure it is vegan.

Miso: A salty, thick paste made from fermented soybeans. Available in light and dark varieties, and also in combination with other grains like barley and brown rice. I use brown rice and barley miso, since it has a mellow, mild flavor. Available in health food stores and grocery stores.

Non-dairy milk: There are many choices for non-dairy milks, including soy, rice, almond, oat, multigrain, potato-based, and hemp varieties. Soy and rice are the most popular, and often the least expensive. Look for fortified varieties, and if using soy milk, be sure to buy those using organic non-GMO soybeans. Some are sold refrigerated or packaged in aseptic TetraPak containers for longer shelf life. Experiment with different milks to find ones you like, depending on the use. For example, I prefer rice milk for drinking straight and in cereals, but I prefer soy milk for baking.

Nutritional yeast: Light, thin yellowish flakes that can be used as a nutritional supplement, but also have a cheesy, nutty flavor which works well in vegan foods. Nutritional yeast can be used in recipes or sprinkled directly on food such as pasta, bread, and popcorn. It is rich in protein, minerals, and vitamins (especially B vitamins, including B12), and is easy to digest. Nutritional yeast is grown on molasses, but is inactive (unlike baking yeast), and also differs from brewer's yeast and torula yeast. Look for the Red Star brand of nutritional yeast (sometimes called Red Star Vegetarian Support Formula or Red Star Yeast T6635+) to ensure it is fortified with vitamin B12. Available in health food stores and bulk sections in grocery stores.

Phyllo pastry: Paper-thin sheets of pastry, also called filo or fillo dough. Phyllo is Greek for "leaf," and this pastry is used in the popular Greek dishes spanokopita and baklava. Most varieties are made from wheat flour, but you can find spelt versions (e.g., Fillo Factory). Check ingredients to ensure there are no hydrogenated oils or animal products. Available in health food stores and frozen sections in grocery stores.

Pine nuts: The seeds from the cones of several varieties of pine trees. They are ivory color, and while they can range in shape and size, they are usually teardrop-shaped and the size of orange seeds. Pine nuts have a soft texture and earthy taste, and toasting enhances their nutty flavor. Keep them refrigerated or in the freezer, since they can go rancid quickly (like many nuts). Available in refrigerated sections in grocery stores.

Pistachios: Green nuts with a delicate, slightly sweet taste and crunchy texture. Pistachios work well in sweet and savory dishes. Brownish green is the natural color of pistachios; red pistachios have been dyed.

Polenta (prepared): Polenta is a porridge-like mixture made from cornmeal and water, and sometimes milk and seasonings. Polenta can be made from scratch and served fresh, ladled thick into bowls or on plates to accompany other dishes. Or, it can be poured into dishes or moulds and chilled until firm, and then sliced and fried, grilled, or baked. Prepared polenta is packaged in a tube, is fairly firm in texture, and available in plain and seasoned varieties. Available in pasta or ethnic foods sections of grocery stores.

Portobello mushrooms: These mushrooms are known for their great flavor and "meaty" texture. They are large with a brown, round, flat cap, and a woody stem that is usually discarded or used in vegetable stocks. Available fresh in most grocery stores.

Potato starch: Sometimes referred to as "potato starch flour," it is a gluten-free flour and made from cooked potatoes. Do not confuse it with potato flour (which is heavy and with a distinct potato taste). Available in most grocery stores.

Pure maple syrup: A natural sweetener from the sap of sugar maples. I use pure maple syrup in many desserts and baked goods. It's not to be mistaken for the cheaper "maple-flavored" syrup sold as pancake topping. Pure maple syrup is 100% maple syrup, with no artificial flavors, colors, or additives. Available in grocery stores; organic varieties are available in health food stores and some grocery stores.

Pure vanilla extract: Made from steeping pure vanilla beans in alcohol and water or a glycerin water base. Look for pure vanilla extract, checking the labels to ensure it's not artificial or imitation varieties, which contain artificial colors and flavors, and do not have nearly the same flavor as pure vanilla. Available in grocery stores and organic varieties in health food stores.

Quinoa: Pronounced "keen-wa," this ancient grain is small in size but big in nutrition. Quinoa is a complete source of protein, and is high in calcium, iron, and phosphorous. Uncooked quinoa resembles flattened couscous, creamy beige in color with a little ring around each grain that comes out like a tail when cooked. This ring holds the majority of quinoa's protein and gives it a slight crunch. Quinoa cooks quickly (see Cooking Whole Grains, page 228), has a light texture, and can be digested easily. It must be rinsed for a few minutes before cooking to remove its natural bitter coating. Available in health food stores and some grocery stores.

Red lentils: These are small, pink-colored lentils that turn golden when cooked and have a mellow flavor. They cook very quickly (see Cooking Beans, page 229), but do not hold their shape after cooking, so they are best in soups. Available in health food stores and grocery stores.

Roasted red peppers: Most grocers carry jars or bottles of roasted red peppers packed in oil, vinegar, or water. They are tasty and quick to use, saving you the time of roasting them yourself. Look for varieties without chemicals or preservatives such as sulfites.

Shiitake mushrooms: These mushrooms have a brown, sometimes flat cap with a light underside and a thin, stiff stalk. They have a distinct earthy flavor and a chewy, meaty texture. Available in most grocery stores.

Silken tofu: A smooth and silky variety of tofu sold in small, rectangular, aseptic boxes. An alternative processing of the soy milk creates a different texture than that of regular soft and firm tofu. Since silken tofu becomes so smooth and creamy when blended or puréed, it is often used to create smoothies, dips, and desserts. Its packaging allows for a long shelf life, even without refrigeration (although I prefer to refrigerate). Mori-Nu silken tofu (soft and firm varieties) can be found in most grocery stores, health food stores, and some Asian specialty stores.

Spelt flour: Made from spelt grain, this flour is available in both whole-grain and refined forms. It is a good substitute for wheat flour, although the amount may need to be slightly adjusted. If possible, buy a whole-grain spelt flour that has been sifted, to make your baked goods a little lighter and more tender. Available in health food stores and some grocery stores.

Tahini: Sometimes called sesame seed butter, this paste is made from puréeing white sesame seeds. It is often used in Middle Eastern recipes such as hummus and baba ghanouj. As with all natural seed and nut butters, the oil in tahini rises to the top because there are no additives to suspend the oils, so stir the oil through the nut butter before using and then refrigerate. Available in health food stores and most grocery stores.

Tamari: A soy sauce made from fermented soybeans, and without the colorings and additives found in many commercial brands. Tamari is also wheat-free unlike most soy sauces. Available at most grocery stores.

Tapioca starch flour: Sometimes simply referred to as tapioca flour, this is a gluten-free flour that is made from the cassava root. It works well in gluten-free baking to help sweeten flours such as rice, amaranth, and quinoa, but is also useful as a thickener (much like arrowroot or cornstarch) for sauces and pies. Tapioca flour is not the same as instant tapioca; it is finely ground into a flour that is easy to dissolve.

Available in health food stores and natural foods sections in grocery stores.

Tempeh: A soy food product that originated in Indonesia, tempeh is made from soybeans that have been cooked and combined with a culturing agent. The process turns the mixture into a solid cake form with the soybeans pressed together. Tempeh is higher in protein and vitamins than tofu, and unlike tofu, is also high in fiber. The culturing process also makes tempeh a more digestible soy food. When buying tempeh, look for a firm cake that has a thin whitish bloom. It may have a few greyish or black spots, but should never have any pink, yellow or blue coloration. Tempeh leftovers can be covered with tight plastic wrap and refrigerated for up to 4–5 days, or frozen for several months. Tempeh should be steamed, sautéed or otherwise cooked before eating. To reduce any bitterness, simmer it in vegetable broth for about twenty minutes before using. Available frozen in grocery or health food stores, and in varieties that include grains, flax, and vegetables.

Toasted sesame oil: Pressed from toasted sesame seeds, this oil has an intense sesame flavor and a dark golden color. Be sure to use it when recipes specifically call for it. The flavor is so strong, in fact, that you need just small amounts to season dressings, sauces, and other foods. (Lighter colored sesame oil is not produced from toasted seeds and thus does not have the same rich flavor.) Available in health food stores and grocery stores.

Unrefined sugar: Unlike common white and brown sugar, unrefined sugar retains some nutrients because it is partially refined or not refined at all. The term "unrefined sugar" can include such products as Sucanat, Turbinado, and evaporated cane juice. Unrefined sugar has a golden color (light to dark beige), and some types (e.g., Demerara) have granules that are a little larger than standard white sugar.

Be sure to check the label to ensure it is unrefined; organic sugar, for example, is now popular but is not necessarily unrefined. Finer granules are easier to bake with; Sucanat and most varieties labeled "unrefined sugar" work well.

Vegan marshmallows: Marshmallows made without gelatin (which is derived from animal bones and connective tissues). Available in some health food stores and from online sources.

Vegan Worcestershire sauce: A Worcestershire sauce made without anchovies. I have found two brands available in health food stores, one by Annie's Naturals and the other by The Wizard.

White rice flour: Flour made from grinding white rice. White rice flour is gluten-free, but because it is made from white rice rather than brown, it is not as nutritious as brown rice flour. It is sometimes preferable in baking or cooking, however, depending on the texture required for a recipe. Sweet rice flour is also available; it differs from white rice flour in that it is ground from sweet rice, and has a finer texture that is sometimes preferred in gluten-free baking. Available in health food stores and natural foods sections in grocery stores.

Wild rice: Not actually a grain, but a water-grown grass, wild rice has a purple-black color, a lovely nutty taste, and a chewy texture. It opens up and curls when fully cooked, exposing a white interior. Available in health food stores and most grocery stores.

Xanthan gum: A fine powder that is particularly useful in gluten-free baking to help bind ingredients and add stability and elasticity. Xanthan gum is also useful to thicken frostings and desserts, and is also often found in store-bought salad dressings and sauces. Available in health food stores and some grocery stores.

INDEX

DREENA BURTON is the author of the bestselling cookbooks *The Everyday Vegan* and *Vive le Vegan!* (both published by Arsenal Pulp Press) and hosts the popular blog *vivelevegan.blogspot.com*. She is also a regular contributor to *VegNews* magazine and *Vegan. com*, and is featured on the *Everyday Dish* cooking DVD. She lives in British Columbia with her husband and two children. Contact Dreena at *dreena@ everydayvegan.com*.